Norms Under Siege

The Parallel Political Lives of
Donald Trump and Silvio Berlusconi

Norms Under Siege

The Parallel Political Lives of
Donald Trump and Silvio Berlusconi

Edoardo M. Fracanzani

Winchester, UK
Washington, USA

JOHN HUNT PUBLISHING

First published by Zero Books, 2021
Zero Books is an imprint of John Hunt Publishing Ltd., No. 3 East St., Alresford,
Hampshire SO24 9EE, UK
office@jhpbooks.com
www.johnhuntpublishing.com
www.zero-books.net

For distributor details and how to order please visit the 'Ordering' section on our website.

ISBN: 978 1 78904 466 9
978 1 78904 467 6 (ebook)
Library of Congress Control Number: 2020941136

A CIP catalogue record for this book is available from the British Library.

Design: Stuart Davies

UK: Printed and bound by CPI Group (UK) Ltd, Croydon, CR0 4YY
Printed in North America by CPI GPS partners

We operate a distinctive and ethical publishing philosophy in
all areas of our business, from our global network of authors to
production and worldwide distribution.

Contents

Also by the author

A Letter to Cavour. Anomalies of a Nation; original title: "Lettera a Cavour. Anomalie di una Nazione." Published by Armando Edizioni, Rome, 2009. ISBN: 978-8860815491

The Origins of the Conflict. The Political Parties, the Judiciary and the Rule of Law in Italy's First Republic (1974-1983); original title: "Le origini del conflitto. I partiti politici, la magistratura e il principio di legalità nella prima Repubblica (1974-1983)." Published by Rubbettino, Soveria Mannelli (CZ), 2014. ISBN: 978-8849841022

To Carla and Isabella

Introduction

How to learn about institutions and political cultures by comparing two controversial leaders

"Hic sunt leones," the ancient Romans apparently used to write on certain maps, "There are lions here," as a warning that unexplored areas of Africa might hide dangers; uncharted territory we might call such areas nowadays. When Donald Trump was sworn in as president, a significant number of Americans, likely a majority in fact, had the feeling that the country was entering a phase of politically uncharted territory. A couple of decades earlier most Italians had a very similar feeling, as Silvio Berlusconi broke into the political game and won the elections at his first attempt, thus becoming prime minister.

Comparing Donald Trump to Italy's Silvio Berlusconi is not a novel idea. Anyone observing Berlusconi's style of government in Italy during the 90s and the following decade would easily recognize as familiar Trump's political modus operandi and rhetoric. In fact, the resemblances between the political trajectories of Trump and Berlusconi are striking. Both men started their careers in the real estate business and claimed to have built an empire thanks to their abilities and skills; however, Trump inherited a significant part of his wealth at the least, while Berlusconi can claim with stronger grounds to be a self-made man. Both later became celebrity entrepreneurs in the entertainment business: the Italian tycoon as the owner of three private national networks, Trump as the host of a popular reality show. Their business dealings often required special connections with politicians, and at times, reportedly, even with shady individuals with ties to organized crime; in conducting business, neither seemed to display great concern for ethical standards. Trump and Berlusconi entered

1

the political arena making a grand and noticeable entry: the current American president captured the attention of the media by using unprecedented language in characterizing immigrants as "rapists and murderers," while Berlusconi shocked most Italians declaring his support for a political party founded on the ashes of fascism. Curiously, the moment they entered the political game is symbolized by a descent, presumably from some "higher place" somewhere: Berlusconi always referred to this moment as his descent into the field, borrowing from the jargon of sports, as he often would; Trump famously descended the escalator in Trump Tower before a group of (apparently paid) cheering supporters. Both claimed to be the only individual with the skills necessary to end the problems of their country. While in office, they both had to face accusations of pursuing their own personal interest, even when such personal stakes appeared to be in conflict with official government objectives. In staffing their administrations, they seemed to price public flattery and personal loyalty above any other quality, even at the cost of having mediocre, corrupt, or unqualified professionals serving within their teams. In conducting foreign policy, both leaders showed a strong preference toward strong men and dictators, Russia's Putin most of all, while often having difficulties dealing with other democratically elected leaders from all sides of the political spectrum, especially in multilateral settings. Both proved to be skilled communicators, particularly effective in conveying clear messages through simple, at times vulgar and, especially for Trump, rudimentary language; in many cases introducing a disconnect from the traditional political speech patterns, especially in Italy, where traditional politicians would often speak through convoluted phrases. At the same time, they both exhibited a high degree of disregard for the truth and facts, right down to the cover-ups they used to justify or downplay their sexual scandals. Berlusconi explained that he tried to interfere with the police's handling of a young prostitute because he thought (on what grounds it is still not clear) she was the niece of the Egyptian president. Trump initially claimed to know nothing about the non-disclosure agreement and payment to a porn star made by his attorney in order to prevent her from going public about an affair they (allegedly) had. In general, Trump and Berlusconi demonstrated that they valued people of the opposite sex for their physical appearances more than any other quality. Moreover, physical appearances played a significant role in their personas as well: they are obviously obsessed about their hair and while Berlusconi seems to have a problem with his height, Trump appears to hate any reference to the size of his hands or the length of his fingers. Both leaders seemed to appreciate their public personas being associated to their ostentatious buildings: Trump Tower in New York City and Villa San Martino in Arcore, Milan, as main residences and Mar-a-Lago and Villa Certosa as vacation resorts by the beach. While in office, both dedicated a lot of energy to pushing a major project of public infrastructure they could be remembered by: a wall on the southern border for Trump, a bridge connecting Sicily to continental Italy for Berlusconi.

Trump and Berlusconi often lacked to demonstrate a particular preference toward an ideology or specific policies, if not for its immediate impact on their image or on the political equilibrium of the moment. A possible exception could be what appears to be Trump's obsession with the US being "ripped off" and "laughed at" by its allies on the international stage. Both always boasted about their intuition, gut feeling, judgment, and ability to negotiate; they often declared to value personal relationships in the conduct of business, internally and internationally, with little regard for institutional and formal rapports. During the political tenures of these two leaders, their country became polarized and divided to an extent that has very few precedents: possibly the civil war in the US and the last stage of WWII in Italy, when the fascist regime in the northern part of the country was fighting the Resistance. Even in the 50s and 60s, when the political wedge in Italy between the filo-soviet communists and the Christian Democrats was deep and led both sides to attack each other with all the tools of political propaganda, the ideological divide did not prevent the representatives from both parties from cooperating on specific issues. In the era of Berlusconi and Trump, the real source of the dispute between the two sides seems to be the individual leader of the Right rather than ideas and policies, which is probably one of the reasons why many analysts in both countries have warned against a "personality cult" poisoning the political debate. It did not happen by chance. As we will see, the rhetoric of division has been a useful, probably indispensable, tool for the political positioning of the two leaders.

Of the many things Trump and Berlusconi have in common, one may tell us more about the societies where they operate rather than about the leaders themselves. The fact that they could break many long-standing norms and still maintain such strong support among voters made apparent how some traditional values and norms were no longer regarded as such by a significant part of the electorate. Trump could refrain from releasing his tax returns and still not be politically damaged, demonstrating that voters did not really care about his finances and potential conflicts of interests; Berlusconi was sworn into heading the executive branch in Italy even while owning almost all of the private TV channels, thus controlling directly a significant share of the news. Both Trump and Berlusconi bragged about their ability to take advantage of loopholes in the legislation in order to pay fewer taxes or not to repay debts, underscoring that such an attitude was just smart. Both lied extensively and made unreasonable promises to the electorate (having Mexico pay for a border wall comes to mind), but were able to win elections nonetheless. Both Berlusconi and Trump could mobilize a core of supporters, at all times between, say,

20 and 30 percent of the electorate, who would approve of them no matter what they did. Trump famously said that he could shoot a person in the middle of Fifth Avenue and not lose a vote. Berlusconi had a very similar connection with his base. The mainstream press faced an extremely difficult challenge in holding them accountable; in most cases, the two leaders would avoid interviews by journalists they considered not friendly and, even when they accepted to be questioned, they would disregard any question they did not like, or respond with attacks and even insults. They would regularly play the role of victims of the media, of the opposition party and of the judiciary (or the "deep state") and manage to offer an apparent justification for any detrimental news reported. Both proved extremely skilled as "Teflon politicians," able to get rid, undamaged, of most scandals that would seriously hurt the career of other, more traditional, politicians.

If the similarities between the two are numerous and evident, there are many reasons it may be worthwhile to set them side by side and observe with as many details as possible the political phenomena behind their rise. The first reason could be of special interest to US readers: if indeed Trump and Berlusconi are expressions of a similar political phenomenon, understanding the deed of the latter may be very useful as a guideline for the future developments of "Trumpism" in the US, especially if the current president wins another term in 2020. Berlusconi first won the elections and became head of government in Italy in 1994, about a quarter century ago; maybe there are some lessons to be learned from his trajectory, and possibly they can be applied to the current and future US political developments. Secondly, for those who think that Trump's politics is highly detrimental for traditional Western liberal values, a better understanding of how a politician could maintain a loyal base of supporters in the face of the lying, the scandals, and the norm-breaking behavior can be useful to prevent such a phenomenon from happening in the future. In the US, Italy, or elsewhere. The last, but probably not least, reason for studying Trump and Berlusconi is that the comparison provides an interesting perspective in the different institutions and political cultures of the US and Italy and may help us to understand if and how these institutions are able to resist populist attacks while providing some hints as to how they can be effectively reformed.

* * *

In many analyses of recent international political developments, the election of Donald Trump is treated as one of a series of events within a wide populist wave that has swept the Western world. In June 2016, most people were shocked by the result of the referendum in the UK, where a majority of voters favored the so-called Brexit, the country leaving the European Union after more than 4 decades of gradual economic and administrative integration with the other countries of the area. This result followed an electoral campaign in which the proponents of "leave" associated EU membership with extra-European immigration. Shortly after, in the last presidential elections in France, held in the spring of 2017, all major political parties that had traditionally governed the country for the last half a century had such low performances in the popular vote that they did not even make it to the run-off. Though the final victory went to Emmanuel Macron, who can reasonably be identified as a centrist, the other party participating to the run-off, the National Front, a right-wing movement with deep racist and anti-Semitic roots, founded by Jean Marie Le Pen, achieved almost 34 percent of the popular vote. In Italy, the last general elections in March 2018 witnessed the victory of two parties widely characterized as anti-system. One of them, the Northern League, founded in the early 90s on a platform of secession of the northern regions from the rest of Italy, later largely shifted to a rhetoric of nativism and anti-immigration. The other party is the Five Star Movement, created less than 10 years ago, from scratch, by a professional comedian whose main message was a break from traditional political parties and the use of the internet as a means to, in some unspecified way, establish a new, direct democracy. During the previous years, the party of Viktor Orbán had conquered political power in Hungary, shortly after the country had entered the European Union, and established a sort of "soft authoritarian" state, implementing a systemic occupation of the Hungarian institutions. An example later followed, and to some extent exceeded, in Poland. Among the last manifestations of populism in Europe we can remember Austria, where the young leader of the People's Party, Sebastian Kurtz, became chancellor based on a strong anti-immigration platform; and Germany, where the last elections marked a dramatic reduction of votes for the traditional parties and Angela Merkel struggled to maintain her position as head of the government. More recently, in Brazil, a majority of voters elected as president Jair Bolsonaro, a former army captain and right-wing extremist who openly and publicly defended torture and military dictatorship. Even a country such as Canada doesn't seem to be immune to populism, as Rob and Doug Ford proved able to maintain a significant number of supporters notwithstanding their inclination toward authoritarianism and a significant degree of contempt for the rule of law and norms in general.

Are Trump and Berlusconi part of a wave of populism that is sweeping across the western hemisphere? Actually, this question makes more sense for Trump, given that his rise in the US happened more or less at the same time as this populist trend. Berlusconi, on the other hand, entered politics when Bill Clinton was president and when, on the contrary, liberalism, or neoliberalism, was in rather good health both in the Americas and in Europe. Back then, populism seemed a political phenomenon far away in time (mostly dating back in the 30s, 40s, and 50s) or in space, characterizing mostly third world countries, certainly not the economically developed world. But what is populism, exactly, anyway? As is often the case with political labels, it does not seem to have a rigorous meaning. Moreover, it certainly expresses somewhat different concepts in the US as opposed to Europe. In the old continent, the term usually carries a negative connotation; in fact, history's greatest examples of populist leaders are usually regarded as demagogues, leaders who achieved and maintained power by exploiting the worst and irrational prejudices of the common people: Mussolini, Hitler, and so on. In the US, on the contrary, populism is not necessarily negative and, indeed, parties have been founded bearing that specific name; politicians in many cases have no problem in defining themselves, or leaders they support, as populists. In America, the term populism seems to refer to a political approach that puts the people at the center of the discourse, possibly in opposition to the elites, particularly the economic elites. After World War II, most leaders identified as populists in the United States were on the right of the political spectrum: Joseph McCarthy, George Wallace, Richard Nixon, and, more recently, Donald Trump.

The current wave of populism appears to be closely connected to the pace of globalization, an acceleration of the world circulation of goods, information, and people that started in the 80s and that has gradually changed the political and economic geography of the world, carrying significant consequences in all the societies of Western countries. A notable one is the reduction of the relative bargaining power of unskilled workers and a significant increase in the immigration flows from areas with lower economic development, with all its economic and social consequences. In fact, most attempts to provide an explanation for the rise of populism in the West insist on two sets of reactions from part of the society. The first one is the economic anxiety resulting from rising inequality and relative economic uncertainty, while the second is the cultural backlash associated with immigration from different areas which causes a perceived reduction of traditional cultural identity and ethnicity.

While populism certainly has been spreading in the Western world in the last few years, Trump and Berlusconi appear to represent, at least partially, a distinct political phenomenon. From one point of view, they lack the traditional background of the prototypical populist leader, someone who denounces the corrupt oligarchies in the name of the virtuous people: while they made political gain from attacking traditional elites, they were and are, in fact, part of the elites themselves because of their wealth, power, and celebrity status. From another perspective, in many cases, populist leaders seek to change the system, which they describe as rigged in favor of the few. Trump and Berlusconi, while themselves denouncing the "system," thrived in it; and to the extent that it was rigged, it was actually rigged to their advantage. In social science, the concept of "free rider" describes an individual who manages to disregard norms and rules while others, or most of the others, abide by them. In all human societies, a number of laws and norms ensure that each individual restrains his immediate interests and desires so as not to provoke aggressive reactions from fellow humans and, in this fashion, enjoys the benefits of social life and cooperative enterprise. From the individual's standpoint, however, the best possible situation is the one where all or most of the other members of society abide by the rules, while he does not, thus getting access to the benefits of society while not having to restrain his self-serving actions, even at the detriment of others. Societies, of course, tend to discourage such situations in a number of ways, but they do not always succeed. To some extent, crime (or norm-breaking) does pay in some instances. A case can be made that Trump and Berlusconi are the ultimate free riders, because of their ability to fully take advantage of society while minimizing the cost of adhering to the rules. If this characterization is correct, they desperately need the system that made their success possible, however rigged it may be and the last thing they really want to do is reform it. Arguably, this reasoning is confirmed by the fact that policy-making under their leadership has not matched their populist rhetoric at all.

* * *

When highlighting the similarities between Trump and Berlusconi, it is important to consider that although the US and Italy are both mature, high per-capita income economies with liberal-democratic traditions, the two countries are different in many regards. While the US is arguably the most powerful country on earth, Italy has no significant role on the international stage. Someone once said that it is an economic giant, a political dwarf and a military worm (considering the relative economic decline of Italy in the last 20 years, its claims to be an economic giant are becoming increasingly less founded). Its institutions are very different from the American ones, even though they are both informed by the same principles: separation of powers, popular elections, majority rule, individuals' rights such as freedom of expression, etc. The political culture of the two countries is also different to a substantial degree.

Italy was formed as a political entity in 1861, when it became a constitutional monarchy inspired by the liberal principles of the state that unified the peninsula, Piedmont, and of the politician who, more than any other, contributed to its creation: Camillo Benso di Cavour. In a time when France was being ruled by Napoleon III, the Austrian empire by the Habsburg dynasty, and, soon to be united, Germany by the Prussian king, Italy was one of the very few relatively large countries, together with Great Britain and the US, to enjoy liberal institutions. According to the charter introduced in Torino in 1848, and then extended to the rest of Italy, the king would appoint the head of the executive branch based on the electoral results: the prospective prime minister had to achieve a confidence vote of Parliament in order to govern the executive branch lawfully. Of course, electoral rights were rather limited back then, based on gender, income, and education.

During the first few years of Italy's political life, the governing elite had to face a number of serious obstacles: dramatic internal social differences between the poor South and the North, a delay in economic development if compared to other European countries, minor wars in 1866 and 1970, followed by a major one in 1915. However, during these decades, the political leaders seemed to have learned the lessons of Cavour, a profoundly liberal reformer, and managed to rule the country rather effectively while maintaining Italy's liberal institutions until the early 20s. Soon after World War I, following the political polarization exacerbated by the Soviet revolution in Russia, Benito Mussolini achieved his goal to become prime minister and, shortly after, duce (leader) of Italy; founding a new ideology (to the extent that fascism can really be defined as an ideology) in the process.

Of course, the fascist regime ended up in an alliance with Hitler's Germany and was entangled in a disastrous war that left the country in ruins, both materially and morally. After the defeat, the political power went to the parties that had emerged shortly after the temporary introduction of the universal suffrage, back in 1913, most of which had actively opposed Mussolini's regime: the Christian Democrats on one side, at times allied to a number of other centrist parties, and the Communist and Socialist parties on the other. These two political coalitions reflected the world polarization at the start of the Cold War, when the two main powers that defeated Germany and Japan, namely the US and the Soviet Union, extended their ideological and military influence across the globe. The first political elections under the new republican constitution, in 1948, marked the victory of the Christian Democrats, thus confirming the positioning of Italy well within the western hemisphere and in, soon to be founded, NATO.

Italy's new constitution was a mix of three main elements. The first one was the country's political heritage and experience; the institutions were forged after the ones Italy had before fascism, with a Parliament at the center of the system holding the keys to both the legislative as well as the executive branches: the appointed head of government had to achieve, and subsequently maintain, a majority in Parliament. A big difference with respect to the past was that the king was gone: a referendum in 1946 had sanctioned the end of the kingdom and the person in charge of appointing the prime minister after the elections would be a President of the Republic, elected essentially by Parliament, with no executive powers. A second element of the new constitution was its declared rejection of fascism and a few mechanisms to prevent its return: the members of the elected assembly in charge of drafting the new constitution remembered well how Mussolini's regime had been able to establish a dictatorship in a way that was legal, to a good extent. A number of articles would make it more difficult to alter the charter in the future. The third element stemmed from the political equilibrium of the moment: a compromise between the Christian Democrats and the Socialist and Communist parties that had formed the anti-fascist alliance.

From the ideological perspective, there is a major difference between the politicians who voted the Italian constitution into effect and the US founding fathers over a century and a half earlier: both prevailing political cultures in Italy had relatively limited interest for institutional engineering, outside, of course, the effects on the immediate short and medium-term political competition. The Communists and the Socialists embraced the Marxist tradition and ultimately considered the constitution, as the law in general, as a "superstructure," an expression of the capitalist mode of organizing the means of production, rather than the stable rules for deciding who exercises power in the name of the people. The Catholic tradition of thought, on the other side of the political spectrum, was still somewhat dominated by dogma and objective religious reality. Most of the Christian Democratic leaders believed in the centrality of the party as the democratic tool to mediate between the people and the state, rather than the traditional liberal institutions, with all their checks and balances.

The results of the 1948 elections marked a pattern that would repeat itself for several decades. The Christian Democrats would win a plurality of votes, most times a little more than 40 per cent, and thus, with the alliance of smaller centrist parties, could obtain the majority of Parliament necessary to control the executive and the legislative branches. Communists and socialists would get around 35 per cent of the votes combined (but with no other party to form a coalition with) and would stay in the opposition until 1963, when the socialists, no longer embracing the Soviet Union as an ideological reference, agreed to support a centrist government. While it would be an overstatement to characterize the governments led by the Christian Democrats during these years as highly efficient, Italy's society in the 50s and 60s was able to develop at an unprecedented speed. The northern part of the country, already the one with a higher degree of industrialization, grew to such an extent as to reduce the difference with the most industrialized countries and even exceed Great Britain, in the 80s, for per-capita income. The economic development had an obvious effect on the population, especially on the poorest regions, which shifted from rural to urban and from largely illiterate to highly educated within a generation or two. From a political standpoint, during the 50s and 60s, the Communist Party never seemed to represent an actual reliable alternative for power, in the sense that its Marxist heritage and its perceived anti-system nature prevented a majority of Italian voters from considering it as a real, safe electoral choice. They thought, not without grounds considering the party's ideology, that if the communists won the elections, they would not only introduce a change of policies but rather a change of regime altogether. The lack of competition can be damning for the quality and value of products provided by companies in business markets, but just as much can be said of the political supply provided by parties. The Christian Democrats knew that, no matter what they did, they were relatively sure that they would retain power for lack of a credible alternative. This political system has been described with the expression "imperfect bi-party system": while there were two major coalitions competing in opposite sides of the spectrum, one of them did not have reasonable chances to run the government.

In the mid-70s, the weaknesses of the political system became more evident; the electoral strength of the Christian Democrats was gradually shrinking and with a socialist party not solidly in the government coalition, it was hard for the centrists to maintain a majority in Parliament. To make things more difficult for the ruling party, a number of corruption scandals exposed many of its leaders. At the same time the communists, more distant from the Soviet Union since the 1969 invasion of Czechoslovakia, were slowly growing electorally, and the prospect of their party winning the elections seemed a realistic possibility for the first time since 1948. The crisis was somewhat solved, between 1976 and 1979, by a coalition of Christians Democrats and the Socialist Party supported, indirectly, by the communists, who did not vote against it. However, this solution, the so-called "historic compromise," was abandoned in the aftermath of the kidnapping and murder of the Christian Democrat Aldo Moro, one of the country's most influential politicians, at the hands of the left-wing terrorist group the Red Brigades. After 1979, the control went back to the Christian Democrats, who could now count on a firm alliance with the new socialists, as their new young leader, Bettino Craxi, managed to dramatically shift the party to the right. The new coalition (Christian Democrats, socialists, and three smaller parties) ruled the country until the early 90s, when the extent of the corruption of the system became more evident than ever following a number of criminal investigations and indictments by magistrates, mainly in Milan, the economic and financial center of Italy. The scandals, together with the result of a new referendum that changed the electoral law upon which the system was based, created an impossible scenario for the traditional parties, which were swept away. This is when Silvio Berlusconi, by this time the owner of half of the national TV channels and an ally of the Socialist Party's strong leader, came in; he presented himself as a political outsider, ready to fix the country's problems after the failures of the inept and corrupt political elite.

It is apparent from this brief outline of Italy's history that its institutional experience is quite different from that of the United States. While both countries now belong to the group of liberal democracies of the high-income world, Italy does not even come close to the level of stability provided by the institutions of the US. In fact, no large nation in the world, with the possible exception of the UK, matches the United States in this regard, as the country managed to function for over 200 years with, arguably, only one real constitutional crisis: the secession of a number of states from the Union, and the civil war that followed, in the 1860s. This testifies to the effectiveness of the principles applied by the American founding fathers in the constitution, achieving a successful compromise in the trade-off between the attribution of power and the need to keep it in check in order to prevent its abuses. In general, the US electorate could always count on two parties, each with a reasonable policy plan for government, competing for two branches of government.

In the US system, the executive and the legislative are effectively separated because they can count on an independent source of their power, deriving from the vote of the electorate that chooses both in distinct elections. In Italy, on the contrary, the members of Parliament, who are elected by the citizens, retain the power to vote the bills into laws, but they also determine whether the head of the government gets to keep his (so far Italy has had no female head of government) job. So the relevant question becomes who controls, and to what extent, the members of Parliament. In this regard, the UK has a very similar system, but the British also have majoritarian electoral laws that favor the formation of two competing parties and, maybe, more importantly, they never had a significantly anti-system party with deep roots in the electorate. In general, it is safe to assume that senators and representatives care about their re-election and that whoever and whatever can influence that outcome will have a significant impact on them. The chances of re-election, in turn, depend, at least to a significant degree, on the electoral system. In the US, the congressional electoral system is based on majoritarian districts where one representative, the one who achieves the most votes, gets the seat; such a mechanism ensures that the elected candidate will always pay a lot of attention to the opinions and will of her constituency. In Italy, on the contrary, during most of its history, members of the House were elected with a proportional system: the competing parties would present lists of candidates in a large district (often represented by 30 or more members of the House) and would achieve seats based on the proportion of the votes given to the party. In this kind of election, it is very important for the candidates which relative position within the party's list they occupy: the higher up they are, the higher the chances of getting a seat. For the individual candidate, the position in the list can actually matter a lot more than the electoral result of the party. Of course, this situation gives a lot of power to the individuals who are in charge of preparing the lists, the ones who control the party and can thus determine the chances of election of the candidates. In most cases, the Italian citizens had no idea what the name of their representatives were, let alone their biography, inclinations, and voting history.

Shortly before Berlusconi entered into the political arena, the system had been dysfunctional for many years. The first clear sign that the parties were no longer able to represent societal needs effectively manifested in the 70s, when a referendum was set to establish whether Italy would introduce divorce legalization. The Christian Democrats strongly campaigned against it but lost, making it evident that the society, on certain issues, was less conservative than its leaders. A series of elections shortly afterward clearly indicated that a large percentage of voters were unsatisfied with the ruling party and seemed to consider the possibility of having the communists (who, in the meanwhile, had distanced themselves from the Soviets) in power. The problem, however, was not only the corruption of the Christian Democrats, but, rather, with the overall system of representation. The party system may have worked well in the aftermath of the war when a population still largely rural, relatively poor, and with a high percentage of illiteracy, could benefit from being oriented by the political elites. But by the end of the 70s, the situation was completely different: Italy had closed the gap with other industrialized countries in terms of per-capita income and human development, voters were much more informed and independent and resented a political elite that seemed very distant from the needs of the society. Especially the citizens from the highly industrialized North.

In these years many academics and the most enlightened politicians saw that the country needed a radical institutional reform, possibly of a kind similar to the one France had introduced in 1958 when a presidential republic had replaced a party system virtually indistinguishable to that of Italy. However, besides the fact that there seemed to be no Charles De Gaulle in Italy during those years, after the experience of fascism the country was wary of empowering a single individual with the executive branch and no reform was ever even tried. In the mid-90s, when

Berlusconi founded his party, there was a great divide between society and the political class. The common perception was that politicians did not properly represent anyone but themselves, public services were considered inefficient and inadequate, while taxes were high and unevenly distributed. Moreover, the traditional parties in Italy were nothing like the GOP or the Democrats in the US, where these organizations play a major role mainly during the political campaigns but have no large permanent staff. In Italy, the parties were big organizations, with millions of members, offices all through the country, significant assets and thousands of employees. According to an estimate, about one million people, out of a workforce of about 20, were professionally dedicated to politics in the 90s, draining significant resources from the society.

* * *

From the point of view of a European, some elements of the American political debate are puzzling and many of the issues that contribute to the ideological polarization between left and right in the American political debate are nearly absent from Italy, or, in fact, from virtually all European countries. It is the mostly certain positions of the Republican Party that seem so distant from the values of the old continent, particularly in the last few years. Such things as universal health care, gun control, environmental protection regulations are widely considered no brainers by nearly all European politicians, on all sides of the political spectrum, and, unlike in America, they are not so ideologically charged. While it is possible to listen to a few European politicians argue for the prohibition of abortion, this is largely regarded as an extreme position. In the same way, virtually no one advocates for abrogating gun control, or public health-care, or against the need to protect the environment from global warming. It may appear almost a paradox, but many right-leaning parties in Europe could be regarded as positioned to the left of the US Democrats on many issues: labor laws, health care, unemployment subsidies, criminal justice, gun control, and many others. Another difference between the American political debate and the Italian one is that, while in the US most of the weight of the evangelicals appears to be on the side of the conservatives, in Italy it is historically more evenly divided between the right and the left. Overall, the influence of organized religion appears to be much more significant in the US than in Europe.

Another peculiarity of the US within the contemporary mature economies is the low amount of taxes, particularly income taxes on the richest individuals, which corresponds to the relatively low level of public expenditure on entitlements such as, again, health care, unemployment subsidies, childcare, retirement plans, and the sort. Such lower wealth redistribution is consistent with the philosophy of small government traditionally supported by Republicans. What appears to be extraordinary is that this party has been able to achieve competitive electoral results even though, given the current US distribution of wealth, most voters seem to have a specific interest in raising the taxes of the wealthiest individuals and, accordingly, being able to fund social programs that may benefit them and their families.

The central thesis of a book published over a decade ago, "What's the matter with Kansas?" (published in Great Britain under the title "What's the matter with America") was precisely this apparent paradox: why would a substantial part of the electorate accept economic policies that seem contrary to their interest? The answer that the author provided, in short, was that many voters cared more about certain cultural issues and were ready to overlook their immediate economic wellbeing so long as they could get satisfaction on other things. What things exactly? A political marketing consultant might suggest calling them the three "Rs" of the Republicans: religion, rifles, and race. Starting with the last one, cultural resentment linked to ethnicity is by no means restricted to the US. Many European countries (and non-European ones, such as Australia) have seen an increasing percentage of their population raising concern, especially in the last few years, about the significant flow of immigrants from Africa and other areas of the world with different religions and cultural values. What is peculiar to the US is the historical presence of a large part of the population of non-European descent and the fact that part of the white population, especially in the states of the South, apparently still has a problem with it. After the civil rights acts of the 60s and the development of the "Southern strategy" by Republicans, associated with the loss of a huge portion of its electorate by the Democrats in the South, it has become apparent, particularly during the Obama presidency, that the problem is still not completely solved and that this phenomenon is still politically exploitable. After all, it had a non-secondary role in allowing Trump, a promoter of the birther movement, to become president. In different ways, usually by recurring to dog-whistle messages, more rarely by dubious or almost openly racist statements, certain Republicans manage to maintain this part of the electorate on the party's side. The same is true for the second "R," guns. While a number of Democratic senators and representatives often argue in favor of the right to bear arms, and against some bills designed to limit it, gun enthusiasts generally know that their go-to party is the GOP, with its "special relationship" with the National Rifle Association. The last "R" stands for religion. Within the West, a significant presence of evangelicals is another distinctive element of the society of the US, especially in connection with a number of political issues about which evangelicals hold very strong views. Abortion is not a frequent subject of debate in most European countries, while it certainly is in many states of the Union, where Republican administrations have challenged the Supreme Court with measures enacted with the evident purpose of restricting the practice of abortion. Another aspect of religious influence that is very difficult to detect in Europe is the presence of literal biblical traditions in the education system: while there are several religious schools and universities in Italy as in other neighboring countries, nobody thinks of proposing creationism as an alternative to evolution as a scientific theory. According to many scholars and observers of society, the presence of a strong evangelical element in US society is associated with a current of anti-intellectualism that supports a widespread suspicion of universities, often seen as liberal indoctrination machines to the detriment of religious values.

It has been argued[1] that the thesis of the author of "What's the matter with Kansas" is not really confirmed by available statistics and voters' demographics: it turns out that if you measure the split of working-class votes in the political divide during the last decades, there has not been a shift from the Democrats to the GOP. However, one could point out that the cultural issues used by the Republicans for electoral purposes may have prevented a further loss of votes within the low-income voters; the mere fact that about half of the working class in many states keeps voting Republican, possibly against their economic interests, still requires an explanation. Regardless, and maybe more importantly, when identifying the voters most likely to be attracted by the arguments of the GOP, the most significant demographic factor could be the level of education rather than income. You might expect those voters with lower analytical capabilities to trade the three "Rs" in exchange for economic policies that may benefit them when picking their candidate. In this regard the shift has been remarkable: up until the sixties, most college graduates voted Republican; nowadays the situation is wholly reversed. In the last congressional elections, while white men voted Republican 60 percent to 39 percent and white women were split even 49 percent to 49 percent, white men without a college degree voted republican 66 percent to 32 percent and white women with no college degree 56 percent to 42 percent.[2]

Of course, all this is common knowledge among the politics practitioners and, while it is seldom debated within the conservative circles, for obvious reasons, liberals often raise it in columns and TV shows. Usually, the conclusion goes something like this: "OK, but we are not going to get the votes of blue-collar, poorly educated whites from the fly-over country by looking down on them and explaining how irrational they are." This is both true and a rather resignedly way to deal with a problem, but it may be something that the left has in common on both sides of the Atlantic: much lower self-confidence than the right in its ability to shape the public discourse and change the opinion of voters. Both Trump and Berlusconi are masters in this regard.

Nevertheless, if the "What's the matter with Kansas" interpretations were correct, the GOP would have probably boxed itself in a long-term losing strategy with no obvious exit. On one side, it is building a base largely made of demographics that are shrinking: white voters, older ones, the less educated. On the other, it is distancing itself from the part of society that is more intellectually and economically dynamic: Hillary Clinton was not wrong when she said that, in 2016, she got the votes of districts representing two-thirds of the GDP. Republicans often complain that the mainstream media, as well as a substantial majority of the academic world, appear closer to the values of Democrats; they should not be surprised that most of the intellectuals are not fond of anti-intellectualism. After the 2012 presidential election, the Republican establishment seemed aware of the problem and the "autopsy" that the party produced illustrated very clearly that it should change course in order to increase its appeal to minorities, women, younger voters... then Trump came and won doing exactly the opposite. There are many signs, however, that while Trump led the party to victory in 2016 (though, it is important to keep in mind, Hillary still won the popular vote by a significant margin), his electoral and positioning strategy may be a disaster for the party in the future, as it exacerbates many of the problems the GOP already had. This, of course, may be a concern for the party much more than for the 74-year-old leader.

If a significant decline of the Republican votes would be a problem for the party, it probably would not be healthy for the country overall. What would take the GOP's place? In the wake of the 1994 Italian elections, the ones that led to Berlusconi's first government, a well-known political science scholar, Norberto Bobbio, wrote a small book[3] about the essence of the left and right of the political spectrum as it developed historically in the Western political tradition. Bobbio plausibly associated the left with the principle of equality. In this way, for example, we can affirm that eighteenth and nineteenth-century liberals were to the left of absolutists for believing in *equal* rights for all citizens. Or that socialists were to the left of liberals for their struggle toward economic *equality*, or that European social-democrats were on the left side of the political spectrum because of their policy toward a robust welfare state as a means to reduce income *inequalities*. While this definition seems to work reasonably well for the left, it does not follow that the right should be automatically associated with its opposite; in fact, that would sound unfair: the right certainly did not consistently stand for inequality. So what is the basic and general aim of the political right? It can be argued, at least with reference to the modern right in Western countries, that the central value is personal responsibility.

Personal responsibility is an extremely important principle in policy-making, particularly in the US, where this concept has deep cultural roots, stemming, possibly, from the historical experience of the first communities of immigrants in America, who had to rely largely on themselves to a higher degree than individual Europeans in order to survive and thrive. The same could be said of the pioneers who colonized the western frontiers throughout part of US history. This may also be the single cultural feature that most helps to explain the extraordinary success of the US in the generation of wealth, knowledge, innovation, and culture in the last century or so. The significance of the principle of personal responsibility may be a major factor in explaining why the center of the political spectrum in the US appears somewhat shifted to the right in comparison with most European countries. Not only Republicans but also many Democrats, possibly a large majority of them in fact, would look with disapproval at many of the labor protection policies that both the left and the right implemented in Europe in the 70s and 80s.

A case can be made that both Berlusconi and Trump impersonate living violations of the principle of personal responsibility. In fact, their whole lives, before and after they entered the political arena, are a demonstration of how, under certain circumstances, a refusal of being responsible and accountable for one's own actions and statements can still pay, as their financial and political fortunes testify. This would provide a clear explanation for why some of the fiercest antagonists of these two leaders, in the US as well as in Italy, have been and are conservatives of the purest breed. One characteristic feature of Trump and Berlusconi is their apparent complacency when saying the most outrageous things and, when confronted with arguments pointing to the unreasonableness of their statements, their doubling down on them. As if they derived satisfaction from the expression of their power, intended as the absence of restraints. Of course, they make outrageous statements because they can, and they can because their political base allows them to. In fact, the base seems to largely enjoy the unconventional and provocative rhetoric of the two leaders. That same base that is ready to justify and rationalize any corrupt act, any lie, and any misleading or offensive pronouncement, apparently suspending their critical thinking and accepting implausible, even bizarre arguments. Why do they?

Part of the answer could be the attack on political correctness that Trump and Berlusconi brought to the political discourse. After years of having to exercise restraint on their opinions concerning such things as minority rights, the role of women in society, and the like, many voters certainly welcomed someone who could voice their point of view publicly and loudly. But there may be another significant element to explain the bond between the two leaders and their loyal base, largely skewed toward the poorly educated: their wealth and power notwithstanding, in a certain way they are not really part of the elite. Berlusconi and his new money, with his manners of a TV loud-speaking salesman, was never really accepted in the traditional clubs of the Italian industrial and financial aristocracy; he was tolerated at times, especially when he achieved political power, but never fully integrated. The same can be said of Trump: his self-centered aggressiveness and vulgarity did not play well with many members of the economic and cultural establishment. Therefore, in a quite paradoxical way, even if they are technically part of their countries' ruling class, they are not elite in a perhaps more profound way. This gives them the extraordinary advantage that they can attack the elite and not be perceived to be hypocrites: their attacks seem, and, at least in part probably are, genuine. Their supporters sense it and respond to it; especially those voters tired of listening to members of the cultural elite (people like actors, journalists, academics) telling them what to say and what not to say and think, how to behave.

* * *

The following chapters explore how the political actions of Berlusconi and Trump have an impact in their country, in the presence of different institutions and different political cultures. If Italy's experience with Berlusconi is any predictor of what will happen in the US with Trump, the news is not very good. Italy's political system was far from perfect before Berlusconi became the central political figure, but his "descent" into the political arena certainly made things worse. Today's Italy is struggling with economic stagnation and with a highly dysfunctional political system where nobody seems to find a way to introduce the institutional reforms that would be necessary to reverse the current course.

The idea of comparing empowered individuals such as presidents, kings or military commanders as a means to better understand the societies where they operated is quite ancient and has possibly its best-known practitioner in first century AD historian Plutarch. Having lived and worked as a public servant in both Greece and Rome, Plutarch could use a very good knowledge of the institutions as well as the political culture of both to better study and describe the deeds of the statesmen, in pairs, one from each of these two ancient civilizations he chose to compare in his "Parallel Lives." One of the criticisms of Plutarch's main work is the excess to which the ancient historian emphasized the similarities between the Greek and Roman personalities he described. The idea in the following chapters is to highlight both differences and similarities; but mainly to understand how a related political phenomenon could take place in two countries that are similar enough to make the comparison meaningful, but with the necessary differences to render it interesting, and try to extract some lessons and some suggestion to study this phenomenon further.

Chapter 1

Life before politics. The enthusiastic salesman and the ambitious deal-seeker

When New York Times reporter Nick Tosches asked convict Michele Sindona which banks the mafia uses, the answer was: "this is a dangerous question. In Sicily the Banco di Sicilia, sometimes. In Milan a small bank in Piazza Mercanti."[1] The small bank in Milan was the Banca Rasini, where Luigi Berlusconi, Silvio's father, had spent most of his career as a clerk and then as director. Sindona knew a thing or two about the mafia, and about international financial dealings of all sorts as well. Born and raised in Sicily, he moved to Milan where he quickly became a prominent financial consultant. In the 60s he managed to purchase a bank, the Banca Privata Italiana, together with other financial institutions and companies of various kinds, in Italy and abroad. In 1972 he sought to expand his business in the US and, while also establishing significant connections with the Republican Party of Richard Nixon, bought the Franlin National Bank of Long Island, one of the largest American financial corporations. By that time, the Italian central bank was already investigating Sindona's business and, after detecting several wrongdoings, ordered an independent official to step in and shut down his bank. Soon enough, mismanagement of Sindona's operations became evident also in the US: the Frankiln Bank had been granted a loan by the Federal Reserve but went bust shortly afterward in one of the biggest financial bankruptcy schemes in US history. By the end of the decade, the executive nominated to run Sindona's Italian bank, Giorgio Ambrosoli, an honest public servant who would refuse repeated attempts to bribe him and resisted various threats, was murdered. A few years afterward, shortly after the interview with the Times reporter, Sindona himself died by poison while in prison.

The Rasini bank may provide a possible explanation for one of the biggest mysteries in Italy's recent history: the origins of Mr Berlusconi's fortune, or at least the sources of the initial funding of his entrepreneurial activities. Until the early 80s, most corporations that Berlusconi controlled were owned by other corporations, owned by tens of other entities, in turn, owned by corporations in Switzerland or other countries where corporate confidentiality was taken very seriously. In some other cases, the corporations were owned by Berlusconi's relatives, or employees, or accountants he hired; occasionally even unwittingly. Another recurrent feature of Berlusconi's early business dealings were the cash payments, even for large amounts of money. Sometimes capital stocks of corporations would be paid for through cash deposits in the checking accounts of the company, often for millions of dollars. Later, during the 90s, the funding of many of his companies was thoroughly investigated but it was impossible to establish the ultimate origins of the funds. It is very hard to explain the lengths to which Berlusconi went in creating tens or hundreds of corporations, often with offshore owners, other than with the intention of hiding the actual origin of the funds and the identity of the owners.

Berlusconi dedicated the first part of his entrepreneurial career to real estate development in his city, Milan. One significant aspect of his early business activity, besides the inclination toward little transparency, is his association with Marcello Dell'Utri, a Sicilian who had moved to Milan while maintaining close ties to his home town, including his acquaintance with many shady characters, often deep into the mafia. This gentleman, who years later will repeatedly become a member of Parliament for Berlusconi's party, will also be indicted and convicted for mafia-related crimes, but was never abandoned by his former boss, who knows and values loyalty. Dell'Utri is also the person who introduced Berlusconi to a prominent mafia boss, Vittorio Mangano, convicted of multiple murders. Mangano was hired (officially to maintain the estate stables) and lived in Berlusconi's estate in Arcore, close to Milan, before being arrested on organized crime charges.

Another early business associate of Berlusconi's was Umberto Previti, a Rome attorney who will be convicted and sent to prison much later for bribing magistrates on behalf of Berlusconi's corporations. The two met as Previti was the lawyer of Countess Casati-Stampa, the owner of the Arcore villa that Berlusconi was interested in buying. According to many accounts, Previti tricked his heiress employer into selling the estate for a ridiculously low price.[2] It appears that Berlusconi was quite effective in convincing people to join his side: in 1979 Massimo Berruti, a young officer of the Guardia di Finanza, a law enforcement agency that deals mainly with tax crimes, was in charge of an inspection at Edilnord, the real estate company controlled by Berlusconi. Asked why he had granted a guarantee to the corporation, which according to the bylaws was owned by residents of Switzerland, Berlusconi stated he was just a consultant. The auditing did not find any wrongdoing, but shortly afterward Berruti left his government job and quickly became a high executive of the Berlusconi group and, years later, a member of Parliament in Forza Italia.

One of the most significant moves by Berlusconi before entering the political arena was probably joining the Propaganda 2, a masonry lodge that was at the center of some of Italy's biggest corruption scandals between the late 70s and early 80s. Masonry was quite significant in Italy in the nineteenth and early twentieth centuries; it had a role in promoting Italian unity and nationalism, often in contrast with the Pope and Catholicism, and in 1915 masons contributed in pressuring the Italian government into World War I. The P2 lodge, however, had special features of its own. Its founder, for starters, was quite a character: Licio Gelli, a volunteer in the fascist military units that went to fight in the Spanish civil war alongside General Franco, later joined Mussolini's Republica Sociale Italiana and played a role as a government agent. However, before the end of the war, he also sided with the anti-fascist partisans and it is not completely clear where he stood. In later years, he described himself as a fascist and anti-communist but was also suspected, at times, of being an agent for the Soviets and the CIA. In the 60s he joined the Italian masonry and then created his own group, the Propaganda 2. Somehow he managed to recruit hundreds of prominent politicians from all parties except the communists: high-ranking officers from the armed forces and the secret services, corporate executives, journalists, bankers, judges, and government officials. In 1981 the prosecutors from Milan who were investigating Sindona ordered a search of Gelli's villa and found the list of members of P2. The list was given to the government and later, amid press rumors, made public. As the Italian constitution bans secret associations, as was the case with Gelli's lodge, participation in it was immediately considered a violation of norms and law, though not a specific crime. The individuals involved and their political orientation suggested immediately that it was an organization of conservative ideology, if not outright authoritarian, most likely with an anti-communist agenda. The P2 political leaning was confirmed a few months later, when Gelli's daughter was found with documents that showed the lodge's program to reshape the Italian institutions in a conservative direction and push back the communists. The press, of course, was all over the P2 as it looked like a secret association of powerful individuals out of a conspiracy theory novel, but it was real nonetheless. Soon enough, it became apparent that the lodge and many of its members were at the center of numerous corruption scandals and right-wing terrorism episodes, such as the bombing of the Bologna railway station in 1980, which caused more than 80 deaths. Among the members of the P2 was the entrepreneur Silvio Berlusconi.

What was he doing there? In light of his political positioning in later years, it is not surprising to see him in a group of anti-communist activists. Until then however, he had not shown any particular political interest outside the contacts with local officers he needed for building licenses or other business-related issues. When he was questioned by the prosecutors regarding his joining and role in the lodge, he downplayed it, saying he did not regard it as significant and that he didn't remember even paying the required membership fee. However, its political orientation notwithstanding, the lodge was also a place where important people could be met and business deals be done. Among the members, for instance, were a couple of officers of pension funds that owned significant real estate properties, sometimes hundreds or even thousands of apartments and buildings. It turned out that many of Berlusconi's most significant deals in the 70s were done with state-owned enterprises controlled by members of the P2. But the secret network benefited Berlusconi in a second important way: after the unearthing of the lodge, a congressional investigation found that the loans granted to Berlusconi's companies by the Monte dei Paschi di Siena, one of the most ancient banks of the world, were of extraordinary size and exposure risk. The managing director of the bank, of course, appeared in the list of members of the P2 found by the prosecutors.[3] Membership of the masonry lodge also caused Berlusconi's first publicly exposed misstep with the justice system as he was found guilty of lying under oath (he then benefited from an amnesty).

Berlusconi's contacts and friendships in high places were also a major factor in his ability to develop his TV and entertainment business. Until the 70s, the only entity that could legally air its programs was thought to be the state-owned Radiotelevisione Italiana (RAI), which had started its broadcasting back in the 50s. By the mid-70s, however, a sentence of the Constitutional Court established that radios could broadcast at a local level while

Parliament should pass a law to regulate private broadcasting companies at a national level as well as appropriate licensing by the state. Quickly, hundreds of "free" radio stations were set up all over the country and soon enough they were joined by local television channels. Berlusconi at first set up a TV channel to serve an area of Milan where he had real estate interest. But soon he had a better idea: he bought or associated other small TV stations to form a real network that covered a significant part of the country. He would prepare all sorts of entertainment programs and distribute the recordings among the stations of the network so that they would broadcast them roughly at the same time and create the effect of a national channel, even though he was bending the rules that banned national broadcasts. He also purchased successful programs in the US, such as the soap opera *Dallas*, and produced new ones on his own, especially quiz shows that would feature famous hosts, very popular with the Italian public. Other entrepreneurs appreciated the idea and two additional national networks, set up by established publishing corporations, joined in the private broadcasting business. But Berlusconi had powerful allies, particularly Bettino Craxi, the young leader of the Socialist Party, and, starting in 1983, the head of the executive branch. His friendship would grant Berlusconi significant help in terms of favorable legislation but also, most likely, financially: later investigations discovered that the socialist-controlled Banca Nazionale del Lavoro would grant extremely generous loans to the tycoon, even against regular practices.[4] The other two broadcasting companies, struggling with debts, eventually sold their channels to Berlusconi, who became the owner and monopolist of the national private Italian television. There was, however, a legal problem: the ban to broadcast nationally. It was quickly solved thanks to a decree signed by Craxi that allowed the three networks to continue their activity and, later, by a controversial law voted for by Parliament that essentially froze the status quo. Five ministers, all from the left of the Christian Democratic Party, resigned as a reaction to the coalition parties forcing a vote on this bill. But it was passed nonetheless and it preserved the role of Berlusconi as the sole owner of national private television for years to come (parts of the law were later found to be unconstitutional by Italy's Constitutional Court, and the legal battle continued for years).

* * *

Many of the elements of Berlusconi's career as an entrepreneur also characterize Donald Trump's rise to prominence in the business world: a heavy reliance on cronyism, a proclivity to bending (and occasionally breaking) the rules, the adoption of a rather low ethical bar in the pursuit of their objectives. However, a big difference is that Berlusconi couldn't count on family money at the beginning of his career. Donald Trump's frequent claims that he built an economic empire by himself relying only on a "small" loan from his father of 1 million dollars has been abundantly debunked. We know Trump started receiving money from his father's companies by the time he was a toddler and during the years he used family funds to bail out of difficult financial situations. His father Fred, however, had indeed built a significant fortune and though he may have inherited some properties and cash (his father, Donald's grandfather, who immigrated to the US from Germany, was an adventurous entrepreneur and set up businesses, often successfully, in many places), he was enough of a skilled entrepreneur to create one of the largest real estate empires in the US from his New York base. Fred's recipe for success, based on all available reporting and biographies, included a lot of hard work, a rather frugal lifestyle, and a heavy reliance on political connections and cronyism in general, together with significant investments in lawyers and accountants to assist him in lawsuits and occasionally protect him from governmental investigations.

One thing Fred had in common with Berlusconi's style of setting up business entities was the lengths he went to in order to create a web of companies with the evident purpose of either distracting the funneling of money in certain directions or avoiding, if not outright evading, taxes. In an instance narrated by Michael D'Antonio in his Trump biography, he reports a testimony of Fred before the New York Commission of Investigations, and shows he would create corporations for the only purpose of shifting profits from one entity to the other: one of Fred's corporations, for example, would purchase building machinery and tools and then lease the same items to another Trump company for a much higher price ("a truck valued at $2,600 rented for $21,000").[5] These testimonies also demonstrate how easily Fred would change his official version of things when needed, with little regard for consistency. This modus operandi within the Trump family was largely confirmed many years later by The New York Times report on the Trumps' financial dealings:

President Trump participated in dubious tax schemes during the 1990s, including instances of outright fraud, that greatly increased the fortune he received from his parents, an investigation by The New York Times has found…Much of this money came to Mr Trump because he helped his parents dodge taxes. He and his siblings set up a sham corporation to disguise millions of dollars in gifts from their parents, records and interviews show. Records indicate that Mr Trump helped his father take improper tax deductions worth millions more. He also helped formulate a strategy to undervalue his parents' real estate holdings by hundreds of millions of dollars on tax returns, sharply reducing the tax bill when those properties were transferred to him and his siblings.[6]

Among the values that Fred seems to have passed on to his son is the importance of conducting business in an aggressive fashion and without being distracted by scruples, which is apparently what distanced him from Donald's older brother:

> Fred Jr., seven and a half years older than Donald, had also worked for his father after college. It did not go well, relatives and former employees said in interviews. Fred Trump openly ridiculed him for being too nice, too soft, too lazy, too fond of drink. He frowned on his interests in flying and music, could not fathom why he cared so little for the family business. Donald, witness to his father's deepening disappointment, fashioned himself Fred Jr.'s opposite—the brash tough guy with a killer instinct. His reward was to inherit his father's dynastic dreams.[7]

In one of the first journalistic portraits of Donald, in 1981, People magazine reports a statement of his: "Man is the most vicious of all animals," he notes, "and life is a series of battles ending in victory or defeat. You just can't let people make a sucker out of you."[8] Such a world view would probably find the approval of Roy Cohn, the New York lawyer and formerly an aid for Senator Joseph McCarthy, very close to Trump, and someone who apparently had a deep influence on him as his mentor during the early business dealings of Donald in the 70s. In 1973, when the Trumps were accused of violating the Fair Housing Act by discriminating against African-Americans who sought to lease their apartments, Cohn was the attorney who countersued the government in a typical Cohn-Trump legal move: never give an inch, never admit wrongdoing, play the victim, counterattack whenever possible. "'Roy,' according to an attorney in his office, 'couldn't have given less of a shit about the rules'...He didn't pay his bills, all but daring his creditor to sue him for what he owed—tailors, blacksmiths, mechanics, travel agencies, storage companies, credit card companies, stationery stores, office supply stores. He didn't pay people back, 'friend or foe,' wrote his biographer Nicholas Von Hoffman."[9] Besides a cynical conception of life, Trump seems to have picked up another of this character's features: his ability to achieve actual results without focusing on analysis and hard work on a given matter, but rather by concentrating on the public representation of his point of view, and whining while using threats and bullying tactics.

> As a litigator, Cohn had eaned a reputation as 'an intimidator and a bluffer' attorney Arthur Liman would write, 'famous among lawyers for winning cases by delays, evasions and lies.' He was unorganized and largely disinterested in specifics, relying less on preparation and more on belligerence and his vast, nonpareil network of social connections that spanned and stretched from New York pay-to-play clubhouses to the backrooms of Washington as well as the Oval Office[10]

Cohn was eventually disbarred a few years later, but his peculiar way of practicing the law seemed to pay off for quite a long time: he was extremely influential in New York and he made a fortune as an attorney.

While Donald's claim to be a self-made man is clearly not credible, considering the amount of wealth he was given or inherited, his record as a businessman is mixed at best. The many enterprises that went wrong, such as the Trump airline, his bankrupted casinos, Trump University, hardly suggest developed management skills. Actually, the business activity that Trump seems to be passionate about is negotiating, *deal-making* as the title of his most famous book goes. His negotiating skills as an entrepreneur are not easy to evaluate with the information publicly available: based on what we know, however, his style seems to rely heavily on threats, bullying, and a lot of bluffing, at times in a rather ineffective way. In the 90s, after the failure of many of his projects, he had a hard time convincing anyone into financing his companies. As Alan Lapidus, Trump's former long-time architect, declared to the magazine Foreign Policy, based on his knowledge of the internal workings of the organization, in the aftermath of Trump's earlier financial troubles "he could not get anybody in the United States to lend him anything. It was all coming out of Russia. His involvement with Russia was deeper than he's acknowledged."[11] A skill that he seems to possess, however, is self-promotion and personal brand building. He adopts a style that involves frequently misleading and outright lying, such as calling reporters pretending to be a spokesperson for himself to promote his image, or saying that his new Manhattan building has 68 stories while it really only has 58, or trying to defend his refusal to maintain his pledge to preserve a work of art when demolishing an old building.[12] But the results speak for themselves: he managed to become a star entrepreneur, a celebrity TV host, and President of the United States.

Something that Trump had in common with Berlusconi during his business career is his apparent carelessness in choosing associates and partners, having no problems engaging in deals with shady individuals, even with ties to organized crime: from John Cody, the construction union boss convicted on racketeering charges and a friend of Roy Cohn's, to Felix Sater, a Russian-born entrepreneur linked to Russian crime and also convicted of racketeering (Sater's company, Bayrock Group, was a partner of Trump's in the building of Trump SoHo, in lower Manhattan). Trump's availability to deal with controversial individuals does not stop with corrupted oligarchs, especially from former Soviet republics: several civil lawsuits filed in different US cities allege that a Kazakh official laundered money by buying units of Trump SoHo. A Trump-branded condo in South Florida was largely purchased by Russian nationals and a Ukraine citizen involved in a money-laundering scheme. In another instance, the Trump organization closed a deal with the family of Ziya Mammadov of Azerbaijan, known as a corrupt politician. The money of dubious origins from other parts of the world was not neglected either:

> In Vancouver, the Trump Organization partnered with the son of Tony Tiah Thee Kian, a Malaysian oligarch who was convicted of providing false reports to the Kuala Lumpur stock exchange. That project, which was guided by Ivanka Trump and is one of the few Trump-branded properties to open since Mr Trump took office, became the subject of an FBI counterintelligence inquiry, according to CNN.[13]

The sales of the Trump Ocean Club International Hotel and Tower in Panama were mostly handled by Alexandre Ventura Nogueira, who worked with a Colombian national who was later convicted of money laundering. "Mr Nogueira told NBC News last year that he sold about half of his Trump condos to Russians, including some connected to the Russian mafia, and that some of his clients had 'questionable backgrounds.'"[14]

* * *

Based on these summarized accounts of the lives of Berlusconi and Trump, a few of the traits the two leaders seem to have in common may have significantly impacted their later actions as politicians. The first common feature seems to be a deep urge to succeed and the employment of all possible means to reach this goal. This urge, in both cases, was initially directed toward the business world, where the main standard of success is the ability to make profits. In this regard Berlusconi seems to have been the more effective of the two: he couldn't count on family money and, at first, as far as we know, on strong political connections, but he was able to create and develop companies that proved extremely successful in time. Nevertheless, there are quite a few unanswered questions regarding the original financing of his companies and the heavy reliance on political and social connections to boost his business. In the case of Trump, there are many reasons to doubt his management skills: his failed businesses, the reliance on family money for bailouts, his continuous lying, and hiding his actual worth. It is quite evident, however, that his self-promoting tactics and media manipulation worked with many people, and were what enabled him to build a public persona that would ultimately allow him to run for the highest office and even win.

Another common feature in the modus operandi of these two entrepreneurs appears to be shamelessness. That is, the ability to say or defend even really implausible things that they believe may work in their favor without any apparent restraint whatsoever. Most people, especially in public, tend to be careful about their statements, about being, or at least appearing, consistent and truthful. Even if one does not feel the moral imperative to not deceive his fellow humans, she or he usually wants to preserve her reputation in the belief that it is worthwhile to maintain credibility, that people will believe her in the future. On the contrary, Trump has no problem calling a newspaper pretending to be a PR guy to promote his playboy skills and Berlusconi could innocently pose as the successful owner of a real estate company for the press one day and deny any actual responsibility for the same company the next day when inspected by the tax authorities or other government agencies. Surprisingly, it worked, at least in their case. According to a journalist who knew him quite well, Berlusconi could tell any kind of story in defending his position and give the impression to his beholder that he really believed what he was defending, no matter how implausible. Trump seems able to stimulate a very similar mechanism. It is often difficult to guess whether it is a studied act or if it is a natural, instinctive predisposition. Shame is a human state of mind that is closely connected to ethics. Although shame can be triggered by different situations, in many, possibly most, cases, one feels ashamed when exposed over the violation of an accepted norm of behavior. According to scholars who study emotions, in many social situations, it is possible to envision:

> shame as a kind of gauge, compass or buffer that bolsters and protects a person's core moral self. For both Rawls and Taylor, never feeling ashamed indicates a person's lack of commitment to or recognition of different value schemes and hence a lack of certain crucial moral attitudes one may take toward oneself (such as self-respect or self-esteem). Our intuition about the sociopath or some other shameless person who cannot feel shame supports such accounts. We regard such sociopaths as dangerous, as incapable of internalizing moral standards, as impervious to community sentiments about moral norms...Feeling ashamed may warn us that we risk losing the esteem of others...[15]

Such a state of mind seems to be absent in Trump and Berlusconi and this enables them to make any kind of self-serving statement they see fit, without any regard for facts. Trump, based on some public statements, seems at times to simply be unaware that certain behaviors are commonly considered unethical, for instance when asked by TV host Stephanopoulos about whether someone should be warning the FBI in case a foreign agent offers dirt on his political opponent, he says, seemingly surprised, "...nobody goes to the FBI..." In another instance, as National Review's Mona Charen wrote, Trump:

> ...may not even fully grasp the difference between corruption and honesty. After spending several minutes denying that he did anything to pressure the Ukrainian president, and

calling such allegations a "witch-hunt" and a "hoax," he cited something that he claimed the news media "refuse to report on." This was a May 2018 letter sent to Ukraine's prosecutor general by three Democratic senators, Patrick Leahy, Bob Menendez, and Richard Durbin. The letter, the president alleged, "expressed concern about the closing of four investigations they said were critical. In the letter they implied that their support for US assistance to Ukraine was at stake, and that if they didn't do the right thing, they wouldn't get any assistance. Gee! Doesn't that sound familiar? Doesn't that sound familiar?" It does, but the letter doesn't support Trump's version. The senators' missive (reported out by CNN, incidentally) concerned reports that Yuri Lutsenko, the former prosecutor general, was blocking anti-corruption probes, including Robert Mueller's investigation. That was the topic the senators addressed, and in no way, shape, or form did they do so in the mafia-don style that Trump himself employs so frequently, and demonstrated with President Zelensky. They never said or even implied that US assistance to Ukraine was at stake. They wrote, "As strong advocates for a robust and close relationship with Ukraine, we believe that our cooperation should extend to such legal matters, regardless of politics. Ours is a relationship built on a foundation of respect for the rule of law and accountable democratic institutions."[16]

Psychiatrist Drew Westen has a similar opinion:

The reality is that Trump seems simply unable to understand that anything he does is wrong. I am writing now with my other hat, as a psychiatric diagnostician. He does not code his words and deeds into true and false, or right and wrong, because he appears to lack the normal capacities for moral emotions such as guilt, remorse, or empathy. To him, as to other malignant narcissists, "good" and "bad" mean "good and bad for me."[17]

It is probably not a coincidence that among the early acquaintances of Trump are some prominent individuals who share his ability to overlook ethical rules in their business or political conduct, such as Roy Cohn. According to Vanity Fair reporter Marie Brenner, who described the "ruthless symbiosis" between the two, "Roy was a master of situational immorality...He worked with a three-dimensional strategy, which was: (1) Never settle, never surrender. (2) Counterattack, countersue immediately. (3) No matter what happens, no matter how deeply into the muck you get, claim victory and never admit defeat."[18] Similar considerations could be made about another long-time associate of Trump, Roger Stone, convicted in relation to the investigation of Special Counsel Robert Mueller, a Republican campaigner for decades and self-defined "dirty trickster." Some of Stone's rules are: "Attack, attack, attack—never defend... Admit nothing, deny everything, launch counterattack."[19] (Another of Stone's rules with which Trump may easily agree is: "The only thing worse in politics than being wrong is being boring.") Another associate of Trump, also indicted (and later convicted for multiple crimes) within the Russia investigation is Paul Manafort, the former chairman of the Republican presidential campaign in 2016, who, not surprisingly, was also a partner of Stone in a rather successful Washington lobbying firm which relied on the participation of another GOP controversial "dirty trickster": Lee Atwater.

What all these persons have in common, besides having been Republican operatives, is that they appear to have chosen a method for conducting business or politics or, in general, any activity, unrestrained by ethical rules to gain effectiveness. It is, after all, a tension that every human has to deal with: how to balance the need to achieve personal advantages, material or otherwise, with the commonly accepted moral standards. It is the well-known distinction proposed by John Rawls between the concept of *rational* and that of *reasonable*, where the *rational*, in line with the traditional theory of action in social sciences, is the drive toward achieving utility for oneself and the *reasonable* describes the attitude of taking into consideration the needs of others and therefore the appropriateness of following certain norms of behavior, which often imply a limit in the pursuit of one's own needs or wants. Individuals may choose to adopt a behavior within a spectrum that goes from strictly abiding by the norms to disregarding them completely. A radical case may be that of criminals, who consciously decide to break laws and norms to achieve some personal advantage. Of course, in all these cases, the choice of disregarding ethical norms may work very well from the individual standpoint, but it doesn't if too many people make the same choice, as society as we know it would simply not function if most of its members did not adhere to norms. It may work, however, for a limited number of "free riders," at least as long as the other members of society allow them.

Both Trump and Berlusconi were exposed to politics since the early stage of their careers as contacts with local government are of paramount importance for a real estate entrepreneur for several rather obvious reasons: development is a highly regulated business in a big city and the government provides licenses and permits. But it also sets long and short-term urban development policies, which can benefit certain companies and hurt others, so campaign contributions can be very important for a builder in determining his fortunes. Of course, the kind of politics the two leaders were exposed to was not really the kind of politics which is instrumental to the development of an idea of how society should be organized. It was rather the struggle for power, the *politique politicienne* as the French call it (in French, as in Italian, there is only one word to translate the two English concepts of "politics" and "policy," so at times it may get quite confusing. The French introduced the expression *politique politicienne* to describe the "lower" aspect of the political struggle, the one that deals not with ideas but raw power, horse-trading, and propaganda).

Another element that Trump and Berlusconi seem to have in common is their apparent resentment of the elite. Money and fame only get you so far in a country's "aristocracy," other things can be as, or even more, important: cultural values, personal charisma, ethical standards, adherence to rules, a family history of dedication to the community, good manners, and taste. This last element, in particular, may have been one that strongly contributed to distancing the two leaders from the traditional elite of their countries. Trump's taste as displayed in his homes has been labeled as "dictator chic." Describing his Trump Tower house in Manhattan, Peter York writes:

> No matter how you looked at it, the main thing this apartment said was, "I am tremendously rich and unthinkably powerful." This was the visual language of public, not private, space. It was the language of the Eastern European and Middle Eastern nouveau riche. Why does all of this matter? Domestic interiors reveal how people want to be seen. But they also reveal something about the owners' inner lives, their cultural reference points and how they relate to other people. With its marble-inlaid dining table, painted ceilings and gold flourishes quite literally everywhere, Trump's aesthetic puts him more in the visual tradition of Turkmenistan President Saparmurat Niyazov...Atop Trump Tower, Trump's apartment projects a kind of power that bypasses all the boring checks and balances of collaboration and mutual responsibility and first-among-equals. It is about a single dominant personality... This, of course, is a startlingly un-American idea[20]

Berlusconi's style was just as ostentatious, if somewhat slightly less flashy, "Berlusconi is an intruder and takes with him a culture of intruder in terms of taste, consumption styles and aesthetics. There is a lot of kitsch, a lot of trash and an infinite series of jokes to characterize his speech patterns and his behavior, all very far from the sophisticated world of old money people."[21] His often vulgar speech patterns and his passion for coarse jokes in public contributed to distancing him from the traditional public behavior of prominent politicians and businessmen. He is also the person who changed TV for millions of Italians, bringing a new style of television programming that, while for many was more entertaining, also brought a wave of vulgarity into the homes of spectators to an extent that did not exist before his channels. As far as Trump is concerned, a typical example of his contrast with what could be termed elite is the story of how he acquired the Mar-a-Lago estate in Palm Beach, Florida, and the conflicts he had no problems in raising to have the county bend to his will. When Trump bought the estate in the 90s it seems that the traditional society of Palm Beach did not exactly welcome him and he was reportedly rejected by the most exclusive club in town. As Mark Seal writes, "There is nothing the old elite hates so much and fears so profoundly as Donald Trump's club,"[22] nevertheless they found themselves overwhelmed with endless lawsuits, a relentless team of lawyers, loud late-night parties, public relations campaigns and a series of "dirty tricks."

At the same time, there are signs that the two entrepreneurs suffer the lack of acceptance from the elite, what possibly constitutes a reason for resenting it, and declaring it "sour grapes." In June 2018, at one of his typical rallies in Minnesota, Trump, as if he were laying on a psychoanalyst's couch, started ranting about the elite and how he has more money and success than the elite, so, he implied, why shouldn't he be the elite. "Why are they elite? I have a much better apartment than they do. I'm smarter than they are. I'm richer than they are. I became president and they didn't…"

Chapter 2

Descending into politics. Looming crises and the ability to seize the moment

If you had asked any political journalist or pundit in early 1993 Italy or 2015 America whether Berlusconi or Trump were on the path to quickly becoming head of the executive branch, most, if not all, answers would have been a dismissive denial. Of course, we now know they would have all been wrong. In both cases these two countries' political systems were going through very particular circumstances that would allow the two leaders to find an improbable path to power. Trump and Berlusconi were very effective in spotting the opportunity and organizing the right communication strategy to exploit it for their benefit. They saw their chance and used their intuition and experience of the establishment of power alliances and the creation of narratives and brands to seize it.

A simple way to assess political systems is to think of their main three essential elements: supply, demand, and institutions, or rules of the game. The last element consists of all the constitutional and ordinary laws, as well as regulations of various sorts, that determine how political entrepreneurs and the society overall interact to empower certain individuals to represent the citizens and to implement policies. The political supply is generally represented by political parties, their elites in particular. Of course, political parties shouldn't be thought of as monolithic entities, particularly in democratic systems, as their dynamics are highly complex and are mostly the result of the interaction of multiple individuals and groups of individuals. But to describe a bird's-eye view of political events, the characterization of a party as a single actor can provide clarity to the model. The political demand is, of course, that of the citizens, the voters in particular: it includes the issues they feel more passionate about, the policies that should be implemented, and a variety of other things according to their view of the world and society. These three elements should be conceived of as highly dynamic: each has the potential to affect the other two to some degree. Laws and regulations, of course, determine how and when citizens may send signals to the elite, by voting, by expressing anger, by participating in a rally or deciding to give a contribution to a candidate; they also provide rules as to how candidates can run in elections, how long they will serve in office, how they are allowed to communicate to the public. It is self-evident that these rules may have a deep impact on the way the parties develop their strategies. On the other hand, the political entrepreneurs who constitute the supply, which includes elected representatives, can usually influence, to varying degrees, the rules of the game, mostly by voting bills into law and shaping agencies' regulations. Some rules, such as those written in the constitution, are more difficult to change. Parties' elites can also strongly influence political demand through their communication strategies. Usually a party, in its attempt to influence the preferences of the citizens, has a lot more agency with those that tend to identify with its general platform rather than others, particularly in the presence of strong loyalty bonds. But even then, that capacity may be limited: if the party goes too far, part of its electorate may change affiliation and switch its preference to a competing party. Political demand has a deep impact on the other two elements: for starters, it selects a significant part of the parties' elite, typically through elections. But in general, the political parties take into account the public's preferences constantly, as they are always competing for approval. All these dynamics were at play in Italy when Berlusconi made his political move.

Berlusconi's first significant public intervention in political affairs was in 1993 when he was asked by a journalist which candidate he would support for Mayor of Rome. He shocked much of the establishment and the public by siding decisively with the candidate of the right. The reason the announcement was found shocking is that the politician he said he would support, Gianfranco Fini, was the head of a party widely considered to have fascist roots: it had been founded as Movimento Sociale Italiano (Italian Social Movement) back in 1946 by a group of former officials and activists of Mussolini's Social Italian Republic, the political entity that had governed northern Italy with the support of Hitler's Germany from 1943 through to 1945. One of the ideological foundations of the new Italian Republic in the aftermath of the war was its anti-fascist spirit which was the glue that held together the Christian Democrats, the communists, and the socialists as well as most of the other parties that represented Italian society after the war. The MSI was effectively ostracized for virtually all the duration of the so-called "First Republic," until the early 90s. Hence, when Berlusconi openly declared support for Fini, most observers were outraged: cartoonists pictured Berlusconi wearing Mussolini's military-style boots and the fez, the traditional hat of the fascist militias. When journalists asked him why he made such a choice, he would point out that, with the new election system for the cities, it came to a binary choice and that the real danger was with the left, the former communists, who may have changed their name but not their illiberal ideology. With that intuition, he positioned himself as the prominent adversary of Italy's political left; hence, as the defender of Italian traditional values. This was possible only because of the recent developments in the Italian political system.

The year 1992 was a crucial one in Italian history. Many of the country's old and unresolved problems were surfacing together creating perhaps the biggest crisis since the end of the war. One aspect of the crisis was economic: for many years, particularly during the 70s and 80s, the administrations practiced very generous spending policies toward the retirement system, health care programs, industrial investments, infrastructures, and many other things. Tax evasion was endemic among small companies and independent professionals and the state never made serious attempts to enforce the law, while no one in government wanted to raise income taxes on employees, who were already probably paying more than their fair share. The consequence was an ever-increasing public debt that, during the 1992 financial crisis, caused the markets to claim increasingly higher interest rates until, at one point, it seemed that they were unable to lend money at all, causing panic among the officials responsible for fiscal and monetary policy, while the lira devalued significantly against most currencies.

A second problem that became manifestly urgent in 1992 was organized crime, particularly in certain regions of the South such as Sicily, home of the mafia. In that year the crime syndicate killed a Christian Democrat, Salvo Lima, probably the most powerful politician on the island and the man who, thanks to the mass of votes he could control, made Giulio Andreotti (later indicted for mafia-related crimes) one of the most powerful individuals in the party, hence in the country. It turns out that in 1992 the Court of Cassation, Italy's highest court of appeal, confirmed the conviction of hundreds of mafia bosses, first among them Mr Toto Riina. Obviously the mafia members were not enthusiastic about the prospect of going to prison and they had apparently been promised a different deal by people in high places, so when the Cassation decided against them, they reacted. A few months after that sentence, the mafia also killed two well-known magistrates who had worked for years to indict the bosses and were among the promoters of the trial that led to their final conviction: Giovanni Falcone and Paolo Borsellino. These last two murders were organized in the most breathtaking way: Falcone, together with his wife and security escort, was killed by hundreds of pounds of explosives that blew up his armored car while he was on his way from Palermo's airport to the city. Borsellino was also the victim of a high-powered bomb set in the middle of Palermo. Italian public opinion was stunned by the degree of violence and unprecedented defiance of the state that the mafia was displaying, while the government looked weak and unable to perform basic tasks, such as finding an agreement between the parties to elect the new President of the Republic, as each party and even different groups within the parties would engage in various negotiations, to either block a candidate or have their own prevail. The Sicilian bombs put an end to all that and Parliament quickly elected an old-school Christian Democrat, Oscar Luigi Scalfaro, a former magistrate widely considered a defender of the rule of law. Organized crime was an old problem for Italy, one that emerged at the very beginning of the Italian state. The fascist regime, which did not tolerate well competitive power centers, managed to at least curb the mafia to a degree in the 20s and 30s, but the bosses rose again with renewed strength after the war and even advocated for Sicilian independence, which was avoided by Rome by granting a special statute of autonomy to the island, included in the constitution. Actually, the mafia, as well as Camorra and 'Ndrangheta (the crime associations in the southern regions of Campania and Calabria), are just one aspect of the larger problem of the Mezzogiorno. This area of the country, since the unification in the 1860s, struggled to keep up with the North in terms of economic and human development. By the founding of Italy, while illiteracy in Piedmont or Lombardy was in line with the European average of about 50 percent, in many areas of the South it reached 90 percent and while, by the turn of the century, the northern regions had significantly narrowed the gap with France and Germany in terms of economic development, the populations of the South had to resort to mass migration to seek better opportunities. During the years of accelerated economic growth, in the 50s and 60s, while the North was on its way to becoming one of the wealthiest regions of the world, the South kept lagging behind, no matter the amounts of public investments that the government would inject into its territory. The result was the transfer of millions of workers and families to the North, especially Milan, Turin, and Genoa, the cities of the so-called "Industrial Triangle." But the gap between these two areas of Italy was not only economic, but also cultural, particularly as it related to the ability to foster what social scientists call social capital; the spreading of organized crime, as well as the economic backwardness, was most likely a symptom of the social capital gap. One of the best studies of the cultural differences between the North and the South of Italy, Robert Putnam's "Making Democracy Work," consists of an assessment of the effectiveness of regional governments during the 70s and 80s and it highlights the enormous gap between the areas of the country as regards the ability of local institutions to solve problems and how the cultural roots of such a gap go way back in time.[1] The difficulty experienced by the society of the South to express an effective elite did not just have negative effects at the local level. In fact, the scarcely dynamic private entrepreneurship in these regions had one major consequence (besides the massive migration of workforce to the industrial regions of the North): a strong overrepresentation of southerners in public employment, which created a sort of division of labor between the two areas of the country in which the people of the North would carry on the industrial development while the South would largely be responsible for providing human resources for the administration of the state. By the early 90s, the South-North gap had also originated a political backlash: the rise of the Leghe (Leagues), parties that advocated the introduction of strong federalist elements, especially from a fiscal standpoint, to limit the flow of resources from the North to the South. In some cases, the representatives of these parties, which arguably constituted the only significant novelty in Italy's political supply since the dawn of the Republic, supported outright secession: the creation of the state of Padania which would include the northern regions, separated from the rest of the peninsula.

The third element of the 1992 crisis was the unearthing of the corruption schemes that had affected the party system for many years. The public, to some extent, knew that there was corruption in the political system, but the new investigations by the prosecutors in Milan showed that the illegal practices were so widespread and shared by all levels of government and all hierarchies of party officials, that they should be considered systemic. It is important to stress that most of the corruption cases uncovered were not aimed at personally enriching individual politicians, though this may also have happened in many cases (when bribes are paid it is not easy to account for their final use). A lot, possibly most, of the money collected by party officials was used to fund the party itself: maintain its staff, advertising for electoral campaigns, and so on. One of the most recurrent crimes prosecuted in the operation "Clean Hands," as the press called it, was illicit party financing when entrepreneurs or managers would give money to a party without the declarations required by law. Just like the mafia for the Mezzogiorno issue, the corruption charges of so many politicians were the symptom of a larger problem: the inadequacy of the institutional system to properly represent the people and propose and implement policies of modernization of the state and its society. The combined effect of the parliamentary system and the proportional electoral law ensured that the parties were the empowered entities, largely without accountability. The constitution put Parliament at the center of the system: any executive depended on the will of the Senate and, especially, the House of Deputies, that were called to grant a confidence vote in the ministers and could withdraw it whenever they pleased (one of the results of this system was an average duration of cabinets of about one year in office). The proportional electoral system, on the other hand, made sure that representatives were elected based on not only the vote of the people but rather and foremost, their relative position on a list. And the position within the list would be decided by the party oligarchy, which would, not surprisingly, use this power to favor the preservation of the oligarchy itself. The situation was further complicated by the presence, on the left of the political spectrum, of an electorally strong Communist Party that was widely regarded as anti-system, or at least not completely reliable as a player in a liberal-democratic republic and therefore not a viable alternative to the parties in power. By the early 1990s, these parties had become power centers with an extensive control of the country that wasn't limited to the strictly political realm: the government, in fact, exercised its authority, directly and indirectly, over most of the banking system, the health care programs, telecommunications, pensions funds, many other areas of the economy and even much of the cultural production. Families that needed help with a pension, or participating in a public contest for a government job (close to 20 percent of all employees worked for some level of government) knew that the recommendation of a party officer could do wonders to advance their cause. At the same time, citizens strongly resented the political elite. Most administrations had proved weak and ineffective in terms of policy design and implementation and it was evident that they were slowing the country down, especially if measured against the economically dynamic societies of the northern regions.

Of course, many members of the political elite recognized these problems and institutional reforms had been on the table for many years. But, as has been noted, it was something of a paradox to ask a system that proved unable to effectively implement reforms to introduce the most important and consequential reform of all: that of the institutions.[2] However, although the political elite had proved unable to act, there was an institutional mechanism that had been used during past years to move things forward: the constitution allowed for a popular referendum to repeal an existing law. The proposal had to collect half a million signatures and pass the exam of the Constitutional Court as some issues, such as taxes, were excluded from the possibility of repeal by popular will. In the past, the referendum card had been played to decide matters such as the legalization of divorce and abortion, in 1974 and 1980 respectively. In 1993, thanks to the initiative of a former Christian Democrat, Mariotto Segni (a rare case of a high party official ready to defy his fellow party members, someone who in the US would be labeled as a maverick), a referendum was proposed to repeal the electoral law with the intent to switch to a majoritarian system. The result of the vote, in 1993, was clear: almost 83 percent of the people who voted expressed the will to change the existing law, a stand that was widely interpreted as a desire to change the system and renew the political elite. In the preceding months, the electoral law for the election of city mayors was also changed: in the past, city elections were a small scale version of national ones, with the local legislatures as arbiters of the government and the parties deciding which candidate to put in office based on their relative position in the electoral list. With the new system, the citizens would elect the mayor directly and she or he would be accountable before the voters. The citizens seemed to greatly appreciate the new way and were getting ready to choose the senators and representatives based on the new electoral law in the aftermath of the referendum; everyone expected new national elections to be held very soon, while an increasing number of members of Parliament were being indicted with corruption charges by the magistrates in Milan and other cities. Which political parties would prevail in the next elections? In the North big chunks of voters were abandoning the Christian Democrats for the Northern League, the party that had surged against the traditional elite and seemed, at times, to seek secession of the Padania from the rest of Italy, or at least embrace a strong federalist reform that would ensure that the wealth produced in the North would stay there, instead of being wasted in what were considered inefficient services and useless investments in the South. But the ultimate expected winner was the PDS, the Democratic Party of the Left, born from the ashes of the Communist Party, which changed its name after the fall of the Berlin Wall and the socialist regimes in Eastern Europe, just a few years before. The city elections held in 1993 showed that the left was ready to take charge. On the other side of the spectrum, Mariotto Segni, a conservative, had gained wide popularity by promoting the referendum and by contributing to the creation of a new political system. He was ready to lead a center-right coalition to defeat the left and implement additional reforms. This is when Berlusconi made his move.

* * *

In the following years, many would speculate that he decided to enter the political arena to save his companies, at the time burdened with heavy debts and with the prospect of remaining without political protection after the fall of his friend, Bettino Craxi; the former head of the Socialist Party was now a fugitive abroad, after an indictment followed by a conviction for corruption-related crimes. It may very well be that Berlusconi was worried about his business prospects, particularly if the left won the elections; but, overall, his limitless ambition and his apparent necessity to be at the center of everything was more than enough to explain his candidacy to head the Italian Government. His televisions and newspapers had supported the popular wave against the traditional political elite during the "Clean Hands" season, and he was well aware that the public wanted to get rid of the old-style politicians. He had a former marketing employee set up a poll company and the head of his adverting team, Marcello Dell'Utri, organize auditions for political staff within the managers of his group and select candidates for Parliament among his executives: in no time, he had a fully prepared operational party ready to compete nationwide. The new electoral system promulgated after the referendum would favor those parties that could engage in alliances to maximize the possibilities of achieving most votes in each district, therefore Berlusconi proposed an alliance with two significant forces: the MSI, widely considered neo-fascist, which changed its name to Alleanza Nazionale (National Alliance) to distance itself from its ideological roots, and the Northern League. These two parties were, from a cultural and policy standpoint, at odds with each other: National Alliance had most of its support in the South and Center of Italy and favored state intervention in the economy (and other areas) while the League's electorate was in the North, it strongly opposed the transferring of funds to the South and saw the Rome-based state as the enemy: "Roma ladrona" ("Rome, the big thief") was one of the commonly cited slogans. Berlusconi cunningly limited the alliances on geographical bases: his party would run with the National Alliance in the South under the name "Pole for Good Government" and with the League in the North, with the name "Pole of Freedom" in an attempt to appeal contemporaneously to the cultural inclinations of the two electorates. Ideological consistency was not high on Berlusconi's scale of priorities and this arrangement would maximize the chances of election of the candidates who would support him, while avoiding a direct alliance, in the same districts, between two antithetical forces. To give some structure to his party, which had been created in a few months out of nothing, Berlusconi established a network of local committees: anyone could create one from scratch in his city, becoming its president, by simply applying and purchasing the president's kit: a case with flags, pins, various gadgets, and instructions on how to support the party's leader.

The declared ideological foundation of the new party was

conservative liberalism, the kind of conservatism associated with Ronald Reagan and Margaret Thatcher in the 80s, which included a reduced role for government in the economy and a strong effort against communism associated with some degree of social conservatism. He promised to cut taxes under the "natural limit" of 33 percent and curb public spending to reduce the debt and restore order in Italy's public finances, while he said his policies would create a million jobs enabling a new "Italian miracle." But all this was possibly not the most appealing aspect of his political pitch. He named his party "Forza Italia," "Go Italy," which is what soccer fans chant when they support the national team, and adopted the color blue, also associated with Italy's official sports teams. His television networks, of course, had a major role in the electoral campaign, as most of his popular TV show hosts openly invited viewers to vote for Berlusconi. Many in the traditional political establishment dismissed the strategy as a ridiculous populist attempt; a prominent leader of the left, Massimo d'Alema, declared that such propaganda tools will never work, "We are not in Brazil," he said.

Nevertheless, it did work, as many groups of Italians embraced Berlusconi's messages and put him in office. Who were these voters? Many of them were anti-communists, or simply anti-left. Mostly they were former voters of the Christian Democratic Party who had for long perceived the Communist Party as a danger for Italy's institutions and were extending that fear to the current left of the political spectrum. While groups from all social segments voted for Berlusconi, the categories that Forza Italia tended to over-represent were small business owners, professionals, and autonomous workers such as plumbers, taxi owners, store-keepers, people with an income higher than average, though often with lower education levels; many of these citizens had a significant role in sustaining the Italian economy and they resented, to a good extent, the inefficient services of the government that were being financed with their taxes. These voters also resented a long-standing Italian cultural tradition, mainly in the left obviously, that regarded entrepreneurs as social blood-suckers who only cared about profits and exploiting workers. Some of them, a minority no doubt, were anti-left for less than noble reasons. By the end of the 70s and the beginning of the 80s the Communist Party, after contributing to the political stability of the executive in the years of the "National Solidarity" (1976-79), found itself in the strange position of being the most determined political force in the struggle against political terrorism and organized crime in a quite paradoxical situation that saw the anti-system party working harder than any other for the preservation of the rule of law and ultimately the system itself.[3] During these years the communists were being perceived to a degree as an effective, rule-abiding, serious institution (in no small part thanks to Enrico Berlinguer, its charismatic, hard-working and honest leader, who acted relentlessly to advance Italy's democracy even if that meant cooperating with conservative politicians). Such was the perception of the party that public servants who distinguished themselves for being straight arrows were frequently addressed as communists[4], usually by people who did not have the rule of law on top of their priority list. In some cases, the anti-communist feeling came from a disdain toward those who wanted to fight tax evasion, quite endemic among many Italian small business owners and professionals (employees were largely excluded from evasion as their income tax was withheld by their employers). This group simply loved Berlusconi. The new leader of conservatism found additional voters among those citizens who are not particularly interested in politics, or not very knowledgeable about it, who would not read papers frequently (or at all) but who would watch TV copiously, especially Berlusconi's networks. A narrative, in Italy and elsewhere, after Berlusconi entered politics, explained that a defining role for his electoral victories was played by the fact that he owned about half of the national TV broadcasting in the country. Certainly, he used it fully for his advantage as the news, and virtually all the programming of his networks in the period close to the elections, was concentrated in enrolling voters on his behalf. A recent study even suggests that his TV channels, with their light popular and culture-free programming, shaped a new citizen-consumer-voter, culturally very much inclined to vote for him.[5]

Italy's political elite had been unable to reform the institutions in such a way as to ensure a more functional system of representation, in line with a modern society. The resulting dysfunctional governments led to the multiple crises of 1992 which, in turn, favored a quick evolution of the political system: a significant change of the electoral law, a renewed and strengthened resentment by the electorate toward the traditional governing parties, the almost complete disappearance of a significant part of the political supply. Berlusconi, in great part due to his superior command of communication techniques and tactics, was able to successfully insert himself in this new environment by appealing to many clusters of voters: conservatives who were extremely worried about the prospect of a victory of the left, liberal centrists who were hoping to finally introduce reforms in line with the highly industrialized areas of the country, and significant chunks of voters with very little information but who felt culturally close to the owner of the TV they watched and loved, who looked up to the success and riches Berlusconi was able to achieve.

* * *

Just as Berlusconi in Italy was able to take advantage of a unique crisis of the political system and create a successful electoral space that would put him in office, Trump inserted himself in a crucial time for US politics. In his case, there was no significant institutional development; the architecture of the US political rules is quite stable and has been abundantly tested through time and updated with progressive, and relatively minor, changes. The problem with the US political system lays, rather, in the interaction between the political demand and supply, particularly in the dynamics between the elite of the Republican Party and a significant portion of its voters. The origins of these dynamics are to be found probably as far back as the realignment of the US electorate of the 1960s.

Before the mid-60s, the electorate of the two main parties could be roughly described in the following way: white southerners, especially from lower-income groups, and the working class of the northern, highly industrialized, states would support the Democrats, while the Republicans could count on the higher educated, the business community, big chunks of the middle class and a significant portion of the black vote. It was an alignment that had its roots in the aftermath of the civil war when Lincoln's Republican Party gained the support of the African-Americans, and in Roosevelt's New Deal, a major element of which was a strong public intervention in the economic system. The sixties, and particularly the commitment of the Kennedy and Johnson administrations to civil rights legislation, changed all that. While just a few years back Richard Nixon could include the black vote as a source of advantage in his electoral strategy in 1960, as he hoped to create a coalition of "fiscal conservatives, educated suburbanites, and Negroes,"[6] in the following presidential election, Goldwater would mention the electoral opportunity of appealing to white voters with racial resentment, of "hunting where the ducks are" and represent states' rights (implicitly rejecting civil rights legislation). As has been noted,

Republicans comprised less than 10% of southern representatives until the 1960s, but increased their southern representation to over 20% by the 1970s and reached over 30% in the 1980 elections, about where they remained until after 1990. By the 1990s, Republicans held more than half of southern districts. Southern Republicans replaced conservative Democrats, leaving House Democrats more liberal on the whole and reinforcing the conservatism of House Republicans.[7]

Before this new, post-Civil Rights Act realignment, the partisan divide could be characterized as mainly economic: Democrats would stand for significant state intervention in the economic system in the New Deal tradition, while Republicans would seek to reduce it and rely on the powerful forces of free enterprise and free markets. Starting in the 70s this economic ideological divide would persist, but new issues would become just as important, if not more so: race resentment as well as, increasingly, social and cultural matters such as: "religious freedom," abortion rights, gun owners' rights, family values, homosexuality, anti-crime policy, environment preservation: all the familiar elements of today's political debate. In the same time frame, the Democrats, who had held a huge advantage in terms of party affiliation with the electorate since the 30s, lost part of this edge to Republicans. Their lead had allowed the Democrats to maintain a majority in the Senate, until Ronald Reagan's election in 1980, and in the House until the mid-term elections of 1994, when Newt Gingrich's strategy seemed to pay off, permitting him to become the Speaker.

As the cultural and social issues gained importance in the partisan divide, the system became increasingly polarized: the distance between the political positions on these issues of the supporters of the Republican Party on one side, and the Democratic Party on the other, became greater, especially dating from the late 80s and early 90s, in coincidence with the tenure of Gingrich and his leading role in the GOP. This phenomenon has been observed both for the party elites — the party officials and staff, the elected officials on all levels of government, and the party activists—and for the voters with party affiliation. The increasing degree of polarization had been a constant theme in many debates with observers of political affairs long before Trump entered the political arena. It is also confirmed by many studies by political scientists: most surveys and analysis confirm that the country became more ideologically divided, especially during the 80s and 90s, based on partisan lines.[8] Until the 70s, Republicans were not more likely than Democrats to support legal abortion or to be significantly more conservative toward women's role in society. A 2004 analysis "both reviews and provides new evidence for three instances of issue evolution that have occurred since the 1960s: race, abortion, and women's rights. At the time of each issue's 'critical moment,' there was either a negative or nonexistent correlation between the public's preferences on the three issues and their party identification."[9] Studies also show that most of the distance between parties derives from the GOP moving farther to the right, rather than the Democrats shifting to the left.[10] Again, the same phenomenon affects the party elite as well as the electorate. Among the effects of this increasing polarization, besides making TV debates livelier, is the extreme difficulty in working toward agreements between the parties to promote bipartisan legislation, a rather important condition for developing policy in the US system of government.

Why is all this happening? To make some significant hypotheses, it may be helpful to use the simple model already proposed, the one based on three elements: rules, supply, and demand. Of course, when we describe the political demand, we are oversimplifying an extremely complex social phenomenon. In fact, it can be argued, there are as many demands as one can identify segments of voters, each with its needs, inclinations, passions, and irrationalities; and one can identify virtually any number of segments, or clusters, of voters as one goes through the extremes of the continuum between adherence to reality and the explanatory power of a model. Moreover, not all the individuals and entities that contribute to the shaping of political demand are created equal. Some, such as media enterprises, have the power to significantly influence other voters, often rather effectively. Others, such as large corporations, wealthy individuals, or civil associations of various kinds, can influence voters directly, by promoting ideas or policies, and also indirectly, by donating large amounts of money that can be spent by party officials to better position themselves. The political supply is also a complex phenomenon, although in this case, the number of actors is significantly smaller as we are dealing typically with the party elites, and, within the elites, more specifically, with those individuals that have the power to influence party lines and to participate in elections as candidates. When shaping political supply, or, put in other words, when defining world views on issues and policy proposals, these individuals will be guided by two main factors: on one hand their own beliefs about how society should be organized and their conviction concerning the most effective policies to get there; on the other hand, whatever they think will grant them the most consensus from the electorate to win elections, which does not always necessarily coincide with the first element. Since the demand can be quite articulated, as different groups wish for different things, the supply must take into account all these factors to maximize its chances of achieving electoral strength.

As for the third element of our model, the rules or institutions, in the US, at least in the time frame that we are considering, did not change significantly, certainly not to an extent comparable to that of Italy, where a major change of the electoral law in the early 90s effectively altered the patterns of democratic representation. In the American system, the main changes in the last few decades have to do with redistricting, including the effort by many politicians to facilitate the electoral outcome for their party through what is commonly known as gerrymandering. Other instances of change in the US rules affecting the political system are connected with campaign financing and the legislation that affects it; the Supreme Court decision known as Citizen United Vs FEC, for example, certainly qualifies as a significant moment in this regard, as it prevents the government, to an extent, from effectively restricting campaign expenditure by corporations and other organizations.

* * *

What seems to be particularly interesting in the period we are considering is the trend of the GOP and its interaction with its supporters, which probably constitutes the most dynamic and consequential aspect of the political system in the recent history of US politics. To better explore this development, we should first take a look at the evolution of the debate on economic policy.

As we have seen, until the mid-60s the main divide between the two parties involved the economy; essentially how the two parties would consider the intervention of the state in the economic affairs conducted by corporations, or the producers, and families, or the consumers. The established view of the Republicans is that, in general, the lower the amount of interference, the better: an excess of regulation goes to the detriment of economic growth as it increases the costs of businesses and discourages productive investments. In the same way, an excess of taxes constitutes a disincentive to work, invest, and produce, therefore lower taxes are preferable as they promote economic growth, while public expenditure in welfare programs, particularly entitlements, should be enacted with great caution as it could incentivize laziness and be an obstacle to fostering personal responsibility. Perhaps more importantly, the Government should not spend more money than it raises with taxes; outside very special circumstances, such as wars, the budget should be balanced and not add to the national debt, which will have to be paid for by future generations.

As far as regulations are concerned, while it is plausible that several rules may slow down business affairs and therefore have a negative impact on growth, it is pretty much an established conclusion among economists and public policy professionals that a certain amount of regulation is a necessary measure. Just to name a few banal examples, without anti-trust laws entire economic sectors may shift toward monopolies, a situation that may cause inefficiencies and harm consumers, who can be forced to pay higher prices for worse products. Regulations in the food and drugs businesses are widely accepted for the negative impact that using profit-seeking as the sole organizing criterion may have on consumers' health (the problem could be if the US is not lagging behind in this area of legislation, if compared with other rich nations, such as the EU countries). The financial sector is another sector where the presence of regulations is considered widely necessary to avoid fraudulent schemes and, perhaps more importantly, the risk of loss of confidence in the system that may cause great economic recessions such as the ones following the 1929 stock exchange crisis or the 2008 real estate crash. In general, as societies grow economically, they become more sophisticated, with more specialized areas of production and new areas of business. In general, the higher the sophistication, the higher the need for new legislation and regulations. One of the last examples of this trend is the current debate on the need to regulate big internet companies, such as Facebook and Google, which concentrate an enormous amount of information, therefore power, while being hardly accountable to anybody; such need was not even conceived of just a few years ago. How does the regulation issue relate to electoral politics? Unfortunately, the public debate on regulation is a very difficult one to develop productively, given that it is highly technical, in many cases quite boring, and followed mostly by professionals, pundits, journalists, and politicians. The consequence is that the way this debate is often proposed to the general public tends to be overly simplified and mostly presented as a trivial binary choice by Republicans: regulating is bad, repealing regulations is good.

The situation is quite different with the other important economic issue in the political divide: taxes and public expenditure. These have a significant and potentially dramatic direct impact on peoples' lives, as taxes reduce their available income while public spending may increase their actual standard of living, so we can expect voters to be more attentive to this particular debate. From a strictly electoral viewpoint, tax increases are normally tough to sell as most people are not keen to see their income reduced, while entitlements can be easier to present to voters. Of course, voters belong to different groups and their reactions to actual policies regarding these issues will depend on the specifics: will tax increase or reduction affect the poor or the rich? The investor, the corporate employee, or the company that pollutes? Nevertheless, as a general rule, we can assume that cutting public spending and reducing taxes on the highest incomes makes more people unhappy than the converse. Moreover,

...A generation of political science research has shown that dismantling large-scale social programs is hard. The status quo bias of political institutions, the well-known tendency for individuals and organized groups to fight fiercely against losing what they already have, and the increasingly understood processes of entrenchment that occur as programs become integrated into economic and social life...[11]

are all elements that discourage politicians from proposing welfare or entitlements cuts.

Frontal assault on the welfare state carries tremendous

political risk...First, social programs are popular, and it is hard for elected representatives in a democracy to do unpopular things. The second source of welfare state resilience is what has come to be called entrenchment—the ways in which various individuals and groups become invested in particular programs and thus gain increased incentive to defend them.[12]

An additional, though banal, reason that cutting welfare programs is usually unpopular is that there are far fewer rich people, those most likely to pay the cost, than the middle or lower class, those that usually benefit the most from social public spending. This elementary truth may have made the economic issue a rather uncomfortable one for Republicans in many political campaigns as well as, or maybe more so, in the implementation of actual economic policies. If we look at the federal budget during Republican and Democratic administrations in the long term, say from Nixon until today, the result has been rather clear. Republican administrations have been consistently less fiscally conservative than advertised, if the expression "fiscally conservative" means working for a balanced budget. The constant elements seem to be significant tax cuts, particularly in the high end of the income ladder, associated with increases in defense spending and occasional minor cuts in welfare programs that do not come close to offsetting the lower revenues. Why this inconsistency? Simply stated, a plausible reason is that while there is a strong push for Republicans in office to reduce taxes, as donors and interest groups strongly pressure them in this direction (with the reduction especially concentrated in certain income brackets), there is no significant incentive to reduce expenditures: many GOP voters, in fact, a significant part of them, have a stake in government programs that cover health care, social security, and other services and cutting them significantly may have a high political cost. The consequence, so far, has been a twofold strategy by the GOP:

on one side display rhetoric that values personal responsibility and does not encourage laziness, in welfare, and lower taxes, especially for corporations and small businesses. On the other side, while indeed lowering taxes to meet the expectations of part of their constituency, Republicans tend to limit the cutting of social programs to avoid a potential backlash from other clusters of voters. The result is an increase of the fiscal deficit, which in fact can be observed clearly in every Republican administration, from Reagan to G.W. Bush and, now, Donald Trump. Even during the Reagan years, the Republican administration "had a limited direct effect on the major elements of the American welfare state: Social Security; Medicare and Medicaid; tax breaks for private social policies, such as employer benefits; and even most anti-poverty programs. Most of these policies survived, continued to grow, and in some cases were notably strengthened."[13] On the contrary, democratic administrations have proven much more "conservative" in terms of debt increase. To be sure, during the Obama years the US debt reached a peak, but this was largely due to the necessity of contrasting the deepening of the economic depression that had started in the previous administration, and the spending programs within the "stimulus" were largely bipartisan. During the Clinton administration, notably, the US had a rare phase of actual debt reduction in absolute terms, the declared dream of every conservative. This trend was quite evident already a decade and a half ago:

When it comes to White House economic policy, the Republican and Democratic parties have switched places since the 1960s. By now the pattern is sufficiently well established that the generalization can no longer be denied: the Republicans have become the party of fiscal irresponsibility, trade restriction, big government, and bad microeconomics...A simple look at the federal budget statistics shows an uncanny tendency for the deficit to rise precisely during Republican presidencies.

There is no mistaking the link between the Reagan and Bush tax cuts legislated in 1981 and 2001, respectively, and the dramatic shift in the long-term budget outlook that each engendered. In between the two, record surpluses were achieved by the end of the Clinton Administration.[14]

These lines were written in 2003, they were being confirmed beyond doubt by the generous fiscal policies of the George W. Bush administration.

This, of course, doesn't mean that Republicans don't care anymore about fiscal conservatism. Many of them do, and there are entire organizations that invest money and other resources to see these policies implemented and the candidates who seem more likely to support them elected. Among the prominent conservative donors, the Koch brothers, for example, have been promoting a rather radical agenda of unapologetic free-market philosophy for years, mainly through their organization Americans for Prosperity (contrary to other conservative advocacy groups, such as the Chamber of Commerce, which appears to pursue the interests of large corporations irrespective of the promotion of free-market policies).[15] Actually, the rise, since the beginning of this century, of think-tanks and foundations that support the actual reduction of government intervention in the economy may be considered a symptom of the inconsistency of the GOP and much of the conservative world on these matters. Also, notwithstanding the large amount of money employed, their presence in the media, and their occasional success in getting certain candidates elected, the Koch, it can be argued, achieved little in terms of pushing the GOP toward balanced budgets, as was evident during the large spending programs of the Bush administration and, even more so now, with Trump, who, in July 2019, accepted a budget deal that allows for additional spending of $320 billion and significantly adds to the national debt.

An issue that appears to be connected to the shift of the Republicans on fiscal conservatism (at least on its actual implementation) has been the GOP official position on health care, particularly on the Affordable Care Act, introduced during the Obama presidency. Republicans fought this program like, possibly, no other. For starters, it is widely considered Obama's signature piece of legislation and, given the effort the GOP put into obstructing his presidency, it is hardly a surprise that they would not support in the least an initiative bearing his name. But there is probably another, deeper reason the Republicans spoke so vehemently against it: this is legislation that can work. Indeed the program partially reached its objective of making health care available at a reasonable cost to millions of Americans who could not afford it, and many appear to like it today. The Affordable Care Act was attacked on many fronts, on technical grounds as well as on principle. Mostly, the arguments have to do with the mandate that the legislation introduces, which affects the free choice of consumers. This is true, but the point is that health care is not really a market like most others. As an expert on this subject says:

> The primary problem in American health care is not that too many healthy people have to subsidize the premiums of the unhealthy; it's that too many Americans are largely insulated from the cost of care they receive through expansive third-party insurance payments covered by employer-provided plans and Medicare. These consumers never really participate in any meaningful way in the health-care marketplace. They get the services they believe they need, and their insurers pay the bills…It is a completely opaque non-market, with very weak price and quality competition. The predictable result is an overbuilt, fragmented, and inefficient system of delivering services to patients[16]

The difficult position of the GOP on health care became quite evident during the Trump presidency: the GOP could not pass a repeal of the act and many Republicans were put in a difficult spot during the mid-term 2018 elections, when possibly the most important issue to cause the blue wave was health care and Republicans did not have a clear message on the issue: they certainly could not defend the ACA after years of criticizing it, but they were also very uncomfortable when asked what they would replace it with, as no coherent Republican reform proposal has been presented to the public

One important argument against the supporters of Obamacare, which could be extended to public health-care or indeed all welfare programs, is the one made by Kevin Williamson on the National Review: the notion that health care is a right is wrong, he says, "Declaring a right in a scarce good is meaningless"[17] as its availability depends on the actual possibility of producing it for everyone in the first place. It is an economic issue, rather than a legal or ethical one. The argument appears well-founded in principle; for example, a significant part of the Italian 1948 constitution, where it announces that such things as a job is a right, does not make much sense: if the jobs were not there to be distributed among the unemployed, what does it mean to declare it a right? However, in the current reality of the developed world, we know that we have the ability to produce enough wealth to provide health care (or other things such as higher education) to all, probably without imposing unbearable sacrifices on anyone. In fact, practically all developed countries with the exception of the US have some sort of system in which health care is made available to virtually every citizen. However weak on the merits, to some extent conservative arguments against Obamacare did have an impact on the public; according to a paper published by the American Journal of Medicine, "the benefits of Medicare have been enhanced to decrease the cost of prescription drugs and to eliminate co-pays for preventive services. Despite these positive changes, a near majority of Americans still oppose the ACA, even though they approve of most of its features."[18] This study suggests that at least part of the explanation is the TV ads campaigns against the ACA run by the Republicans in the 2012 and 2014 elections. A significant example of the dissociation between rhetoric and actual policies in the conservative field.

So, in short, the Republicans have significant difficulties in dealing with the traditional economic divide and siding consistently with the reduction of government intervention in the economy, at least as far as cutting welfare programs is concerned, as such actions may incur a significant electoral cost. The Republicans may use a certain amount of rhetoric against welfare programs in line with their traditional take on the role of the state in the economy, but are rather hesitant in acting when in power, possibly for fear of the potential backlash from the electorate, a part of which may be hurt by such measures. As time goes by, the difference between the declared intentions and the actual policy creates areas of inconsistency for the GOP, as in the case of health care or as evident in observing the fiscal policy of Republican administrations.

* * *

It seems that in the same time frame in which the distance between the traditional GOP stand on economic issues and actual policy implementation became more evident, the position of both the GOP elite and Republican voters became more radicalized. Several studies suggest that, first, the party elites shifted to the right and then, seemingly as a consequence, the electorate did too,[19] suggesting a top-down effect. But is it even plausible that the GOP elites could shape its electorate in such a way as to shift the main issues from the economy toward the social ones? The answer is probably yes. In our simple model of political systems, the interactions between the political supply and the demand are dynamic: each one influences the other. How can the supply influence the demand in particular? Or, put in different terms, how can the party elite influence, to some extent, its electorate ideologically? One mechanism that works in this direction is heuristics: usually, voters have limited information and limited time to study such things as actual policy matters or the candidates' position on them. So, to make sound voting decisions, they largely rely on heuristics, that is detecting clues that enable them to make a decision without investing a significant amount of time studying the matter. Studies confirm what appears to be intuitive: party affiliation is the strongest heuristic voters use to make decisions when voting.[20] A conservative voter is highly likely to identify the Republican Party as her default choice at the ballot and, while the specifics of a given race and details about the candidates' character, history, and their policy views may have an impact, in absence of other very significant information she will seemingly vote for the GOP candidate. As Jonah Goldberg bluntly, but effectively, puts it: "For most Americans, conservatism basically means the stuff Republicans are for, and liberalism means whatever Democrats are for. I don't mean this as a criticism, just a statement of fact...Associating a body of ideas with the institutions (political parties) that are directly charged with putting ideas into action is a pragmatic way to cut to the chase."[21]

This rather natural human attitude of avoiding hard and time-consuming information gathering by resorting to heuristics grants political parties significant maneuvering space; they have the possibility to influence, to a significant degree, voters who tend to identify with them by showing that the party leans in a certain way about a given issue. If such an issue does not openly break with the traditional party line, if it does not blatantly conflict with the interests of the voter, chances are it will contribute to shifting the voter's position on it. According to many scholars, this mechanism might be especially effective for conservative voters, the ones most likely to vote for the Republican Party in the US. Is there an actual difference between the progressive electorate and the conservative one in this regard? In the words of Bill Clinton, in electoral politics, "Republicans like to fall in line and Democrats like to fall in love."[22] The authors of an analysis of the differences between the two main American parties think that the phrase is:

> ...highly evocative of the behavior of modern American political parties. While it purports to describe the attitude of partisans, it captures something essential about the structures of the two parties, as well. For generations, the Democratic Party has been described as the less organized of the two, with interest groups occasionally aligning—but often warring— over the choice of nominees, policy stances, and the direction of the party. The Republican Party, meanwhile, is typically lauded for its internal discipline and top-down command structure.[23]

While sometimes such assertions could be considered as stereotypes, "much research demonstrates that epistemic motivations to reduce uncertainty predict right-wing or conservative ideology."[24] As another study confirms, "Indeed conservatives are found to be more loyal to their group. Furthermore, conservatives are thought to be more sensitive to authoritarian figures and rely more on authority acceptance."[25] There may also be an additional reason that grants the Republican Party an edge in the ability to influence its electorate: low-information voters are the ones most likely to rely on heuristics as they are the ones that seemingly would face the higher costs of analyzing issues and policies. We also know that, according to a clear trend, low-education voters have been increasingly overrepresented in the GOP electorate for some time.

But is this actually what happened in the case of the GOP and its electorate during the election cycles of the last few decades? Did the party elite influence the views of conservative voters as to become more polarized over social and cultural issues? When Newt Gingrich was elected as US Representative for a Georgia district, in 1979, the GOP had not been in control of the House (or the Senate for that matter) since the 50s. While Ronald Reagan's victory in the 1980 presidential election opened the way for a Republican majority in the Senate, the House seemed to be destined to be ruled by the Democrats, as testified by the expression "permanent majority," used at the time. Gingrich brought a new philosophy for the Republicans to deal with the Democrats: instead of working with them to influence legislation, they should oppose and fight them on every front in the most public way possible, to reduce the voters' support of Democrats and increase appeal toward Republicans. Being an effective tactician, Gingrich demonstrated that his method could be successful in various instances, achieving increasing support from his colleagues. The followers of the future House Speaker:

insisted that their party stop working with majority Democrats to make small contributions to policy and instead should oppose the Democrats at every step in the legislative process, avoid accommodation, draw clear ideological distinctions between the parties, and go on the attack with national themes in more aggressive attempts to unseat Democratic incumbents. Vote no and sharpen the criticism was the theme—a 'rule or ruin' strategy, it was dubbed by one House Republican.[26]

What were the main issues in Gingrich's rhetoric during the 80s and 90s? Certainly the traditional republican economic stands: reduced regulations, lower taxes, and lower spending (except for defense), but, as we have seen, the Republicans in this period started relying increasingly on social issues, starting with the ones that could drive evangelicals closer to conservatives: abortion rights, traditional family, private education, etc. While tax reduction was something Gingrich could feel confident about (certainly enough to create a wedge in the GOP when President Bush felt forced to break his campaign promise, "Read my lips," in 1990 and support tax hikes to limit the deficit), for the other economic issues, the reform of welfare, the reduction of expenditures for entitlements in particular, his experiences with the public were not positive ones. For example, when the House majority led by Gingrich proposed to cut aid for families with dependent children or the national school lunch programs (created within Roosevelt's New Deal) as one of the steps to fulfill the GOP's "Contract with America" in 1995.[27]

But even if cuts to certain welfare programs proved politically risky, the new Republican Speaker of the House had demonstrated that combative tactics could be profitable. Especially in those cases in which he could denounce instances of corruption within the other side of the aisle; better still if the case could be presented as the GOP contrasting the left-leaning condescending elites. Of course, the benefit of riling the conservative electorate around the social and cultural issues was that Gingrich could guarantee strong support for his party without risking the backlash that could be triggered by welfare reduction programs. Many scholars agree that the demand-supply dynamics in the recent history of the GOP were much more top-down than bottom-up: the elite largely introduced a higher level of polarization on certain topics and the conservative electorate followed. A study by scholars from Columbia University and Dartmouth College, for example, clearly suggests that the polarization of the elites preceded that of the voters: "The Nation's political Parties, at the elite and activist level, have become more ideologically coherent than they were in the mid-70s. The partisan polarization that has occurred at the elite level has become increasingly evident in the mass electorate."[28] Another scholar agrees: "After declining throughout the 1950s and 1960s, partisanship began to reassert itself in Congress during the 1970s. By the end of the 1980s partisanship in Congress had risen dramatically and has remained at a high level ever since..." After reviewing the evidence the study continues to conclude that "changes in mass partisanship have largely mirrored the partisan changes taking place among the elites since the 1970s."[29] As Edwards Carmine suggests:

> ...institutions matter in politics because they shape incentives and impact who can learn from whom. To win public power, the parties must compete, and a central aspect of competition is their effort to define political choices. The issue evolution model, as well as focusing on partisan elites' framing of issues, gives the role of political leadership its proper due. Thus, any consistent, partisan framing of an issue, cultural or not, might be expected to help voters (under some conditions) do the following things: (a) believe an issue is important, (b) form an opinion on an issue, (c) change their opinion on an issue, or even occasionally (d) change their partisan orientation because of that issue.[30]

It is fairly reasonable to assume that when Republican candidates campaign for elections they mostly seek to appeal to groups that are somewhat already inclined to support them. So they will try to appeal to evangelicals by frequent references to, for example, abortion restriction, or "religious freedom" or natural marriage; they may seek to energize the vote of gun owners by announcing their good score with the NRA or by celebrating the second amendment. Or they may make statements that, in a subtle way, stimulate racial resentment in segments of their supporters (this doesn't mean making openly racist remarks, of course, but things such as opposing affirmative action or siding uncritically with the police in cases of brutality against African-Americans, and so on.) When GOP candidates speak to these constituencies, they seek their support of course, but they also send the message that the party's position on a certain issue leans in a certain way. This may occasionally distance a few voters, but more likely, if the candidate's strategy is sound (and it usually is) it will simply encourage many voters to shift toward those positions that the candidate favors. As the GOP base slowly shifts toward those issues in time, at every election cycle the candidates may tend to radicalize their rhetoric even more, as their base is now shifting to the right on all or most issues and the candidates want to meet the expectations of their electorate. So the radicalization of the base causes a further radicalization of the party elite as well, amplified by the primary election mechanism, while the further radicalized rhetoric of the successful candidates shifts the base even more, hence polarizing the electorate more and more in a continuous loop.

* * *

During the last decade or so, the radicalization cycle of the GOP has been in full effect. The appeal, within much of the conservative electorate, of vice-presidential candidate Sara Palin during the 2008 campaign demonstrated that many Republican voters had become extremely receptive of the anti-elitist, anti-intellectual rhetoric and that many were particularly open to dog-whistle, race-related rhetoric as well as antimuslim, nativist, and anti-immigration arguments together with Christian-aligned cultural elements. All these inclinations in the conservative electorate were reinforced with the election of the first African-American president, Barack Hussein Obama.

Obama brings out the worst in the Republican base. The seeds of anger and resentment, of nativism and victimization, were sown by forces outside his control long before his ascent.

But he harvested them in a way no other Democrat could. The succession of liberal policies; the ostensive shaming of patriotism...the imperiously lecturing tone; the hints of class condescension ('They cling to guns or religion'); perhaps more critically, the dark skin and the African roots and the exotic name—any of these elements, on their own may not have been so provocative. But in this era of convulsion and cultural dislocation, Obama was a perfect villain for the forgotten masses of the flyover country.[31]

The election of Obama can also be considered as one of the main causes of the rise of the Tea Party movement. While its declared purpose was to push for the reduction of taxes and toward fiscal responsibility, most of the Tea Party activists appeared to be very sensitive to race resentment[32] as well as to border security and illegal immigration.[33] An interesting aspect of this movement is that it appeared to be, in many regards, a bottom-up social phenomenon, it seemed to be an instance in which the base influences the elite. As such it contributed to the radicalizing of the US conservative field, mainly through the selection mechanism of primary elections, where Republican candidates in right-leaning districts would be encouraged to adopt radical right-wing rhetoric to maximize their chances to win the nomination.[34] In many cases, Tea Party members, talk radio hosts, and right-wing online media would mobilize to support radical Republican candidates against others, considered too linked to the establishment. Thanks to this wave, Marco Rubio could triumph over former governor Charlie Crist in the primary for the US Senate in Florida, Trey Gowdy could win over Bob Inglis in his South Carolina district, and Justin Amash won the nomination for the GOP in Michigan, just to list a few instances. It is difficult not to find a significant element of anti-elitism in this rejection of the traditional Republican establishment. "The pattern was inescapable: in congressional districts from sea to shining sea, self-styled insurgents found success by racing to the right and distancing themselves from the GOP ruling class,"[35] sometimes making it difficult for the GOP to win general elections as with the Senate candidate in Nevada, Sharon Angle, who was endorsed and abundantly funded by the Tea Party Express and by Mark Levin, but after a successful primary she revealed herself as too much of a conspiracy theorist for the overall electorate.

It is rather apparent that by the time Trump announced his candidacy for the GOP presidential nomination, the party had already radicalized significantly on several issues, like race resentment and immigration. What Trump did was exploit the race card in a much more open and shameless way than in the past. Before him, it wasn't at all obvious that a man with political ambitions could claim baselessly that the sitting African-American president wasn't possibly born in the US and therefore not entitled to the job. He tried it and it worked. So he did the same with another divisive and outrageous declaration, this time on immigration, by declaring that Mexican immigrants are bringing drugs and are rapists (except for some, who, Trump assumed, "are good people"). This also worked, and suddenly Trump became the toughest republican candidate on such things as race, immigration, use of torture, and whatever controversial issue there was to embrace. Of course, many Republicans were appalled by his tactics and declarations, certainly, almost all the party elite (legislators, officials, most activists, and the Republican-leaning wonks) wanted nothing to do with him and part of the electorate was repulsed as well. But he was able to gain the loyalty of a strong base of GOP voters who have loved him ever since and made his triumphs possible in the first primary challenges; then more segments of voters aligned with him as he began appealing also to evangelicals and working-class voters from the northern and midwestern states. As soon as it became clear that he would be the nominee, the rest of the party, both the elite and the voters, rather quickly positioned themselves behind him. In the process, the party shifted further to the right and the degree of polarization in the system increased even more. The last cycle of the radicalizing interaction between the Republican base and the party took place during the 2016 presidential campaign: as Tim Alberta writes:

> One Freedom Caucus member described the "oh shit" moment in the spring of 2016, when he and his comrades realized what was happening. Marauding across the country, Trump was delivering an anti-Washington message rooted not in any narrowly philosophical approach but in the belief that politicians had failed voters. Back home, the conservatives saw their constituents responding in force, much as they had in 2010. But Trump was no Tea Party purist selling a small Government creed. He was selling outrage at the status quo. Trump, they realized, had coopted and broadened their message...they were now part of the broken political class Trump was railing against...

Trump was simply the last development of a cycle that had started long before and that had added to the radicalization of the conservative base, to some degree, at every election. Each time with many of the candidates using anti-elite rhetoric and cultural issues to stand out and gain the support of a base that was growing more impatient at every turn.

Many commentators, especially among liberals, tend to describe Republicans as hypocrites and mostly acting in bad faith because of their positions on economic issues. This is, for example, a frequent claim by economist and Nobel Prize winner Paul Krugman in his New York Times editorials. It is fair, in many cases, to make such assertions if one compares the statements of members of the Republican elite and their actual behavior. But in an analysis of the evolution of the US political system, it is far more important to consider that GOP candidates and officials found themselves in a very difficult position because of a long-term trend that left them little choice if they cared about political survival (and politicians obviously care a lot about that, otherwise they wouldn't last long in their line of work). In the Trump era things got even worse: to survive politically, members of the GOP elite cannot confront Trump and his base and are often forced to make all kinds of embarrassing statements, at times struggling to avoid validating a lie while at the same time trying to not distance themselves from the leader.

Having Trump, an individual who does not seem particularly interested in philosophical principles, as the leader of the party could be what sparked recent debates about American conservatism, its roots, ideals, and its current meaning. If someone wanted to synthesize conservatism in just one founding principle, one that can explain most of the American conservative policies, ideas, and attitudes throughout its history, that principle would arguably be personal responsibility. In his book "The Righteous Mind" psychologist Jonathan Haidt describes how his research team tried to establish a correlation between people's political leaning on the left-right spectrum and moral beliefs on a number of "foundations," as Haidt calls them, or morally relevant axes. At first, he defined one of these "foundations" as fairness, and identified it with compassion and some degree of equality; as expected, left-leaning subjects responding to the team's questionnaire proved much more interested in "fairness" than right-leaning ones. However, the team later realized that people on the right side of the spectrum cared deeply about "fairness," just a different definition of it: one that stressed proportionality, "making sure that people get what they deserve, and do not get things they do not deserve,"[36] which is a rather simple though effective way to express reverence for personal responsibility. It is nearly impossible to explain how the current American conservatives support a president who arguably embodies the exact opposite of the principle of personal responsibility if not by concluding that they mostly lost their ideological references. It appears that Republicans were pulled into a gradual decay of ideas out of their control, a decay that is becoming pathological during Trump's presidency.

The central theme in the book "What's the Matter with Kansas" is the situation in which working-class voters opt to support a political party, the GOP, which in many ways works to undermine their economic interest; in light of the considerations we have seen, this phenomenon appears to be less of a paradox and more of an evolution dictated by the dynamics of the political system. After the new positioning of the two main parties and the realignment of the electorate in the 60s, the GOP increasingly relied on social and cultural issues to fuel its rhetoric. While it maintained its traditional views on economic and fiscal policy, arguing for tax reduction and fiscal responsibility, when in a position of power it only really pursued the tax cuts, thus associating Republican administrations with high deficits and increasing fiscal debts. Such a performance progressively reduced, to some degree, the strength of the economic arguments and, as a consequence, enhanced the relevance of the social and cultural elements in the GOP political supply. After all... "decades of research on public opinion have led to the conclusion that self-interest is a weak predictor of policy preferences... rather people care about their groups, whether those be racial, regional, religious, or political."[37]

An additional electoral tool that Republicans found effective was combativeness: starting in the 80s Newt Gingrich showed his fellow Republican congressmen and senators that a higher level of contrast with the opposing party could achieve significant coverage by the media and, in many cases, also lead to an advantage with the public overall, especially in all those instances in which the attacks could be framed as having the establishment, or the elite, as the target. It has been noted that "...Republicans have a distinct electoral base: their most committed voters see politics in stark us-versus-them terms, resist compromise, and rely on highly partisan news sources in a way not mirrored on the other side of the spectrum..."[38] The loyalty of voters is thus a:

> ...source of Republican confidence: they believe that Republican voters will stick with them even though they don't like major GOP policies. The foundation of this expectation is what political scientists call "negative partisanship"... Voters haven't just become increasingly loyal to their party; their political preferences are increasingly driven by hatred or fear of the other party. Moreover, such tribalism appears far stronger on the GOP side. In 2016, tens of millions of Republican voters cast their ballot for a presidential candidate they acknowledged was unqualified for the job, mainly because they could not bring themselves to vote for his opponent...[39]

While prominent players in both parties occasionally used methods outside the realm of traditional fair play, historically the Republican field seems much more inclined to resort to street-fighters and even seems to have developed a Machiavellian tradition of implementing effective tactics without regard to truth or morals, and, occasionally, the law. It is a tradition that had Joseph McCarthy and then Richard Nixon as perhaps its first most notable representatives and that was to be continued by individuals such as self-defined dirty tricksters Roger Stone and Roy Cohn. It is probably not a coincidence that Cohn was also McCarthy's most prominent aid, while Stone started his "dirty trickster" career with the Nixon administration. It is also probably not a coincidence, in a time when the Republican president makes no effort to hide his disregard for ethics, that a recent debate within the conservative field deals with whether conservatives should adhere to "civility and decency" in their opposition to progressives or, as Catholic writer Sohrab Ahmari claims, these are "secondary values."[40] Ahmari argues that "there is no returning to the pre-Trump conservative consensus" and that, in order to "defeat the enemy and enjoy the spoils," it is necessary to leave aside the politeness which characterizes conservatives such as David French and resort to more decisive measures.

* * *

Both Trump and Berlusconi decided to run for office in a moment in which they saw an opening, special circumstances that opened a window for them to step in and seek a plausible path to power. These circumstances were different for the two countries in which they ran as are their political systems and cultures, even though they both belong in the democratic-liberal tradition of government. Those differences notwithstanding, there are many similar elements in the rise to power of these two leaders. In both countries, by the time they presented themselves before their electorates, there was a looming crisis that originated many years before and slowly progressed without a clear solution. In Italy, a dysfunctional institutional system that wasn't in line with the country's society and its need for modernization did not allow for proper representation of the people at the political level, making it nearly impossible for voters to choose between competing options within the supply of political solutions. In the US, on the contrary, the problem lay in the development of a dynamic between the political supply and the demand on the right side of the political spectrum, where actual policy issues, especially in the economic domain, became secondary with respect to social and cultural themes that, to some extent, distracted the electorate from the most urgent issues and put one of the parties on a difficult path toward inconsistency and, possibly, a progressive disregard for established norms and ethical values.

In both cases, the candidacy of these two leaders created an atmosphere of surprise, often curiosity, as a reaction to a rhetoric so distant from the traditional etiquette; the surprise became almost disbelief when the candidates ultimately reached their goal and won the elections. This disbelief originated from the awareness, throughout the political spectrum, that things were taking a new and unexpected turn and that public affairs at a high level would be treated in a way different from the past. The disbelief was often accompanied by a certain awe, a preoccupation by some about what was to happen in the short and in the long run, about what kind of effect would the new government style have on the political system and the country's culture, while others welcomed with great expectations a new leader that promised to disrupt much of the traditional political establishment. An additional question, by more than half of the electorate, had to do with the ability of the leaders to gather a loyal and seemingly unbreakable base of followers. Many voters had decided to support Trump or Berlusconi based on the clear and rational analysis of their interests: many wealthy individuals, for example, understood that they could count on tax cuts, or on legislation favorable to their needs, religious groups may have seen the opportunity to see their values recognized and validated, and therefore oversee many of the evident flaws of their leader. But many others, especially within the less educated and less informed, seemed to genuinely appreciate Trump and Berlusconi and, in fact, would rationalize their choice by adopting the talking points of their parties and seemed ready to defend them no matter what they said or did.

Chapter 3

The art of narrative creation with a little help from the enabling elite

According to a number of scholars and observers[1], Berlusconi was not only able to set up an effective marketing campaign that put him in office, but he even previously created the cultural conditions that made his political ascent possible through the spreading of new values and even a new aesthetics thanks to his TV networks. In this view, over a decade of commercial programming shaped the culture of Italians to such a degree as to make them permeable to the appeal of the new leader, in a break with the traditional political discourse. The supposed cultural transformation would be an effect of the light, entertainment-focused content of commercial TV, and the search for ratings at all costs. While such a contention would be very difficult to definitely disprove (or prove for that matter), to explain the victories of Berlusconi in the 90s, or that of Trump in 2016, a couple of elements should be sufficient (besides the preconditions in the evolution of the political system we discussed in the previous chapter): their unique, effective style of public communication and their ability and relentlessness in distributing rewards and sanctions to other actors with public exposure in an effort to induce them to enhance (or at least not damage) their image with voters.

This style of communication has as one of its main features the absence of shame. As noted by author Michael Wolff in his best-selling book on the current White House:

> Politicians and businesspeople dissemble and misrepresent and spin and prevaricate and mask the truth, but they prefer to avoid out-and-out lying. They have some shame, or at

least a fear of getting caught. But lying willfully, adamantly, without distress or regret, and with absolute disregard of consequences can be a bulwark if not a fail-safe defense. It turns out that somebody always believes you. Fooling some of the people all of the time defined Trump's hardcore base.[2]

Shame may constitute a significant restraint on people's impulses to achieve personal goals and many scholars of emotions establish a close link between sentiments such as shame and ethical values:

> The emotions of guilt and shame are pervasive in daily life. They help maintain a sense of personal identity, function as a mechanism of social control and provide channels for processing stress or norm-violation into self-punishment. Guilt and shame subtly shape behavior, often by causing people to behave so as to avoid experiencing them. It is unlikely that any society could be maintained without them.[3]

Shame, it appears, like other human features, is unevenly distributed among individuals and both Berlusconi and Trump seem to be very close to the end of the spectrum, where this sentiment is nearly absent. While it is probably not surprising to anyone that some individuals may be less inclined to feel guilt or shame, or even inclined to adhere to norms of ethics, an interesting question is why such a feature can be so successful in the realm of politics, or, put in different words, why so many voters seem ready to approve of such lack of shame.

While there are many astonishing similarities in the way Trump and Berlusconi shape their political message to the public, there are some notable differences between the two leaders regarding their relationship with the media of their country; the obvious one being that Berlusconi directly owns most of the private TV channels, what enabled him to control roughly half of the TV news that went into Italian homes. In addition, he controls a significant Milan-based newspaper, a national political magazine, besides several cable channels and other publications. During the years in which he was head of the government, he could also exercise very significant control over the state-owned TV, thus achieving a quasi-monopoly over the news that Italians would receive through television. And, his statement of this subject notwithstanding (he would constantly complain, against all evidence, that his channels did not support him at all), his ownership of this media empire mattered a lot and had a direct impact on the political profile of the news and programming in general. To be sure, some of his media did make an effort to at least appear politically balanced, such as the news program of Canale 5, headed for many years by journalist Enrico Mentana; it is probably not a coincidence that he was later fired and substituted by a much more militant journalist in view of an important election cycle. Most other newsmen, however, simply supported their employer on every issue and in every circumstance, often in embarrassing ways. After announcing that he would run for office in 1994, Berlusconi famously pressured the editor of his Milan newspaper, and one of Italy's most popular conservative journalists, Indro Montanelli, to support his party. He refused, as he envisioned a conservative coalition led by Mariotto Segni. Berlusconi wouldn't fire him directly fearing a backlash, given Montanelli's popularity among the conservative public. But in the next few days, the journalist was attacked by the editor of another of Berlusconi's news channels, who elegantly explained that, among other things, if he wanted to run the paper his way he should also pay for it himself. Montanelli resigned, and all of Berlusconi's news outlets quickly joined the marketing campaign in his favor.

Many observers, in Italy and abroad, would often point to his direct control of a significant part of the news to explain his electoral triumphs and his grip on political power, but while

Berlusconi's ownership of his media empire certainly enabled him to position a brand new party with the public and organize a massive campaign in a relatively short period, it is probably a mistake to consider it the necessary and sufficient condition for his political success, especially during the years following his political debut. The other significant asset he had, one shared by Trump, derives from his skills in framing public narratives, a skill both billionaires developed during years dealing with the press, with politicians, and with the shaping of public debate in general. While Trump does not own broadcasting companies and newspapers, after he won the GOP nomination, in 2016, he could count on the unconditional support of several journalists and talk show hosts who would defend him and his position with such an enthusiasm that would match and often surpass the ardor of Berlusconi's media employees. Another significant "asset" Trump and Berlusconi share is their indifference to consistency: they would try a narrative and if that did not work they would simply change it and try something else, without worrying about the coherence of their discourse.

But how relevant is TV for electoral politics anyway? As we mentioned, according to a recent study, very important, particularly in Berlusconi's case. Not only for the direct support during his campaigns but rather for its role in the shaping of the Italian culture in the decade before his running for office. The study, published in 2019 by the American Economic Review[4], analyzes voting patterns in Italy in areas previously covered by commercial TV (at a time when they offered only entertainment programs as news was broadcast nationally only by the state-owned RAI) and compares them with areas where such programming was not available. The research found a strong correlation between exposure to TV entertainment and later voting in favor of Berlusconi. But the study goes further and shows that among younger individuals, exposure to entertainment programming is associated with lower cognitive skills and lower levels of civic engagement (which would also help explain the support for Forza Italia years later, as this party's electorate is significantly skewed toward the poorly educated). As The Atlantic writer Yasha Mounk said about this paper, "...If you had asked me a few days ago, I would have been highly skeptical of these claims. They sound far too much like the sort of thing educated people *want* to believe."[5] Nevertheless it is a claim that others have suggested in Italy in the past. In a famous scene from the movie "Il Caimano" (The Caiman), Nanni Moretti, a left-leaning movie director, responds to a young and politically engaged screenwriter who warns that they just cannot let Berlusconi win: "He already won, twenty years ago...with his televisions...he changed our heads." Paolo Mancini, a scholar of public communication and journalism, writes that:

> The progressive weakening of mass parties leaves room for a strong leader, in this case with enormous resources of money and media, who has been able to integrate his politics with the new framework of images and desires. These images are deeply rooted in the content of the mass media. At the same time, this leader has met the expectations of a political culture increasingly and strongly influenced by individualism and particularism. Seventeen years after Berlusconi publicly declared a union between politics and media, the feeling is still strong that commercial television has dramatically changed the idea and the structure of Italian politics.[6]

Undoubtedly, the effects of TV entertainment programs on culture will be studied in all their aspects and the existence of some long-term correlation between the values that these programs propose to the audiences and their political behavior would hardly be surprising. However, there is a more immediate and obvious way in which TV, as well as other media, has an impact on politics: through the way it proposes and frames political issues, ideas, parties, and candidates.

* * *

Long before Trump and Berlusconi decided to run for office, the media had largely forged their publicly perceived personas. Berlusconi was the self-made entrepreneur who, after creating a real estate empire, managed to defy the state-run monopoly of national TV broadcasting by introducing new and modern channels, thus giving more choice to consumers and providing companies with more opportunities to market their products through advertising. Contrary to the state-run programming, made by bureaucrats or politicians, all talk and little action, or by intellectuals, with their condescending attitude and their obsession for educational, and often boring, programs, Berlusconi was giving Italians what they really wanted. He was buying high-budget programs from the US and producing shows locally with the most popular hosts and entertainers. Trump seemingly had to put in a little more of a specific effort, at least at the beginning, to get the attention of the media and generate his public image. And that he did, using his usual tactics: a lot of lying and misrepresentation (including impersonating a fictional Trump aid and calling reporters to promote his persona), offering many opportunities for gospels and entertaining news, and the occasional lawsuit threats when he did not appreciate a story in the press. The strategy, possibly with some ups and downs, worked and in many ways, Trump managed to create an image of himself that was similar to that of Berlusconi: a tough, plain-speaking, and successful entrepreneur, who would succeed in many tasks where inefficient politicians and inept officers could not deliver. Such as renewing the Wollman skating rink in Central Park in the 80s, after years of unsuccessful attempts by the city of New York. But what really made Trump so familiar to many Americans was his central role in the reality TV shows,

The Apprentice and Celebrity Apprentice: after 2016, several scholars investigated Trump's participation in these shows and, in most cases, found a significant correlation between his public exposure as a TV star and voters' support for him.[7]

Even if TV is not as impactful as some of the studies about cultural predisposition suggest, how relevant is it, or the media in general, for the electoral competition within a political system? This question, of course, has been one of the most frequently asked by political operatives and pundits for decades, as well as by researchers of political science. Competition for office in democratic countries can be quite fierce and a good understanding of all the elements that can determine the outcome of a race is of paramount importance. Analysis of the effect of the media on voters and of their role, in general, in influencing public opinion have at times focused on the fact that citizens, or at least most of them, are relatively uninformed about political events and current affairs, and their lack of knowledge allows for ample manipulation by the media. This is mostly true: the vast majority of the people are quite busy working, raising their families and the like, and have very little time left to dedicate to studying public policy problems; they mostly have to rely on someone to study those problems for them and provide them with options when it is time to vote. At the same time, representing the media (or even the "mainstream media") as some powerful entity ready to manipulate voters according to its own agenda would be misleading: for starters, the media is made up of a relatively large number of actors with different and conflicting objectives. Some are right-leaning, others are left-leaning, most prize economic results above all other objectives. The influential 1988 book *Manufacturing of Consent: The Political Economy of Mass Media* by Edward Herman and Noam Chomsky proposes several factors that impact the ability of media corporations to achieve favorable economic results: things such as the capacity to make significant investments, advertising sales, access to the sources of news, and others. According to the authors these elements, or "filters," would strongly influence media company behavior. While it would be difficult to argue against the relevance of the factors mentioned in the book, it is important to remember that media companies, like all corporations, are complex entities and their final "behavior" depends ultimately on the actions of the individuals within it: how they interact with each other and with the external entities. Each individual will be certainly influenced by market forces, but also by other factors: culture, ethical values, personal ambitions, etc.[8] In many cases, journalists, managers, and other individuals within the same media company can have divergent agendas and the way that the news companies frame the issues may be much more complex and difficult to predict than the model proposed by Chomsky and Herman.

Of course, people form their opinion not only based on what they may read in the paper or hear on TV but also, possibly more so, based on the conversations and exchanges of information they practice daily with their network of contacts within their community. Today these contacts can be multiplied, enhanced (some would say, not without grounds, distorted) by social media. Nevertheless, the media, or the traditional media as we may call them, maintain a very significant role in the formation of public opinion. For starters the media select which news to publish among all the possible events that could be reported; whatever is not in the news will not be known by anyone except the small minority that may have direct knowledge. Of course, deliberately skipping news in order to advance an agenda can be dangerous for an outlet, as its public may lose confidence in it as an information source. Most media organizations influence each other in defining which events are newsworthy, but also the definition of how much space or time to dedicate to each issue has relevance and will likely affect how the audience perceives the issue. Much of the political events of the day are presented by interviews and debate with politicians, which gives them the chance to effectively influence what and how events are presented. Ultimately the news outlets decide which politicians to interview or invite on a TV show, but most times such appearances are negotiated with the administration or the political parties in a dynamic scenario where each tries to advance an agenda. Another way in which the media can impact the perception of an issue is by "framing" it in a certain way: that is defining a certain narrative with respect to the issue, shaping its interpretation, making sense of the events reported.

In any case, we should always keep in mind that media companies are entities that provide services to the public and therefore are deeply influenced by the public just in the same way, if not more, as the public may be influenced by them. Many companies in this trade want to make a difference, no doubt, in terms of presenting issues in such a manner as to contribute to the positive development (in their judgment) of society. Nevertheless, they also, and foremost, want to be relevant and want to be able to pay the bills: a condition to achieve both goals is to sell copies (or to have good ratings), as Herman and Chomsky stated. So media companies will always look very closely at what the public is more interested in, possibly a lot more than whatever political agenda they may have. In order to better understand what their audience is interested in, the media companies will monitor closely the interactions with their readers (or viewers, or listeners) but also the stories told by competing companies, and how successful these stories are in entertaining, or informing, or stimulating their public. Just as the political supply and demand influence each other to determine certain outcomes, the same is true for the interaction of the media and the public: it is a highly dynamic world, which changes constantly throughout several interactions and reciprocal influences.

Having said that, the general orientations of the press core are a very significant element of society and play a relevant role in the definition of the policy agenda and the power struggle. A recent book by Matthew Pressman[9] describes the press until the early 60s as quite different if compared to the one we have become accustomed to afterward: back then, a significant part of a newspaper's political news would be dedicated to the government's announcements and transcripts, with quotes from high officials and very little challenging of politicians' views by the reporters. Political issues would be reported with a fair amount of what could be described as deference to the government, or to institutions in general: many statements of fact, together with speeches and official quotes, but little interpretation of the events or the policies. Just a few years later, starting in the 70s, the situation changed to a significant degree: much more analysis and interpretation of official views, more challenging of elected politicians and government officials by reporters. The media began dedicating significantly more space to public protest, manifestations, and, in general, views on public issues different from the official ones, including allegations of wrongdoing by elected politicians, even in absence of formal indictments, a threshold observed in the past for revealing such scandals. Something very similar can be observed in the evolution of the Italian media: until the early 60s, most of the press is rather close to the governing party, the Christian Democrats. In some cases, it is directly controlled by it, as with Turin's daily *Gazzetta del Popolo*. Other outlets, often owned by families of industrialists, as with Milan's *Corriere della Sera*, the main national paper, are usually aligned with the official views and particularly ready to guard readers against the dangers of the left-leaning parties. In one instance the situation is mixed, as in the case of the daily *Il Giorno*, owned by ENI, a government-controlled corporation which is also one of the world's biggest oil and gas producers. In this case, the company (and its press arm as a consequence) is controlled by the left side of the Christian Democratic Party, and the resulting journalism is not immune from instances of great quality and significant investigative reporting. Most of the transition of the Italian media took place in the immediate aftermath of the "counterculture" in Europe, in the years 1968-69. By 1974 the *Corriere della Sera*, in the hands of a new editor, had lost all of its timidity in denouncing public corruption instances and appeared to be looking with curiosity, if not interest, to the evolution of the Communist Party. Many other papers followed the lead, in one way or another, and in 1976 a new daily based in Rome, *La Republica,* would become the second national paper and would mostly act as a check on the government from the left.

This cultural transition of the media, both in Italy and the US, is a reflection of a broader societal change that is commonly associated with the counterculture movements; the 60s in America, 1968, more specifically, in Europe. The main elements of this cultural shift, which, non-coincidentally, roughly coincides with the diffusion of mass higher education in the industrialized world, are lower regard for hierarchies and tradition, a higher proclivity to challenge authorities of all sorts, including religion, and a higher degree of openness to various expressions of life, including sex. Overall, though it was a complex phenomenon, the counterculture movement could be somewhat defined as left-leaning: in Europe, many of its leaders were openly following the Marxist tradition, though many opposed the established Marxist parties; in the US, most leaders and supporters of this cultural change perceived conservatives as their primary antagonists. Consequently, the "counterculture" was also a major factor in deepening the wedge between the left and the right of the political spectrum. In the US the conservative wave at the end of the decade, of which the "Silent majority" was a major element, supported the Nixon presidency and was largely a cultural reaction to the sixties; just like later conservative movements. As Newt Gingrich put it in 1995:

Here's how we did it until the Great Society messed everything up: don't work, don't eat; your salvation is spiritual; the government by definition can't save you; governments are into maintenance and all good reforms are into transformation...From 1965 to 1994, we did strange and weird things as a country. Now we're done with that and we have to recover. The counterculture is a momentary aberration in American history that will be looked back upon as a quaint period of Bohemianism brought to the national elite...counterculture McGoverniks...taught self-indulgent, aristocratic values without realizing that if an entire society engaged in the indulgences of an elite few, you could tear the society to shreds.[10]

If the immediate reaction to the counterculture movement in the US was Nixon and the Silent Majority, in Italy it took the more sinister form of right-wing terrorism,[11] made worse by an apparent unwillingness of the government (or at least parts of the government) to effectively contrast it. A few years later, as we have seen, in another effort to curtail the effects of the 1968 movement, a right-leaning association of politicians, government officials, journalists, and corporate managers created the covert masonry lodge P2, of which Berlusconi was a prominent member.

Some observers[12] see the renewed role of journalism starting in the 70s, characterized by more analysis and less reporting of plain facts and official announcements, as a consequence of the competition by TV, that was acquiring the role of event reporting, often on an instant basis. That may well be, but, of course, there was a politically relevant element to this change: as papers partly shifted their attention from the official reporting to other sources, such as activists and minorities, from culture to counterculture, many media outlets may have been perceived as shifting too much to the left. In Italy this had immediate consequences: in 1974, the popular journalist Montanelli left the

Corriere to found a new conservative paper, later to be bought by Berlusconi, *Il Giornale*. A few years later the P2 took control of the *Corriere* directly, through the Ambrosiano Bank, thus correcting from the inside its perceived left-leaning attitude, until the intervention by the Milan prosecutors. In the US, the papers were mostly strong enough to look after themselves, but one lasting consequence of their evolution may have been the perception by many conservatives of the US mainstream media as biased toward liberals.

Such perception by US conservatives became manifest in the public debate since, at least, the 80s and it seems to have been growing in the last decades. During the Reagan administration, the Federal Communication Commission stopped enforcing the Fairness Doctrine, which required radio stations to present opposing views of an issue. Quickly, the phenomenon of conservative talk radio programs spread across the country, the most prominent being the one hosted by Rush Limbaugh. He and others began a campaign denouncing the liberal bias of the mainstream media and, by the end of the 80s, the conservative political elite was also characterizing the media as biased toward liberal values in a rather systematic way. Was there an actual bias in the traditional media outlet or was it mostly a strategy adopted by conservatives for their own political gain? Bias is a problem as old as journalism of course. A story can be told in a variety of different ways, even without making false or misleading statements, and each way can be politically advantageous or detrimental to different politicians or parties. Back in the old days, say over a century ago, journalists usually thought that news could be reported objectively, by simply laying out the facts "as they were," a position quite similar to that of classic XIX century positivist historians, who thought history could be simply recorded by narrating events, "letting them speak for themselves." Soon, many realized that things were not that easy. After World War I, for example, many news outlets recognized that a significant part of the facts they reported had been filtered by governments' propaganda agencies, often distorting the truth. Both historians and journalists, for starters, have to select which events they find relevant and how relevant each is. This selection, let alone how the event is narrated, is a highly subjective task that depends on the author's personal experiences, inclinations, and, of course, political bias. While journalism associations in many countries adopted codes of ethics to ensure accuracy and impartiality in the reporting of news, it is not at all easy to establish actual processes to achieve this objective. The late Indro Montanelli suggested a simple rule of thumb: given that all journalists have to deal with their prejudices, they should abstain from dismissing the facts that disprove those prejudices as well as overemphasizing those that favor them.

As for the question regarding the supposed liberal bias of current mainstream media in the US, numerous scholars have attempted to measure it by analyzing media content. Many studies show that bias actually exists and that outlets can be ordered on a right-left spectrum.[13] A recent study, in particular, shows that both newspapers' and TV news programs' political bias can be accurately detected and measured: of the outlets considered Breitbart was the one found to be further to the right, while the Daily Kos was the most left-leaning. Most other media (the study included many of the well-known outlets such as The New York Times and the Washington Post), while showing slight slants, were found to be very close to the center and to each other. An interesting point of this inquiry is the different positioning of the news teams versus the opinion side of each media on the spectrum: the one showing the biggest gap, not unexpectedly, was Fox News[14], where the regular news department is rather balanced while the political opinion programs are heavily right-leaning. The overall conclusion of these scholars, however, was that the bias, at least as far as the main news organizations are concerned, is not significant. Another recent study, aimed at determining whether there is a bias in the way stories are chosen by journalists, also in this case found no bias, either toward liberals or conservatives.[15] Other lines of research focused on the narrative about the supposed liberal bias of the mainstream media to understand whether it was originated by a genuine belief in its existence or if it was a strategically used talking point:

> There might be several strategies prompting such claims of liberal bias, but one that seems likely is that criticism represents an attempt by conservative elites to cast doubts about the credibility of news media in the minds of voters. Research claiming links of liberal bias during presidential campaigns to shifts in public opinion about the ideological leanings of the press suggests such efforts are successful among some citizens.[16]

If indeed the narrative about the liberal bias is a strategy, it seems to work to some extent. In fact, the attitude of GOP voters toward the role of the press seems to change significantly depending on who is in charge, "...A Pew poll in 2018 found that 82% of Democrats thought the media perform a useful 'watchdog' role of keeping politicians from doing things they shouldn't. Only 38% of Republicans agreed. By contrast, five years earlier, when Barack Obama was president, the figures were 67% and 69% respectively."[17]

The role of Fox News on national US politics and on the orientations of the conservative public can hardly be overstated; its relevance is comparable, if not superior, to that of talk radio. A study performed 10 years after its launch in the cable news market in 1996 attempted to understand the effect of Fox on actual voting behavior. It considered voting data in over 9000 towns in the US and compared voting trends of presidential elections in areas where Fox was available with others where it was not. The result appeared fairly straightforward, showing a clear effect of relative advantage for the GOP where Fox programming was viewed by the public. According to the authors, Fox News convinced between 3 percent and 8 percent of its viewers to vote Republican.[18] Another interesting media study, a few years later, attempted to understand the extent by which voters, in the aftermath of the 2010 mid-term elections, felt media outlets were informing them correctly about current political events and also if they were in fact misinformed by the media. The findings for the first question, whether viewers and readers felt misinformed, were probably not surprising: a substantial majority of voters felt that they "encountered false or misleading information in the last election, with a majority that said that this occurred frequently and occurred more frequently than usual." The second, and possibly more interesting part of the survey, which evaluated whether citizens were being adequately informed on relevant issues such as the health care reform law, the stimulus, President Obama's birthplace, TARP (the bailout program for certain financial corporations), found that viewers of Fox News were consistently misinformed to a much higher degree than viewers of other cable news outlets or newspaper readers. For example, individuals watching Fox News on a daily basis were much more inclined to believe that the birthplace of Obama was unclear; or that the stimulus legislation did not include tax cuts (it did of course).[19]

As we saw, the new way to do journalism after the 60s, both in the US and Italy, was a lot more challenging for the political elites. Arguably more so in the US than Italy, as the US press has demonstrated a much higher ability to engage in the investigative reporting that contributed to the unearthing of many scandals and politicians' wrongdoings. To be fair to the Italian journalists, the US press could often count on the crucial help of whistleblowers from within administrations to provide the information and the context for politically relevant stories (think of the role of "deep throat" for the Watergate story in the Washington Post). The American administrative state is largely made up of public servants who see their work as a mission and hardly tolerate corruption or wrongdoing within their administration; often enough, they resort to leaking those instances to the press when needed. This is a phenomenon from which the Italian press could seldom benefit. While there may have been exceptions, the usual implicit arrangement between Italian high-ranking state officials and politicians is that politicians wouldn't mess with the officials (by curtailing their power or by trying to implement more efficient processes in their departments) and, in turn, they wouldn't do anything to affect the politicians' public image. A situation such as former FBI Associate Director Mark Felt acting as deep throat was (and is) very unlikely to be seen in Italy. But there are other important reasons for a less impactful role of newspapers in the political arena of Italy if compared to the US. In Italy, historically, just about 10 percent of the population reads newspapers (not counting media specializing in sports and other specific areas) with some regularity, this greatly limited the papers' resources and, of course, investigative capabilities. Great journalistic enterprises, such as the unearthing of Judge Roy Moore's allegation of sexual misconduct, based on hundreds of interviews in Alabama in 2017 by a team from the Washington Post, or the tax report on the Trump family published by The New York Times in 2018, that required months of analysis of official records of individuals and organizations, just cannot be undertaken without significant resources.

* * *

The public persona of Trump and Berlusconi, their image as tough and effective businessmen who know how to get things done, was somewhat consistent, or it appeared to be, with the way they talked to the public when they ran for office. This is particularly true in Italy at the beginning of the 90s, at a time when the Italian electorate was accustomed to a traditional political elite that seemed to make all possible efforts not to be understood by the layperson. Quite often, in general, politicians try to avoid taking clear stands: it is a strategic attitude that allows them to maintain more flexibility in the future; this proclivity alone may already make their public statements ambiguous and complicated to read for citizens. But in the case of many Italian politicians, an additional problem was their cultural baggage, their doctrines, and the vocabulary that came with it. The two stronger parties of the system until the 90s, the Christian Democrats and the communists, accounting together for about 70 percent of the electorate, had strong doctrinal foundations. The Christian Democrats could be either right or left-leaning, but were always embracing the Catholic ethics (occasionally difficult to apply consistently to the administration of modern society) and the vocabulary associated with it, while the communists adhered to the Marxist perspective of social analysis, and used the correlated jargon, with concepts such as "historical materialism" and the distinction between "structure" and "superstructure," categories that had lost much of their appeal well before the end of the twentieth century. So, besides the ordinary difficulties that politicians always have in delivering clear and straightforward messages to the public, most Italian elected officials had to deal with a certain elitism of speech and their own doctrine-derived vocabulary when speaking in public, which made their statements occasionally obscure and, at times, affected by logical inconsistencies, often forcing the speaker to respond to challenges with very subtle arguments, so subtle, in fact, that very few people could understand them. Also, in many instances, politicians spoke publicly or to the media, not so much in order to inform the public about an issue, but rather to send oblique messages (be it a warning, a threat, or an alliance pledge) to other politicians and thus used terms and expressions that made sense only to the initiated. In other cases still, politicians, as they often do, simply did not want to state publicly their position on a given issue and dodged the questions by presenting very complex concepts that left the public wondering. When Berlusconi entered the political arena and started giving public speeches, with his simple vocabulary and common-sense logic, to many voters he made the old politicians look like Martians trying to explain to them the theory of space-time. Trump had to act in a very different environment compared to Berlusconi. American politicians did not have the baggage of doctrines, and the terminology that goes with them, to worry about, and at least since the 80s a superb public communicator such as Reagan had shown everyone how to effectively reach voters. Nevertheless, if there is something that prevents politicians from appearing as straight-talking, it is the restraint brought by an excess of political correctness (PC). Trump understood this very well and took all the advantage he could from it.

Political correctness has been a highly debated concept in the last few years. Usually, by that expression we mean the avoidance of words or expressions that may offend minorities or groups of individuals based on such things as gender, ethnic origins, religion, disability, sexual orientation, or other similar criteria. For some time there has been a debate about whether political correctness is deleterious and to what extent. Unfortunately, in the contemporary politically polarized society, the debate is complicated by the fact that PC is mostly seen in a bad light by conservatives, though also several prominent left-leaning people have shown a disdain for it: for example, comedian Bill Maher (who even had a show named "Politically incorrect" a few years back) and the late British journalist Christopher Hitchens (if he can be labeled as "left-leaning"). The debate about PC usually breaks out when a public figure makes a statement that is in a possible violation of PC, a number of people or organizations acknowledge the violation in protest and many take sides.

Some argue that everyone, including the person who made the controversial statement, has free speech rights according to the first amendment (or other legal grounds in countries different from the US), and therefore those who protest the statement should back off. This legal argument does not make a lot of sense in these contexts: the right of free speech, or free expression, is granted to citizens to prevent arbitrary government censorship, but as a cultural issue, if everyone has the right to express her view, everyone else has the same right to criticize it, even the right to consider it politically incorrect.

Most people would be fine with the principle that it is appropriate not to offend fellow citizens, especially the weakest ones. However, critics do have a point that political correctness sometimes reaches a point that obfuscates the understanding of an issue. Situations in which, for example, a minority entitled to respect and protection is considered immune to criticism for the mere fact of being a minority. Is it not appropriate to criticize Muslim immigrants if they force unwilling women in their families to perform acts, according to their religion? Or is it appropriate, if a statistically significant correlation between a given nationality and a given crime is found, to state it publicly? Probably most reasonable people would say yes, but there are several people, especially on the left, who would have issues with it. In some cases, the urge to prove respect for categories of citizens considered weak proves so strong as to progressively affect our vocabulary: a few decades ago it would have been considered fine to address someone as a "crippled" without meaning any disrespect or harm; later it was found to be more politically correct to address such an individual as a "disabled person." However, someone could point out that the expression "a person with a disability" would be preferable, as to "dilute the link between the individual and the 'disability' and to reiterate that the disability is only a single element of many which make up the individual."[20] In Italy, nowadays, the preferred expression would be "a person with different abilities," to remind us that such a person may have abilities, even though she may lack some of those abilities that most people have. In time such expression may be found to be slightly ironic, therefore not politically correct and a new one would have to be introduced. Such verbal struggles may appear as excessive exercise in minority protection to many reasonable people. During a debate, Maher proposed his definition of politically correct as "the elevation of sensitivity over truth," to which psychologist Jordan Peterson added, "It is the elevation of moral posturing about sensitivity over truth, it is even worse."[21] Examples of both can easily be found in contemporary public debates, but while they demonstrate that political correctness can sometimes be an obstacle to critical thinking, it does not follow that it should be banned altogether from our culture: respect for minorities is hardly a bad thing in itself. As in many other realms, measure and balance may be the solution.

Arguably, no one exploited political correctness fatigue for political gain more than the current US president. Also, it is hard to think of a politician who attacked the very concept of political correctness more than Trump since he launched his campaign in 2015. This caused many conservatives, especially those that constitute his base, to cheer and many liberals to condemn him; in fact, one of the reasons the current occupant of the White House provokes so much excitement within Democratic supporters is the way he displays no respect for established norms of conduct. As Peter Lawler puts it, "Overall, Trump is the best stimulus package political correctness has ever received."[22] The same could be said of Berlusconi in Italy during the 90s and the following years.

Politics can be viewed as the means to solving a fundamental problem of living in society: how to establish power in order to make society function in an orderly way for the benefit of its members, but avoiding, at the same time, that said power is abused by some empowered individuals for their own advantage to the detriment of most. Current, highly industrialized societies, characterized by extreme division of labor, are very complex and require sophisticated levels of legislation, regulation, and administration. Debating specific issues requires language that can be often perceived as technical and sophisticated. Nevertheless, when politicians adopt sophisticated language in public speeches, they distance themselves from a significant portion of the electorate, possibly a majority of it in fact. The challenge, for those politicians who wish to offer a vision for society and seek to improve it, is to express complex matters in as simple a way as possible. Politicians who have little interest in actual social improvement do not have that problem: they can concentrate on delivering oversimplified messages, particularly messages they know their audience enjoys hearing. It is quite evident that the two leaders to whom this book is dedicated belong to the latter category; however, there is a difference between the two. Berlusconi, while quite effective in displaying a clear and appealing speech pattern, maintains a certain level of formality. Trump appears to, simply, not care at all and, outside of written and scripted speeches, he often expresses his thoughts in public as would a guy in a bar talking to a couple of friends, at times using phrase structures, or "word salads," that are more commonly heard from toddlers. John McWhorther, a linguist from Columbia, said on MSNBC that Trump seems to use "what language was undoubtedly like when it first emerged among people who didn't have writing and were getting their first verbal sea legs...It is great for casual circumstances, but he uses that same way of speaking in what most of us would consider formal and important circumstances, he never leaves the realm of the casual."[23] In this way, Trump dismisses complex issues with a few casual remarks, but he also makes himself appealing and familiar to many voters, particularly to the poorly educated. In addition, by adding the total lack of formality to his speech pattern he also expresses dominance. He seems to say: "you see? I don't have to be careful and put effort into the way I express myself. I don't have to think too hard about what I say, as Obama did during his long pauses. I say whatever I want and nobody can compel me otherwise." He can show he is above reproach, he doesn't have to be presidential, as he often brags, and his speech pattern is probably the most evident aspect of it.

The appeal of oversimplified language is strongly connected to the public sentiment usually called anti-intellectualism, which has a significant role in modern US (as well as Italian) politics. Of course, this is hardly a new phenomenon and many statements included in Richard Hofstadter's 1963 classic *Anti-Intellectualism in American Life* are certainly valid today, starting with the fact that anti-intellectualism resides overwhelmingly in the right. In the 50s it was interlaced with anti-communism, today it is wider in its scope and seems to be more intense as the GOP often uses anti-intellectual rhetoric to attack the cultural elites and characterize them as distant from the "Real America."[24] Newt Gingrich, one of the political entrepreneurs who arguably contributed more than anyone to the deepening of the current political polarization, used anti-intellectualism profusely, despite being himself an intellectual, as an academic, and a university professor. Another, similarly divisive, politician in Berlusconi's cabinet team by the name of Giulio Tremonti, also an academic, once proudly said at a rally that: "We are the ones who do not read books," plausibly in order to fully please the crowd of right-wing supporters that was listening.[25] In fact, Berlusconi's party was equally anti-intellectual. One of the few real scholars who joined the group, the classical liberal Giuliano Urbani (who had been among the first to worry about the perspectives of a victory of the left in 1994 and had warned various entrepreneurs of the necessity of creating a conservative alliance), was quickly marginalized, like most other intellectuals unwilling to join the populist attitude of Forza Italia. For conservative politicians, anti-intellectualism has also the advantage of being interpreted as mainly anti-left, as progressives were being increasingly perceived as the "liberal elite" in Italy as well as in the US. A clear advantage of anti-intellectualism display is that it allows those who embrace it to propose simple solutions to complex problems, solutions that can be easily understood without a lot of analysis: such as building a big wall on the border to solve the immigration problem. To many, especially poorly educated voters, it can be an appealing way out of the sophisticated issues of dealing with the government of modern society as well as the ethical problems that arise in policy-making: why bother with the complexity of the elites' analysis when there are banal explanations and remedies for everything? As a nineteenth-century Italian social scientist, Francesco Ferrara, once said: "The despot compromises with the demagogue, does not forgive the economist." The habit of throwing in the word "fascism" when analyzing political phenomena has been largely abused and most of the time it is not helpful to better understand right-leaning parties or politicians. However, the anti-intellectualism which is so characteristic of Berlusconi's and Trump's supporters was also a very important element of Mussolini's regime in Italy. And it is probably not a coincidence that one of fascism's best-known slogans, "Me ne frego," which could be translated with "I don't give a damn,"[26] can be interpreted as a manifestation of such an attitude toward the intellectual elite.

As Trump once said at a campaign rally, "You know, I've always wanted to say this—I've never said this before with all the talking we all do—all of these experts, 'Oh we need an expert—' The experts are terrible!"[27] Certainly the disdain toward expertise and professional analysis by many citizens is not something that was wholly generated by Trump, as it wasn't created by Berlusconi in Italy. Several books in the last few years testify to the increasing development of this attitude within part of the public[28]; but certainly Trump has a major role in encouraging and validating it. And many Republicans have condoned it for years. A typical example is their often-stated position on regulations: the less, the better, which is obviously a deceiving oversimplification. In today's highly sophisticated economic systems, regulations play an extremely important role and their design and implementation require specialized study; nevertheless, a solution often sold to the public is that eliminating regulations is good for its own sake, regardless of the complexity of the specific matter. As presidential historian John Meacham said, "We are almost in a pre-enlightenment, pre-reformation world...the premise of reason, which was the whole insight of modernity, that you could look at data, you could observe reality and then form your views as opposed to be handed your views from on high..."[29]

* * *

A powerful factor that interacted between Trump and Berlusconi on one side and the media establishments of their respective countries on the other, is the entertainment value that these two leaders were able to supply the media with. It started when they entered the political arena, and it seems destined to last for so long as they have a relevant political role. Both made their debut in politics with highly controversial statements that projected them right on the first page of the main papers; both provided a significant boost to the sales of newspapers and to the audiences of talk shows and political debates during their tenures. One major reason they managed to constantly fill the news cycles is that a significant part of the public found them entertaining. Two main mechanisms can plausibly be used to explain why their act is fun to so many people. The first derives from the surprising availability of a political supply that is emotionally in line with certain voter groups and ready to part ways with the politically-correct, traditional style of politics, and state clear messages that had been regarded as outside the political mainstream. It is not just the plain, even crude, language, it is the norm-breaking that shows many followers that there is, after all, a different way to do politics, that doesn't involve candidates looking down on them, and, on the contrary, may own those elitists, particularly the liberals, who are always trying to remind them how inadequate they are. This element would play a role, of course, in explaining how unapologetic certain citizens feel about the two leaders. The second source of entertainment comes from a totally different audience, which includes those that oppose Trump and Berlusconi and find their rhetoric and norm-shattering surprisingly outrageous. To the extent that outrage can be exiting and entertaining, the frequent statements by Trump and Berlusconi were able to provide new interests to those who were shocked that someone could just break with established norms with no apparent consequence whatsoever. Those same people were left scrambling to understand toward which uncharted direction the political culture of their country was moving and with the urge of keeping informed about the details and the context of Trump's and Berlusconi's deeds.

During the 2016 GOP primary campaign, the US media followed Trump very closely and dedicated to his campaign a lot more coverage than any of his competitors. Eventually, the extremely large amount of space given to him by the networks could be explained, at least in part, by the fact that he was leading in the polls (not an unusual criterion adopted by the media), but in the beginning, he wasn't enjoying a lead and he still would get more air time than the other candidates. According to scholar Thomas Patterson[30], the guiding line of the TV shows was the entertainment factor: Trump could really stimulate an interest. As performer Seth Meyers noted, Trump often adopts the technique of stand-up comedians, trying out punch lines with the audiences, noting which one is most appreciated and sticking with it for the following shows. In fact, Trump even admitted it himself: as he noticed that his audience was appreciating him shouting "drain the swamp," he kept saying it at his rallies more and more. Berlusconi's favorite trick during speeches were jokes, especially dirty jokes. But the main item in both leaders' repertoire is controversy. They fully understood that with controversial statements they would constantly capture most of the attention of the media, hence the attention of the public, and they pursued this tactic with enough determination as to keep the focus almost constantly on them and occupying the newspapers and the news channels with their fights, their insults, and their politically incorrect stands, giving new meaning to the maxim that "there is no such thing as bad publicity."

While the ability of Trump and Berlusconi to entertain gives them ample opportunities to dominate the news and to deliver their messages to the audiences, it would be very difficult for them to maintain an image as statesmen, at least with part of the electorate, without the assistance of the so-called "enablers." In fact, the one element that makes it possible to maintain the upside-down world in which they thrive is their ability to create a circle of people with media exposure that would defend and promote whatever these leaders do or state, thus validating their conduct. The "enablers" are members of the cabinet or the administration, party officials, political pundits, reporters, radio or TV hosts, and intellectuals of various kinds that go on the air or publish newspaper columns rationalizing and "normalizing" the statements of the boss. These individuals have the special role of making the leaders plausible in the public sphere: they struggle to extract sense out of all the controversial statements and acts, and insert them, to some extent, into the mainstream of ideas. How could Berlusconi and Trump manage to induce a large number of people, many with a significant public reputation, to play that role? In many, possibly most, cases, there is a purely rational deal: people with public exposure easily sense that Trump and Berlusconi are highly transactional and that they are ready to reward anyone with an audience who is available to enhance their public perception. In a typical example, a newspaper reporter from the Turin-based daily *La Stampa*, Augusto Minzolini, after years of working to present a positive image of Berlusconi was rewarded when the tycoon became prime minister for the fourth time in 2008 by being nominated to the powerful position of director of the TG1, the news section of the main state-owned TV channel.[31] In an interview with Anderson Cooper, the radio host Howard Stern explained that Trump had asked him to speak in the nomination convention of the GOP in the summer of 2016 and that he knew he could get anything from Trump if he had accepted to play that role.[32] The transactional attitude displayed by Trump is evidently very clear to Senator Lindsey Graham, who was a harsh critic of the current president during the primary, but seems to have become a close confidant of his after the election. As he said to journalist Mark Leibovich, "From my point of view, if you know anything about me, it would be odd not to do this…'this' is to try to be relevant…I've got an opportunity here working with the President to get some really good outcome for the country."[33] Given the rewards that Trump and Berlusconi are willing to give to their enablers, it is not surprising that so many journalists who had demonstrated their loyalty and availability to defend any of the leader's statements ascended to government roles during their administrations. And the leaders don't require subtlety: actually the more sycophant a pundit can be, the better; even defenses that would be considered shameful by most people are highly welcome. As when, in June 2017, Trump's cabinet members were assembled to publicly praise and thank the leader for the opportunity given to them to serve in the administration.[34] Berlusconi appreciated the same kind of praise and display of personal loyalty.

However, it would probably be a mistake to assume that all the "enablers" act on a transactional basis. Many of them must believe that, even though some of the statements and actions of these leaders may be wrong, it is best to play along for the long-term objectives of the conservative cause. This is a direct consequence of the extreme polarization that Trump and Berlusconi introduced (or exacerbated, rather) in their political systems. Their highly divisive rhetoric generates a situation where most people feel forced to take sides; this mechanism works for the electorate, but even more so for the elite. The conservative electorate is forced to choose between embracing the new right-wing wave and continue opposing the liberals or adopt a relatively neutral stand. Something similar is true for those who have public exposure, except in their case those conservatives who do not align themselves with the leader are relentlessly attacked, probably more so, in fact, than political opponents from the left: Trump and Berlusconi simply cannot allow adversaries on the right. Clear examples are Indro Montanelli in Italy and William Kristol in the US. The Italian journalist, one of the country's most popular and with solid conservative credentials, was forced to leave the newspaper he had founded and was ultimately marginalized from public life. As for Kristol, one of Trump's fiercest critics on the right, he had to witness his magazine, the Weekly Standard, being shut down while he became rather irrelevant in the public debate. As has been noted:

> ...like the Maoists, the Trumpers aren't really interested in picking a fight with the other superpower. They're much more concerned with controlling the near abroad—which is to say, the Republican Party. That's why they tend to focus their hatred on Republicans and conservatives who decline to get on board, rather than on Democrats and liberals. Jeff Flake is the enemy; Kamala Harris is just a random nonplayer character.[35]

Conservative magazines with ambitions of intellectual

leadership, such as the National Review, quite critical of Trump during the nomination process, were seemingly induced to join the new conservative playbook. While some of its writers occasionally criticize some of Trump's most outrageous tweets and actions, these outlets are very careful not to provoke the GOP base, knowing that a frontal attack to the leader of the GOP can mean going out of business or at least becoming irrelevant. Under Trump and Berlusconi, ultimately, all conservatives have to face a trade-off between access and relevance on one side, and integrity and reputation on the other: at times a rather difficult choice.

The simple method enacted by Trump and Berlusconi, distributing punishments and rewards to individuals with a politically relevant public profile depending on their attitude toward them, proved very effective in at least two ways. For starters, it allows them to pose as the clear leader of the right side of the political spectrum, with very little competition from other politicians of that side of the aisle. The second one is that it provides a significant edge in comparison with the communication effort of the opposing party. Trump and Berlusconi can always count on being in full control of the conservative framing of events and their narratives will be disseminated, in most cases, with very few personal interpretations by the journalists, pundits, and politicians of their side, systematically and effectively. The individuals participating in this process know very well what the boss wants and the way their loyalties will be put to the test, so, once they accept the deal, they will adhere to the message with the highest degree of consistency. Whereas public statements on the other side come from many different independent individuals: politicians, pundits, and journalists, who, usually, have nobody to answer to if not their constituencies or their readers. While these narratives are usually more coherent and almost always much more fact-based, they lack a similar center of control and, as a consequence, may appear, oftentimes, incongruous if considered as the narrative of a party or group. If the extent of controversy that the actions by Trump and Berlusconi generated during the years is taken into account, the effectiveness of their communication methods is quite remarkable. Just a small portion of the justice-related scandals that affected the two would have been more than enough to end a promising political career, as we shall see in the following chapters. Nevertheless, they were both able to maintain their power and not lose significant support from their base, largely because of their communication tactics. One of the main reasons such tactics proved so effective, again, is the overall coordination within the conservative field: on most scandals or sensitive issues all the journalists, pundits, and administration officials aligned seem to follow a very similar script and talking points, this makes the repeated messages familiar and helps them stick with the public. Of course, every person involved has her own style and level of spinning of the facts that she or he is inclined to display, but to some degree, they all participate in the spreading of the official narrative. It is not that there are a small group of puppeteers who organize the communication strategy and pass the talking points along to all participating actors as one would imagine in a "Big Brother"-like regime. Rather, the effectiveness derives from the simple rule adopted by Trump and Berlusconi that shapes all conservative communication according to their needs: they will reward anyone who makes them look good and attack anyone whom they feel is damaging them, the extent of the reward or the attack is proportional to the level of favorable or unfavorable coverage. It is simple and effective, and it ensures that the conservative field speaks with one voice, with very few exceptions. The left has nothing like that, and certainly no leader with the will or the ability to distribute rewards and punishments in a similar way.

* * *

The resulting public debate is not very functional, to say the least. That is if the point of the debate is to better understand the country's problems and seek the best solutions to such problems. Of course, from time immemorial, politicians do all they can to look good on TV, in debates or interviews, and in the columns of newspapers, as their political success was, and is, based on their public perception. Nevertheless, before Berlusconi in Italy and Trump in the US, a code of conduct seemed to dictate some basic rules. Traditionally, a journalist should not be personally attacked when asking a fear question; an uncomfortable question shouldn't be completely ignored in order to give a speech about an unrelated topic, a political adversary should not be intentionally interrupted for the evident purpose of not allowing her to make an unfavorable point. Again, it is not that before these two leaders there was no question dodging or attacking of reporters perceived as unfriendly, it is just that with Trump and Berlusconi it became systemic: in all debates and interviews, the effort is focused on the optimization of the perception of the leaders and their politics, especially when close to an election cycle. So, on TV shows, all or most arguing based on actual facts and policy reasoning becomes secondary to the dramatic effect. The tactic adopted by the "enablers" is to limit as much as possible the ability of reporters or adversaries to highlight things perceived as detrimental to the leaders: one of the most commonly used techniques is to talk as much as possible about whatever is more favorable to the leader, if necessary by disregarding completely the questions from reporters so as to leave as little space as possible for anything perceived as damaging. When this is not possible, because the reporters are not playing along and will not let go of an issue, the same reporters are attacked. The assault, besides covering the unwanted questions, has the additional benefit of providing the audience with a rationale as to why the journalists are trying to put the leaders in a bad light: it is because they hate them, or because the media is biased, or because they lean left. Certainly not because they seek to make the head of the executive branch accountable. Self-victimization, after all, is one of the preferred poses of Trump and Berlusconi and their close supporters. Another technique, this one especially put into practice in Italy, is confusion: when the argument in a debate is not working in the desired way, the participants on Berlusconi's side would simply make noise and cover the other panelists with whatever words, even repeating endlessly the same sentence over and over. Niccolo' Ghedini, a lawyer for the Italian tycoon, for example, would often participate in TV debates, usually to explain his point of view on the legal adventures of his employer, and when the debate did not appear to go in a favorable way he would simply cover other participants' voices by repeating "ma va la!'," which means "come on," on and on. He soon became known to the public as "ma va la' Ghedini" and he was far from the only one in Berlusconi's entourage to adopt this tactic.

An additional distinctive technique that both Berlusconi and Trump used in their communication efforts has been to find ways to communicate directly with the public with no interference by the media: a way to avoid scrutiny about the message and its content. Berlusconi first announced his candidacy to lead the government by taping a message where he spoke directly to the citizens. His own television stations broadcast this tape of course, but public TV also contributed largely to its spreading. Trump, thanks to the development of social media, has twitter at his disposal: since he announced his candidacy for president and made several controversial statements, he was able to accumulate millions of followers that regularly receive his messages, usually multiple times a day; and the media abundantly amplifies the tweets, especially the ones that are found to be more outrageous. Using John Rawls' categories of the "rational" and the "reasonable," it could be argued that the attitude adopted by Trump and Berlusconi is rational but not reasonable. It may prove effective in order to avoid risks for their public image, to dodge the scrutiny that comes with reporters challenging them with potentially pointed questions, but it is unreasonable, or unethical, as it violates a basic norm within the political culture of the West: political leaders must be subject to public scrutiny. During the campaign for the 2001 political elections, when Berlusconi had a clear advantage over the candidate of the center-left in the polls, he constantly refused to participate in a public debate. When challenged about this by journalists he would simply say: "I am winning, why should I accept to give a chance to my opponent?" Following the same pattern, Trump ostensibly refused to participate in a debate during the 2016 primary campaign because he thought the moderators were unfavorable to him. Once elected, he obviously dedicated time and effort to closely monitoring the optics of the daily press conferences at the White House. However, the officials that acted as press secretary or director of communications never fully satisfied Trump's desire for imposing narratives to the press. It did not work with Sean Spicer, or with Sarah Sanders, or with Anthony Scaramucci or the others. The final solution was to quit having press briefings altogether and substitute them with what comedian Steven Colbert has dubbed "chopper talk." Occasionally Trump, while on his way to board Marine One, would stop in the White House garden and answer a few questions from reporters, while the noise of the helicopter would often cover his, or the journalists', voice. Everything seems to be staged to make things confusing and allow for claims of misunderstanding in case something goes wrong. Traditional press briefings are designed to allow for rather clear questions and answers that get on the record, exactly the opposite of what Trump wants. Another characteristic way Trump avoids accountability is by adopting speech patterns that are vague and tend to imply ideas rather than expressing them clearly and taking responsibility for them; as scholars Richard C. Fording and Sanford F. Schram write, his "distinctive speaking style, especially his use of enthymeme where meaning is implied but never stated allowed him to set new precedents in masking his xenophobic, racist and sexist appeals, making him an expert at what others have labeled dog-whistling..."[36] Which is an interesting paradox: one of the reasons many supporters find him appealing is his disregard for the politically correct and his way of "telling it like it is," while he does exactly the opposite by recurring to insinuation and refusing to take responsibility for his statements.

It is beyond doubt that the communication style and techniques of Trump and Berlusconi presented a hard and unprecedented challenge to the press core. The fundamental truth about the mainstream media is that they mainly wish to be, and also be perceived, as unbiased. In a recent article, Politico's John F. Harris introduced the concept of centrist bias:

> ...a quarter-century covering national politics has convinced me that the more pervasive force shaping coverage of Washington and elections is what might be thought of as centrist bias, flowing from reporters and sources alike. It is a headwind for Warren, Sanders, the "squad" on Capitol Hill, even for Trump. This bias is marked by an instinctual suspicion of anything suggesting ideological zealotry, an admiration for difference-splitting, a conviction that politics should be a tidier and more rational process than it usually is.[37]

While Harris is making the point that politicians of both parties who position themselves closer to the wings usually are not favored by mainstream journalism, it is also true that there is another level of "centrist bias": the effort by many reporters not to be seen as siding with one of the parties in a dispute and to present contrasts in a way that is as neutral as possible. It is a psychological state not dissimilar from that of certain law enforcement officers, such as Special Counsel Robert Mueller, who evidently wish to do their job thoroughly but also want to appear as outside and above the political fight. It is just not possible when prosecuting (or reporting on) someone like Trump or Berlusconi: they will simply not allow it, if someone with an audience says or writes something damaging about them, they (or their allies) will attack relentlessly and portray the journalist or the prosecutor as politically motivated, or as a hater, or something to that effect. The solution for many journalists is to do with their reporting what Mueller did with the conclusions of his investigation: present the facts in such a way as to avoid looking like they want to attack the thin-skinned president. An easy way to do this for reporters is to present two sides, with equal dignity, to each story. During the impeachment proceedings, The New York Times published an:

> article by White House correspondent Michael Shear that stated that Democrats and Republicans were living in "different impeachment realities." With neither party able to agree on "basic facts," Shear was at a loss. Taking the GOP's conspiracy theories and bald lies at face value, all he could say was that impeachment had devolved into an "intensely partisan" and "very divisive" fight, with "both sides" sensing that "political vandalism" had taken place. Never mind that one of these realities is, well, reality. More to the point: The Times seems incapable of grasping that the Republican Party does, in fact, live in the same reality as everyone else but is doing everything in its power to get media outlets like the Times to turn a straightforward story of presidential wrongdoing into a story about extreme partisanship. Impeachment, in the Times' style of both-sides reporting, becomes yet another game, a way for the red and blue teams to square off once more.[38]

A similar journalistic style was adopted by many reporters from the *Corriere della Sera* and other mainstream outlets during Berlusconi's tenure. There was even a word for it, "terzista," that was used to describe those pundits and journalists who tried to always portray themselves as outside the political fight and equally distant from both parties.

Chapter 4

The rational voters and the emotional base

The most striking aspect of the Trump and Berlusconi phenomena is, perhaps, the degree of loyalty from the base of supporters that they were able to achieve in the US and Italy. Before Berlusconi, the Italian electorate had a history of supporting, at times with strong passions, ideologies or parties rather than single politicians. Of course, occasionally, there could be a party leader who would prove to be more charismatic, or simply more likable than others, but the leaders' personas were never really significant factors in electoral politics, and not only because of the electoral system which tended to prioritize the role of the party rather than single politicians. Possibly, an additional reason for such a low proclivity toward the personalization of politics was the heavy heritage of fascism, the memory of the cult of personality associated with Benito Mussolini, and how that political experience ended up in a complete disaster for the country. The rise of Berlusconi changed all that. Suddenly Italians, at least a significant percentage of them, were again establishing a bond with a political leader, a bond that was as strong and acritical as it could ever be. In the US, the personalization of politics is much more aligned with the institutional system which, while admitting a significant role for the parties, is based on the single politicians who represent the people. The president, of course, but also the senators, the representatives, the governors, and other officials represent a constituency, and are selected through elections based not only on their ideological and party affiliation but also, possibly more so, on their personal history and character. However, even in the US, it is not easy to find a precedent for the special connection between Trump and his supporters. Some past presidents of both parties, leaders such as Kennedy and Reagan, could inspire their political side and were at times extremely popular, but they could hardly ever count on the acritical support that Trump seems to enjoy. Famously, he said that he could shoot a person in the middle of Fifth Avenue and would not lose votes; the claim seems to describe correctly how Trump's voters, or at least many of them, are willing to overcome any flaw, blatant lie, or corrupt act of the leader, rather than abandon him. Berlusconi could count on a very similar attachment by a significant minority of Italians, always ready to rationalize his lies and inconsistencies even at the cost of stretching the truth. How did the two leaders manage to create such a bond and how can we characterize their electorates? Of course, this is a central question of the political phenomenon associated with these two politicians: it is not surprising that individuals with great ability for the creation of narratives and manipulation, together with a lack of scruples and willingness to disregard generally accepted norms, would try to ascend to positions of power. What is remarkable is that they succeeded by convincing so many people to support them.

The first element that Trump and Berlusconi have in common in terms of their electorates is, obviously, that they both belong to the right side of the political spectrum. This is probably not a coincidence: the two leaders are at the head of populist movements and, arguably, the vast majority of contemporary populist movements in the high-income world are right-wing. While there are notable recent examples of left-wing populisms, they are to be found in developing countries, mainly in Latin America. Many in the US would argue that Bernie Sanders' success in both the 2016 and 2020 democratic primaries is founded on a populist platform of the socialist kind and that he adopted a rhetoric that was a mirror of Trump's but on the opposite side of the political spectrum. That would probably be a misconception. While definitely left-leaning, the policies that Sanders proposes are hardly populist: single-payer health care, minimum wage, free (or virtually free) college, are all perfectly implementable reforms in a wealthy country like the US, just like they were implemented, in a variety of ways, in most other rich countries. If we agree that one of the defining features of the populist leader is the inclination to exploit fears and mislead the aspirations of the masses by emphasizing dubious dangers and promoting oversimplified solutions that do not constitute actual effective policies, then Bernie's proposals are not populist, at least not clearly so. He may occasionally get the math wrong and overstate a little how much a given welfare program will cost or by how much it will raise the national debt, but the policies make sense and are implementable, even though many might not find them desirable. Trump's promised solutions, such as a border wall that Mexico will pay for, or tariff wars that will bring jobs back, are close to being the very definition of populism (at least the European concept of populism). It is not at all clear why populism in the US and Europe grows more within the right side of the spectrum, but the recent experience in this part of the world is rather straightforward. It might have to do with the fact that the right tends to have been more radicalized in recent decades: a popularized study in 2018 by the non-profit organization *More in Common*[1] measures the "wings" in the US electorate based on the position of respondents on several issues. In the assessment of the researchers, the left-wing includes 8 percent of the voters, a segment the study calls "Progressive Activists," while the right-wing, with two separate clusters named "Traditional Conservatives" and "Devoted Conservatives," comprises 25 percent of the electorate.

* * *

What are the relevant variables that should be considered when analyzing the electorate in Italy and the US, particularly those that contribute to explaining the divide between the right and the left? One is geography. On one hand, both America and Italy are characterized by cultural elements that are common to all parts of the country and tend to be preserved by a relatively uniform education system, the media, and other things such as literary heritage, aesthetic patterns, language, political culture, and the like. On the other hand, differences, sometimes very marked, between single geographic areas can be easily identified. On the strictly political level, an interesting analysis of the cultural differences among the US states is the one introduced by Daniel Elazar in the 80s[2], which divides the states into three categories. "Moralist" states are those where the citizens are expected to participate in politics as a means to achieving the common good. In the "Individualistic" states, politics is supposed to deliver only those services that are specifically required by the citizens, in a businesslike fashion. Finally, the "Traditional" political culture characterizes the states where society is viewed as more hierarchical and the exercise of politics is seen as more of a privilege than a duty. The prevailing political culture does not translate into ideology: Utah and Minnesota are both considered moralistic states but are on the opposite sides of the ideology spectrum. According to a study performed in the months following the GOP 2016 nomination process, states that are characterized by a moralistic political culture are much more likely to have given Trump a lower share of the vote.[3] Italy has a clear regional divide, though it may have been mitigated to some degree in the last few years. The center of the country, particularly Tuscany, Emilia Romagna, and Umbria, are traditionally left-leaning: the Communist Party had its best performances there until the 90s and, even afterward, the left-leaning parties could usually count on these regions' electorate. The northeast has almost always been more conservative while the northwest, for many years the economically more dynamic area, has seen an alternation of conservative and progressive majorities. The South has been mostly conservative on a social and cultural level; however, in those areas in which the left has strong electoral results it tended to be a rather radical left. Another important geographical factor in the characterization of the electorate is the urban vs rural divide. In both the US and Italy surveys show a long-time correlation between voters of small towns and a preference for conservative parties and, vice-versa, more progressive voters in the big cities.

Another fundamental element when assessing the electorate is education. Studies on the orientations of registered voters in the US clearly show a strong correlation between a higher level of education and Democratic affiliation in the last couple of decades. This is particularly evident for voters with postgraduate degrees.[4] Such a gap increased dramatically during the last few years, since 2015, when Trump joined the GOP nomination process. A lower degree of education, as one would expect, correlates strongly with voters with a low level of information concerning political issues, a category Trump relied on significantly more than previous Republican candidates.[5] A similar pattern could be observed with Forza Italia voters, whose demographics were significantly skewed toward the poorly educated. As far as gender is concerned, in the US there has been a substantial difference between the party affiliation of women, clearly more attracted by the Democratic Party, and men, more equally divided between the two parties, usually with an advantage for Republicans. In this case, too, the trend was accentuated in the last few years. In Italy, there is no significant difference between genders in this regard, though in some elections during Berlusconi's tenure, women proved more conservative than men on average, while in other instances it seems that women might have found the sex scandals of the leader too much to stomach.

Religion is definitely a consequential factor in electoral politics in the US, where the correlation between Protestant voters and the GOP is very high, while the Democrats have an edge with the Jewish and with the religiously unaffiliated. Of course, evangelicals are, in an overwhelming majority, Trump supporters: as with other clusters of voters, the effect of Trump's candidacy was to accelerate a pre-existing trend where evangelicals were becoming increasingly Republican. In Italy, religious voters have a more complex role. First, close to all religious people are Catholic; a significant exception is that of immigrants from Muslim countries, but these individuals are largely recent immigrants, usually without citizenship and therefore have no right to vote for the time being. A second important difference with the US, where active Christians mostly belong on the right side of the spectrum, is that Italy has a long-standing tradition of left-leaning Catholics. This group characterized a significant part of the Christian Democratic Party; it survived the end of the First Republic in the early 90s, and ended up joining the former communists to create the current Democratic Party.

In the last few decades, scholars of political phenomena, when analyzing electoral behavior, have started paying a higher degree of attention to factors other than demographic and cultural ones. A fruitful subject of inquiry has been the role of emotions[6] and other psychological inclinations of voters. When considering the electorates of Trump and Berlusconi, a very important factor appears to be the authoritarianism. A group of researchers measured the inclination toward authoritarianism of white voters through a survey and found that while 62 percent of those who ranked higher on the authoritarian scale had voted for George W. Bush in 1992, this percentage rose to a whopping 86 percent with the election of Donald Trump.[7] In a very similar way, studies in Italy have found a strong correlation between the authoritarian inclination of voters and support for Berlusconi.[8] Citizens identified as "authoritarian" express a preference toward a hierarchical and more traditional organization of society. Many of Trump's messages and much of his rhetoric are obviously intended to achieve the support of this group of voters. For example, something that the current US president has always been careful to display publicly is his "toughness" and ability to exhibit dominance; if this means defending or even promoting violence, so be it. This is probably why he said in the 2016 presidential campaign that he would bring back waterboarding and "much worse," or why he encouraged his followers at his rallies to punch protesters "in the face" or why he recommended police officers not to "be nice" to suspects taken into custody. Trump's body language at press conferences, when reporters ask him a challenging question or press him on a subject without showing intimidation, expresses all his outrage for the defiance of the journalist toward his dominant figure. These are clear messages to an electorate that appreciates a vigorous exercise of authority without excessive ceremonies or concessions to the politically correct. Berlusconi was also the favorite politician of authoritarian leaning people. Even though he did not seem to feel the urge of appearing tough in the same way as Trump, he certainly thought it important to act in an authoritative, if benevolent, fashion and often seemed to imply that he had some innate right to rule; like Trump, when entering the political arena, he adopted a symbolism that portrayed him as descending toward politics from some higher place. Berlusconi always acted as though he was the natural leader of the conservative coalition, with no need for primaries or any other selection mechanism, while Trump was the only candidate in a primary debate who did not pledge to support whoever won the nomination for the GOP if they lost. This last instance was a particularly enlightening moment: all the other candidates accepted the pledge as a way of indicating that the cause, the party, was something bigger than they were. Trump alone refused to bow to the Republican Party, or anything else. Likely, most voters that would score high on the authoritarian scale admired him for it.

* * *

With this premise, we can now look at the electorates of Berlusconi and Trump and try to extract some conclusions and possible explanations for the ability of these leaders to generate a strong bond with a significant part of the electorate of their countries. A first useful distinction within their voters could be between "rational" ones and those we could regard as "emotional." These two categories may, at times, overlap; for example, a significant percentage of religious voters possibly had a clear rationale for supporting Trump, but, at the same time, many would be displaying an enthusiasm for the candidate that seemed motivated by more than just the prospect of having conservative judges in the Supreme Court. It is likely, in fact, that cold calculations were not the only thing at play when some evangelical leaders compared Trump to Cyrus the Great, the sixth century BC Persian leader who, according to the Bible, led the Jewish people to freedom from the Babylonian captivity. In a similar way, an individual may be inclined toward authoritarianism both at an emotional level, and because she may rationally believe that a hierarchical society is better fit to achieve certain goals.

Several "rational" voters of Trump and Berlusconi can be identified. Maybe the most obvious one is the conservative who believes that the left represents a danger for the society and is ready to support any candidate who could defeat a progressive program. This is especially true in the US, where the vote ultimately resolves in a binary choice. A rather common statement among American conservatives in the aftermath of the 2016 elections was: "Yes I voted for Trump, but just because I thought he was the less evil if compared to Hillary..." Many voters declared a similar rationale in Italy after voting for Forza Italia: "The left is much worse." Which does make sense, even though many may disagree about the extent of the actual threat coming from the current US or Italian left. A second "rational" voter is the one who considers mainly the economics of the electoral transaction: she or he will vote in such a way as to maximize her economic wellbeing. In general, such individuals should rationally vote for conservative candidates if their income is above average and for the left if they are in the low end of the income ladder. In Berlusconi's electorate, one category that was overrepresented was that of small business owners and professionals (people such as plumbers, taxi drivers, but also doctors and lawyers). In Italy, many individuals within these professional categories go to great lengths in order to pay as little tax as possible, sometimes resorting to outright evasion. They voted for the leader who, in many different ways, had always winked at the "smart" businessmen who managed to take advantage of the flaws of the system and promoted several laws that allowed tax evaders to settle with the government and "launder" their capital in exchange for a relatively small fee. A fee much smaller than the actual taxes evaded; though, to be fair, this was an Italian habit in government long before the arrival of Berlusconi: particularly during the 1980s, tax amnesties, instead of being exceptional measures, became a recurring tool of economic policy in an effort to collect some additional cash to partially offset increasing expenditure programs. On the contrary, those who looked forward to free-market policies, such as reducing the role of the state in the economy and fostering competition in certain sectors, were disappointed by the actual policies implemented by Berlusconi. These people were a small part of the public but a significant part of the pundits, who listened with interest to the leader's rhetoric about fostering free enterprise; they soon realized that Berlusconi did not really care to bother the special interests that wanted to maintain the status quo. While he talked a lot about "draining the swamp" of monopolies, state-owned inefficient enterprises, and crony capitalists, he actually enlarged it. Social conservatives, particularly religious voters, constitute a third significant example of a rational voter, in that they seek practical objectives that the two populist leaders seem prone to pursuing to a significant extent. It is well known that an overwhelming majority of evangelicals are Trump supporters; in their case, a major rationale for support is Trump's declared availability to nominate conservative judges, which likely will support with their "judicial philosophy" the evangelicals' cause in matters such as abortion rights, education, "religious freedom," and other issues that evangelicals care deeply about. In Italy the head of the government has no say in the appointment of judges, but also, as we have seen, the religious electorate has a rather different distribution across the spectrum. During Berlusconi's tenure, most former left-leaning Christian Democrats created the party of the Margherita, which eventually joined the former communists to create the Democratic Party. According to surveys performed close to the 2001 elections, which opened the way for Berlusconi's longest period in office, voters of the Margherita were more likely to go to church every Sunday than Forza Italia supporters.[9] Nonetheless, many conservative religious voters did support Berlusconi and the leader did seek support in this important reservoir of votes. These electoral groups expected favorable policies on fiscal matters, particularly tax exemptions for religious entities, but, possibly more so, a conservative legislative program on various social issues such as divorce, same-gender marriage, education, and others.

Several scholars have made attempts to provide accurate segmentations of the electorate to better understand the success or failure of parties and candidates. While many such exercises provide useful insights as to the inclinations of constituencies, they are usually constructs of the subjective judgments of the researchers and do not always help in understanding the dynamics of the electorate's orientations. As far as Trump is concerned, an interesting exercise in voters clustering was performed by the *Voter Study Group* in 2017, which, based on a survey of 8000 individuals, identified five segments. The first segment, which the researchers named "The Staunch Conservatives," accounts for 31 percent of Trump's 2016 voters and includes those that are fiscally and, to an extent, culturally conservative; they are engaged and relatively well informed about political issues and events, they tend to be loyal Republican supporters and older, richer, and more male than female on average. The second most important segment is "Free marketers," with 25 percent. As the name suggests, these voters firmly believe in the forces of the free market, they dislike state intervention in the economy, favor low taxes, and are not as socially and culturally conservative as the first segment. "The American Preservationists," representing 20 percent of Trump's supporters, are possibly those that contribute the most in marking a difference between Trump's electorate and, say, Mitt Romney's in 2012. They are more progressive on economic issues than the first two clusters, but tend to include individuals who disfavor immigration, both legal and illegal, as well as individuals who manifest racial resentment; on average, they have lower educational levels. Another important segment, the "Anti-elite," accounts for 20 percent and groups those voters who believe that the system is rigged; they are not as fiscally conservative as the rest of the electorate on the right side of the spectrum, and are significantly less informed and educated. The last group, "The Disengaged," represents 5 percent of Trump's electorate: it includes very low-information voters with little or no interest in political events, who also feel that the system is rigged and may be skeptical of immigration. While this segmentation provides important analytical information and certainly helps to explain Trump's appeal to the public, it is not always clear where the line should be drawn in terms of the relative weight of each cluster and to what extent the groups tend to overlap. However, most will probably agree that the "Free marketers" and the "Staunch conservatives" tend to include more of Trump's voters we called rational, while the other clusters comprise more of those who tend to make voting decisions based on emotions. But which emotions are we talking about, exactly?

One relevant emotion certainly appears to be a fear of change. Current technological advances together with an unprecedented increase in the international flow of goods and people have created a pace of societal change that is a lot faster than what the Western countries faced in the past. While such change may strongly contribute to enhancing the standard of living of many, probably most, people, certain categories may face harm or may perceive some of such changes as harmful. This is a common phenomenon in industrialized countries, mainly the US and Europe, and, in fact, it has been identified by scholars as one of the main reasons for the growth of populist parties and political movements. It also explains why so many of these movements use communication lines that refer to a more reassuring past, like "Take back control" or "Make America Great Again." The part of the electorate that is more sensitive to this kind of fear tends to be highly skeptical of changes in race relations, as well as immigration, especially of Muslims, who may be associated with the threat of terrorism.

But possibly the most important element of Trump's, as well as Berlusconi's, extraordinary success with a certain class of voters is a rooted resentment toward the elites, particularly among those who are ready to uncritically rationalize in any possible way their support for these leaders, without much regards for their actual policy positions or their character. In part, in both the US and Italy, there has been a long-standing sentiment of elite resentment within the conservative side. In the US, it may go back as far as McCarthyism in the 50s and it tends to exploit a certain widespread view within part of the public that cultural elites, often characterized as left-leaning, should not be completely trusted, and considered distant from the traditional

American values and disdainful, with all their sophistication, of the average American family. In the 50s, during the Cold War and with the prospect of possible atomic weapons confrontation, the threat of communist propaganda could be pointed to as a concrete element to be feared. Nowadays such fears are much more difficult to rationalize and the ideologues, or pseudo-ideologues, of that side point to "globalists" as those who try to force real Americans into changes they do not want. In rational terms, their case does not seem strong to say the least, but facts and reason do not seem the priority, or even a necessity, with many voters. There is a detachment between the GOP base and the elite that became evident with Trump's election but has been developing for years. Its origins lie in the inclination by the Republican elite to attract low-information citizens for electoral purposes since the 60s. A clear and relatively recent example is the choice by John McCain and his 2008 campaign manager Steve Schmidt of Sara Palin for the Republican ticket. In Italy, probably since the counterculture movement of 1968, the conservative side of the political spectrum adopted a similar point of view: the left is getting a hold of the cultural world; as a result, the overwhelming majority of cultural production is dominated by a communist or progressive elite that works against the traditional national values. The accusers would often point to Antonio Gramsci, a founder of the Italian Communist Party who died in Mussolini's prisons, and to his view that it was necessary to achieve a "hegemony," an ideal and cultural influence within Italy's society in order to transform it, and eventually achieve a communist system. Whether or not the left actually managed to establish a "hegemony," both Trump and Berlusconi succeeded in funneling the anti-elite feeling in such an effective way as to ensure a loyalty directed specifically toward them which was unprecedented in both countries. While in the past the claim by conservative politicians of a left-wing conspiracy of the elites may have had an impact on part of the electorate, it was somewhat ephemeral, as such rhetoric could also be seen by many as hypocritical: after all, those who warned against the elites were part of the elites themselves. With Trump and Berlusconi, this changed to a significant degree: because of their history, their manners, and their past relationship with the "elites," their assertions are perceived as genuine and, to a very significant extent, they are.

Right after Trump's surprise victory in November 2016, one of the most persistent narratives in the press was that he had been able to win the support of the white working class, especially in states like Pennsylvania, Ohio, and Michigan, an element that proved crucial to his Electoral College majority. However, later analysis showed that the income of the typical Trump voter was higher than average. Herbert Kitschelt and Philipp Rehm, political scientists at Duke and Ohio state, "found that the common assumption that the contemporary Republican Party has become crucially dependent on the white working-class— defined as whites without college degrees—is overly simplistic." Instead, they contend that:

> the surge of whites into the Republican Party has been led by whites with relatively high incomes—in the top two quintiles of the income distribution—but without college degrees, a constituency that is now decisively committed to the Republican Party…Individuals in the low-education/ high-income group tend to endorse authoritarian economic policies and tend to oppose progressive economic policies. Small business owners and shopkeepers—particularly in construction, crafts, retail, and personal services—as well as some of their salaried associates, populate this group.[10]

These constituencies, which, generalizing a bit, we may call petty bourgeoisie, particularly people with low education and higher than average incomes are (or were) also, by far, the strongest social base of Berlusconi's support in Italy. People such as plumbers, taxi drivers, store owners, and others were the most loyal voters of Forza Italia for an entire season of Italian politics. These people resented the cultural elites that looked down on them, especially those in charge of carrying out the government policies and the media.

In an interesting exercise, Politico's John F. Harris invited his Trump-supporting readers to send in a brief justification for their political position in the wake of the impeachment proceedings in January 2020.[11] Many of the published answers are extremely telling; for example, one reader wrote: "I and a lot of Americans support the president because he is Everyman, not the pretentious power-hungry politicians and righteous 'journalists' roaming the streets of DC and big cities..." But possibly, the most revealing answer of all was the one that read: "To those of us who support what he has accomplished...it feels like he is our O.J.," a phrase that summarizes how a social group may support a leader who, though with a flawed character, is seen as capable of vindicating that same group. As CNN's Chris Cillizza wrote:

> the most amazing trick Trump has pulled as a politician— and now as president—is to convince lower-middle class, predominantly white voters that he is one of them. Wealth aside, Trump is not exactly the average Joe. He was raised in New York City and, with the exception of his resort in Florida, has never lived outside the city. He went to private schools through high school. He dated models and actresses. He starred in a reality TV series for more than a decade. And yet, Trump somehow, in the course of the 2016 campaign, effectively convinced a decent chunk of voters—especially in the Midwest hollowed out by manufacturing losses—that he and he alone understood the challenges they faced in life. Time after time, at rally after rally, attendees would tell the

media that Trump got them—that he effectively channeled their frustrations, their anger and their hopes...Trump may have more money and "better houses" and "nicer" boats than the people he is calling elites. But the average person in the crowd in North Dakota has neither multiple houses nor a boat. They know that Trump does have these things—he talks about them incessantly—and yet, somehow, they believe him to be one of them.[12]

Chapter 5

Two judicial systems and the stretching of the rule of law

"It is better to be red with shame than green with rage." This phrase has been attributed to Berlusconi and whether he actually said it or not, it is rather enlightening of his modus operandi in running businesses, or politics. Apparently, the original version of the statement worked the other way around and was a maxim of Enrico Cuccia, an Italian banker who was particularly powerful in the 70s and 80s: "It is better to be green with anger (for missing a profitable deal), than red with shame (for accepting an illegal or unethical proposal)." Cuccia knew a thing or two about finance and power; otherwise, he hardly could have exerted such an influence on Italian capitalism for so long. Nevertheless, he had been raised as a professional in a tradition of public banking management that saw societal development and the public good as the ultimate goal, and while his conception of how a bank should be governed may be obsolete in the current economies, it was always associated with an ethical approach. Ethical considerations, on the contrary, are something that seems to be totally absent from Berlusconi's thinking, or even an element he may consider as a weakness, something that might prevent you from winning, therefore to avoid at all costs. In any case, the phrase should not be taken literary: arguably, shame does not appear to be a sentiment Berlusconi displays frequently, if at all. Trump is very similar in this respect.

Most people, in their daily conduct, either feel an internal drive to behave ethically or decide not to break social norms so that they can maintain a good reputation and gain credibility with others; which in turn may increase the chances of better personal fulfillment in the long run. The two businessmen-turned-politicians, on the contrary, are able to pursue their interests relentlessly, leaving ethical considerations aside, without any regard for their reputation and credibility. To make their case, they resort to any argument they believe is effective, without really worrying whether such arguments have foundations in facts or reason. Their speech patterns and body language suggest that they genuinely believe what they are saying, even in those cases in which they resort to clear misrepresentations of reality, as if they had a reflex that automatically adapted their notion of reality to the interest of the moment. The trick, surprisingly, proves a lot more effective than one would expect. Somehow, they can make their interest the central issue before their audiences, or at least that part of the audience that supports them, usually by complaining about how badly and unfairly they are being treated. The late Indro Montanelli would characterize Berlusconi's attitude with a Neapolitan, rather vulgar, colloquialism: "chiagne e fotte," that can be translated as "he whines while screwing you over..." Trump famously stated that one of his tactics for winning is to "whine, whine, and whine... until I get what I want." An interesting thing to analyze is what happens when political entrepreneurs with such low regard for norms are confronted with the justice system, a system that, in modern states belonging to the liberal-democratic tradition, is designed to overcome instances in which the subjects are in fact expected not to behave ethically.

A central principle in contemporary mature democracies is that public officials ought to enact policies for the benefit of the citizens, instead of making decisions for their own gain. Since the establishment of the classic liberal political philosophy, democratic regimes put in place a set of rules designed to ensure that elected officials do not take advantage of their power in order to maintain power. Classic liberals were well aware that, while most politicians tend to implement policies to seek social benefits, it is safe to assume that many others do not.

The mechanisms conceived to prevent abuses of power mostly provide opportunities for an empowered official to be checked by other officials under Madison's precept that "ambition must be made to counteract ambition." This is essentially the conceptual basis and the justification for the separation of powers in modern political systems; but if this principle is applied to, and informs all, modern democracies, there are significant differences as to how it is enforced in practice, depending on the specific historical experience and political culture of the country considered. Here we are mostly interested in the separation between the executive branch and the judicial one, and how the latter can exercise a check on two leaders known for their reduced inclination toward self-restraint as Trump and Berlusconi. The judiciary can exercise a check on the executive in many ways, but possibly the most forceful, as well as the most personal one, is the situation in which the head of the executive is being investigated or prosecuted for a crime.

Both the Italian and the US institutional systems were designed using the principle of the separation of the judiciary from the executive branch. But how is the independence of each guaranteed in practice? Two compelling sets of rules, arguably, may contribute to ensuring this outcome: laws and norms. A combination of the two governs all systems. To cite a famous historical example, Nixon was induced to resign in 1974 because a legal mechanism, namely impeachment, was likely going to put him out of office. But this was also possible, most historians would agree, because high-ranking officials in the justice department had refused, based on ethical norms, to obey the president's orders aimed at obstructing the investigations that involved him, and deciding to resign instead. These two sets of rules have quite different effects and implications: the law is rather rigid and while it can be bent, to some extent, through interpretations and application to specific cases, it tends to offer relatively little space for maneuvering. Norms, on the other hand, depend heavily on how much the public values them. While breaking the law triggers several automatic responses by institutions designed with precisely the function of preserving the system, the violation of a norm essentially affects only one's reputation. How much it affects it depends on, again, how much the public feels the norm should be followed. It is interesting, in comparing two politicians who are seldom guided by ethical principles, to observe how the legal system can maintain its capacity to function when the head of the executive branch refuses to adhere to established norms. If one considers the Italian and US judicial systems from the point of view of their ability to check executive power, it is possible to argue that while the former is largely based on the law, the latter relies, to a significantly higher degree, on norms. This is probably not an accident, as it reflects a different cultural element between the two countries: on average Americans, particularly public servants, are more inclined to adhere to ethical rules as compared to Italy's, which, therefore, needs a stricter set of laws in order to preserve its system.

* * *

Italy, in the tradition of civil law, has an "inquisitorial" criminal-justice system. As in other European countries, the prosecution of crimes is part of the judiciary and, as such, is independent of the executive branch. The minister of justice, the equivalent of the US Attorney General, cannot appoint, remove, fire, or interfere in any way with the officials in charge of prosecuting crimes. So, while Berlusconi was in office, when a local prosecutor started an investigation that targeted or involved him, there was nothing the government could do to shut it down. What Berlusconi's party, Forza Italia, sometimes attempted in order to shelter its leader was to promote and vote bills into laws in an effort to improve his situation in the trials, for example by reducing the terms of the statute of limitation. Nothing, however, could prevent prosecutors from investigating him and his cronies. Eventually, he was found guilty of crimes and sentenced; precisely for this reason, he could not run for a parliamentary seat in the last Italian general elections, in March 2018. To understand the relevance of Berlusconi's indictments and trials after he won the 1994 elections and became head of the Italian government, it is essential to take a quick look at the evolution of the relationship between the judicial and executive branches before that date.

The politicians and the lawyers who drafted the constitution in 1946 designed the judicial branch having in mind essentially two things: the previous institutional and administrative experience of the Italian Kingdom before Mussolini (1861-1922), and the imperative of preventing the possibility of fascism, or similar regimes, ever rising again in the future. The result was a judicial branch completely independent and separated from the other two; a judiciary, in particular, that included the prosecution, recognized as possibly the most powerful manifestation of this branch and a potential element of conflict with the executive. The Italian constitution also states that magistrates (again, including prosecutors), when making judicial decisions, are subject only to the law: not to the Ministry of Justice, not to other, more senior, judges. To ensure the actual independence of the judiciary and of the single magistrate, the constitution creates two entities: the Constitutional Court, which has a function comparable with the US Supreme Court, and the Superior Council of the Judiciary. The Council has the power to administer the career of all judges: promotions, assignments, internal investigations, disciplinary actions; the magistrates elect the majority of its members, while a third of them are nominated by Parliament. However, for various reasons, for many years after the approval of the constitution, Parliament refused to pass the necessary legislation to enact the institution of both the Constitutional Court and the Superior

Council, which started their activity only toward the end of the 1950s. Even then, most senior judges and prosecutors were mostly conservative, culturally close to the governing party, the Christian Democrats, and they had ways to exercise control over the younger generations of magistrates. Hence, it was quite rare that the judiciary would investigate and indict prominent politicians (except for representatives of the Communist or Socialist parties, who were prosecuted mostly for crimes linked to the expression of their ideology). Things changed dramatically during the 60s, especially by the end of the decade, when the general movement of cultural change accelerated a shift in the ideology of the Italian judges and stimulated a significant percentage of them to a state of mind more prone to questioning the established order. Many magistrates also shifted to the left, as is evident from the results of the elections of the Council as well as the elections for the Magistrates' Association.[1]

Starting in the 70s, prosecutors became increasingly active in the investigation of politicians. However, notwithstanding the increased independence and the new "ideology" within judges, politicians could count on some rather effective defenses when facing criminal prosecution. For starters, all members of Parliament had a general immunity granted by the constitution. A special commission could authorize the prosecution; however, the senators and the members of the House in this commission proved all but generous in granting authorizations, regardless of the evidence of crimes presented by the magistrates. The elite of the ruling parties also had a second tool to use against legal jeopardy: according to the constitution, the members of the cabinet suspected of crimes would not be prosecuted by ordinary magistrates but by a special Parliamentary Commission. If indicted, they would then be tried by the Constitutional Court in a proceeding similar to the US impeachment. This procedure, not surprisingly, did not prove to be very effective as the members of the commission usually demonstrated more sensitivity to political considerations than to the evidence presented. However, in one of the biggest corruption scandals of the Italian Republic, the commission did manage to indict two prominent politicians of the Christian Democratic Party. During the investigations of the US Senate sub-committee led by Frank Church (the Select Committee to Study Governmental Operations with Respect to Intelligence Activities) in 1975 and 1976, executives from the Lockheed Corporation testified that they had bribed government officials in Germany, Italy, the Netherlands, and Japan. The Rome prosecutors opened an investigation, but as a local agent for Lockheed publicly accused the former defense minister, Mario Tanassi, the file was transferred to the House of Representative and the special commission for the prosecution of cabinet members was tasked with probing the matter. In previous years, the commission always had a solid Christian Democratic majority, but after the 1976 elections, things were a bit different. Though the CD still won a plurality and was confirmed as the first party, its weight was significantly reduced and the distance with the second party became rather thin (in the House elections the DC ended up with 38 percent of the votes against the 34 percent of the Communist Party). Hence, now the commission had eight Christian Democratic members, but also seven communists and two socialists, plus three additional members from minor parties. Ultimately, the commission indicted two former cabinet members: one was later acquitted by the Constitutional Court and the other one found guilty. However, the most prominent politician accused, Mariano Rumor, former prime minister and the one toward whom the evidence seemed more compelling, was saved by the vote of the Christian Democrat president of the commission, whose vote had the power to break the tie according to the commission rules. In the aftermath of the Lockheed scandal the President of the Republic, Giovanni Leone, also implicated, was forced to resign. In the late 80s, a popular referendum eliminated the

Parliamentary Commission indictment system.

During the 80s, the activity of the prosecutors in various cities of the country led to a strong tension with the Socialist Party, which had become a permanent member of the government coalition together with the Christian Democrats and three other smaller parties. Even though the indictments brought to light an alarming number of alleged crimes by politicians, there were no dramatic political consequences. Voters had few alternative choices: either the Italian Social Movement, a direct heir of Mussolini's fascism that could only attract a minority of the electorate, or the Communist Party. The latter had clearly distanced itself from the Soviet Union in a slow process that had started with the Soviet invasion of Czechoslovakia in 1969 and could be considered complete in coincidence with the cracking down of the workers' manifestations in Poland at the beginning of the 80s.[2] However, the majority of the Italian electorate still did not trust the communists. Moreover, the economy was growing, the country had become a member of the G7, the group of the world-leading economies, and by the end of the decade, the income per capita was exceeding that of the United Kingdom. Corruption existed and most Italians tended to despise politicians, but things were not so bad after all.

Nevertheless, in 1992, as we have seen, everything changed. A threefold crisis swept away the traditional parties: a financial meltdown, due in large part to the accumulation of public spending and growing deficits in the previous years, threatened the economy. In the meantime, the mafia, in open defiance to the state, organized the assassination of two prominent judges who were investigating the bosses. Finally, prosecutors in Milan uncovered a series of corruption cases that showed clearly how the problem had become systemic; the press was all in to show the details of the investigations and, in many cases, the confessions of the politicians and the businesspersons involved. By this time, the Communist Party had changed its name abandoning the word "communist": "Democratic Party of the Left" was the new name of the biggest party on the progressive side of the spectrum. The Soviet Union was gone and the former communists seemed to be the only political force spared by the judges (if we do not count the MSI, the party originating from the fascist regime, which seemed doomed to never play a relevant role in the political system).

The majority of the press and the pundits, during the 1992-93 period, attributed a significant role in bringing down the traditional parties to the judiciary, because of the extent of the investigations and trials against the politicians accused of corruption. Actually, the reform of the electoral system introduced following the popular referendum in 1993 was a fundamental factor in changing the traditional dynamics of democratic representation. But there is no doubt that the unearthing, by the prosecutors, of the systemic corruption which characterized the political parties was a major contribution in distancing the electorate from the Christian Democrats and the socialists. This situation enlivened for many years a debate, which had started during the 80s, about the relationship between the judiciary and the other powers. This situation had many observers worried about the possible overreach of the prosecutors and judges, who, some argued, had the power to overrule the will of the electorate by indicting elected officials as they pleased. Of course, this is an aspect of a wider problem about the advantages and drawbacks of the separation of powers and it interests all the countries belonging to the liberal-democratic tradition of government. One of the arguments of those who do not favor a strong interference of the judiciary on the executive is that, often enough, prosecutors tend to grandstand by indicting politicians, as a way to get on the front page of the papers. This is certainly true in many if not most cases, but it is also the mechanism at the base of the whole architecture of the US (as well as other free countries) system of government: as the Federalist Paper n. 51 reads:

> The great security against a gradual concentration of the several powers in the same department consists in giving to those who administer each department the necessary constitutional means and personal motives to resist encroachment of the others. The provision for defense must in this, as in all other cases, be commensurate to the danger of attack. Ambition must be made to counteract ambition... this policy of supplying, by opposite and rival interests, the defect of better motives, must be traced to the whole system of human affairs, private as well as public...

So, while it may certainly be that prosecutors sometimes seek grandstanding and personal career objectives when investigating politicians, it is worthwhile to wonder whether this works in favor of or against the majority of the people. Arguably, it mostly works in favor of the citizens as it provides an effective check on executive power as well as a means to expose wrongdoing, therefore making it less rewarding for those politicians to embrace corrupt behavior. Another frequent accusation to active prosecutors is that they are politically biased and go after certain politicians because they belong to an opposite ideology or party. Of course, this is a plausible situation; furthermore, law enforcement officers can be biased in other ways against various categories of citizens: like all human beings, prosecutors and judges (as well as policemen) are subject to their culture, their prejudices, and their biases of various kinds. The way to avoid injustices is to apply all the rules designed for this purpose: appeal trials, right of defense, etc. A different situation, sometimes alleged by defenders of the executive power, is the one in which law enforcers collude with politicians or other individuals creating a conspiracy to prosecute someone unjustly. This is a situation that can be defined as corrupt, it may be difficult to prove absent specific investigations, but it can certainly be recognizable by a number of clues: how the investigation was originated (and predicated), prior history of that same prosecutor, etc. In Italy, starting in the 80s, in association with an increasing contrast between the judiciary and the main parties in office, the expression "Government of the Judges" started circulating among the critics of what they deemed an excessive intervention of the magistrates in the affairs of the executive. In this debate, advocates for the executive often claimed that actions by law enforcement officials might subvert the will of the people, manifested through the democratic elections that put the investigated politician in office. That is true, of course, but also largely irrelevant: while the work of prosecutors may indeed, given the circumstances, affect the result of an election by causing a politician to lose her or his job, this is precisely how the system is designed: so that elected officials are always subject to the law. There can always be cases of judicial abuse, even against representatives of the executive or legislative power. However, these, at least in countries with an established system of rule of law, are very rare. Probably the main reason for this is that indictments or investigations of public officials tend to be very public, which means that reporters (and other interested parties) will likely read carefully the legal documents, scanning them for newsworthy details. This, in turn, means that prosecutors are particularly careful when investigating a politician and they will usually make sure to have a strong case and avoid all possible mistakes before proceeding, because they know their acts will be closely screened and any irregularity will likely be exposed.

In Italy, starting in the 70s, most cases in which the magistrates investigated or indicted politicians would cause the political party affected to protest and to call for legislative reforms, supposedly in order to protect the system against the abuses by judges who were accountable to nobody or who were said to be colluding with politicians of the opposite side. However, it is very hard to find instances of potential abuse by reviewing today the judicial cases of these decades. Most of these sensitive investigations were initiated in what appears to be a legitimate way: because someone affected by the wrongdoing reported the crime, or because of evidence emerging from unrelated investigations; indictments were usually based on solid evidence. The possible exceptions are a few cases in which Communist officials were indicted (and usually quickly acquitted), for what seemed to be pretexts. Maybe the most bizarre case of judicial abuse was in the early 80s, when prosecutors in Rome indicted various members of the Superior Council of the Judiciary for consuming coffees during meetings; according to the prosecutor of the case, this constituted embezzlement. What contributed in making the indictment suspicious was the timing; it happened right before a procedure that was going to discipline the magistrates found to be members of the secret masonic lodge P2. A second famous case, a few years earlier, also by the prosecutors in Rome[3], was the arrest of a high-ranking officer of the Bank of Italy who had opposed a design to accommodate the financial entanglements of Michele Sindona. Sindona was also a member of the P2, and someone with access to Giulio Andreotti, one of the most powerful Christian Democrats during most of Italy's First Republic.

* * *

Before we go through a brief description of Berlusconi's criminal trials during the time he was the central political figure, we should say a few words about the prosecution of white-collar crimes in Italy. Often enough, in the US, we hear that the typical crimes committed by white collars are difficult to prosecute and that they often lead to acquittals, even in the presence of strong evidence; when they don't, actual prison time for the ones that eventually get convicted is a rare event. As a writer for *The*

Atlantic reports about the Paul Manafort case, "The American criminal-justice system works at every stage and every level to give chances to people like Manafort and deny them to poorer people." This happens for several reasons:

> First, there can't be a sentence without an investigation. After 9/11, the United States Department of Justice and the US Attorney's Offices that it controls shifted resources and focus from white-collar crime to drugs, guns, and immigration... Second, prosecutors have enormous power over who goes to jail and for how long. That power doesn't just involve deciding who gets indicted. It involves deciding *how* he gets indicted. Manafort faced a recommended sentencing range of 19 to 24 years under US sentencing guidelines. But that range was driven only in part by what he actually did. It was driven just as much by how the special counsel's office chose to pursue the case—what charges it brought, what evidence it presented to Ellis, and what part of Manafort's history it cited as "relevant conduct" at sentencing. Federal prosecutors can substantially shape a sentence by the plea deal they offer, choosing which parts of the sentencing guidelines apply. Prosecutors are more inclined to wield that power to benefit people like Manafort, not people charged with crimes involving drugs, blue-collar property crimes, and violence. Third, Congress has given Ellis the power to give people like Manafort a break, but has denied him that power when the defendant is accused of many blue-collar crimes. Last year, Ellis sentenced a 37-year-old man named Frederick Turner to 40 years in federal prison for methamphetamine distribution. He had no choice: Congress passed laws making 40 years the mandatory minimum sentence.[4]

All these considerations notwithstanding, the US justice system would seem as a repressive police state for would-be moneylaunderers, fraud perpetrators, and tax evaders, if compared to Italy's. As in the US, to be sentenced to serve prison time, the indicted person has to be convicted by a court. However, in Italy, convictions can always be appealed and the appeal can, in turn, always be overthrown by the Court of Cassation, a high court that can overrule any trial based on possible wrong interpretations of the law. Only after the conviction is confirmed in all degrees of judgment can the sentence be executed and the culprit be put in prison. It is true that a judge, given certain conditions, can send an indicted person to jail as a precautionary measure, but this is seldom an actual possibility in white-collar crimes. A second element to consider is that the Italian justice system is hardly an efficient one: criminal trials take, on average, many years and the European Court has repeatedly found Italy in violation of the reasonable duration of trial principle, also condemning Italy to financial compensation to those harmed by this slow process. When people indicted can count on the assistance of good law firms, as is often the case with white-collar defendants, the trial can become especially slow and easily end up with the statute of limitations kicking in. Overall, a white-collar offender going to serve actual prison time is a very rare event in Italy.

Berlusconi's judicial troubles started just a few months after he became the head of the Italian government, in May 1994. In November that same year, the prosecutors from Milan notified him of an indictment for bribing police officers back in the late 80s and early 90s; specifically, he was being investigated for paying off officers of the Guardia di Finanza, a special police force, mainly responsible for the investigation of crimes related to tax evasion and money laundering. This event triggered the early end of his first government, as his most important political ally, the Northern League, soon withdrew its support in Parliament, thus causing Berlusconi's resignation. But, maybe more importantly, the indictment was also the starting point of a long (a more than a quarter-century-long, thus far) struggle by

Berlusconi and his supporters to protect him from the criminal trials and preserve his public image in some way. Since then, the Italian political debate has been continuously interlaced with the role of the justice system in the balance of powers and, particularly, as it relates to the position of the defendant Berlusconi. His supporters and enablers would point to the prosecutors and judges, accusing them of biases and of seeking to reverse the outcome of the democratic process by accusing someone chosen by the people. Many others would point to the fact that Berlusconi should defend himself "within the trials, not from the trials," as he seemed to do by adopting such tactics as to publicly accuse the magistrates and pose as a victim of some conspiracy.

That first indictment led to a conviction in 1998. The verdict was then partially reversed by the appeal trial in 2000 when Berlusconi was acquitted of one count, while for other counts the statute of limitations extinguished the crimes. Finally, the third-degree trial, in the Court of Cassation, completely exonerated Berlusconi, who had recently won the elections again and had become, once more, the head of the government. Nevertheless, it was later discovered that a significant witness in this trial, a British lawyer by the name of David Mills, had favored the defendant in court with false statements regarding the administration of offshore companies controlled by Berlusconi's group, and in which Mills was involved as a hired professional. Mills was subsequently charged for accepting a payment of $600,000 from Berlusconi in exchange for his false declarations and was sentenced to more than 4 years of prison, a sentence confirmed by the appeal trial. The Cassation, while confirming that Mills indeed committed the crime, saved the British attorney thanks to the statute of limitations. An interesting twist, during the Mills trial, was the approval of a bill by Parliament controlled by Berlusconi and his allies in 2008, known as the Alfano Bill, from the name of the young minister of justice, Angelino Alfano.

According to this newly approved law, all criminal trials in which a defendant held one of four high public offices of the Republic[5] could be suspended for the duration of their service. Just a few months later, the law was found unconstitutional by the Constitutional Court and abrogated. According to Berlusconi, such law was necessary for a "judicial system such as ours, where some magistrates, instead of applying the law, attribute themselves with an ethical task..."[6]

Just a few years earlier, Berlusconi's government had tried something very similar. According to a law passed in 2003, named after Renato Schifani, a senator for Forza Italia, the five highest officers of the Republic could not be subject to a criminal trial. Significantly even more ambitious than the Alfano Bill, this law was also abrogated as unconstitutional, and, according to many observers, it had been passed by Parliament with the clear intention of interrupting an important trial where Berlusconi was the main defendant: the SME trial. This particular proceeding is extremely interesting as a telling window on the political and business practices in Italy's history. During the depression of the 30s, among the measures of the fascist regime to restore economic and social stability was the creation of the Istituto di Ricostruzione Industriale (Institute for Industrial Reconstruction), or IRI, an entity that would purchase or acquire businesses that seemed doomed to fail, for the purpose of preventing the laying off of workers. IRI was preserved with the introduction of the Republic and had become, to some extent, a sort of cemetery of failed businesses, as it owned several companies that were producing at a loss, costing the taxpayers millions of dollars every year. The Christian Democrats were hesitant to close IRI because of the political backlash they feared from the resulting unemployment of, possibly, thousands of workers. So, in the 80s, under the presidency of Romano Prodi, in an effort to put a stop to this cycle, the government sold many IRI businesses to private investors, hence reducing the losses of the institute. One of the deals, which involved the sale of the electric company SME to Carlo De Benedetti, wasn't favored by the head of government (and Berlusconi's powerful friend), Bettino Craxi, who asked Berlusconi and other prominent entrepreneurs to present an alternative bid. The result was a civil suit that reversed the sale of SME to De Benedetti. However, later investigations found that the judge who made that call, Renato Squillante, may have been bribed by Berlusconi, who was indicted. The billionaire was ultimately acquitted, but Squillante was convicted. His appeal with the Court of Cassation allowed the statute of limitations to kick in saving him from prison (the same judge was also indicted for bribery in another famous case and again, the Cassation got him off the hook).

The SME trial certainly wasn't the only one in which Berlusconi was being accused of having corrupted judges. Another judicial case during these years, in fact, probed the tactics adopted by the tycoon when he tried to acquire an important media group, the one founded by the Mondadori family; a case that, once again, involves a dispute with Carlo De Benedetti. Both De Benedetti and Berlusconi, toward the end of the 80s, owned a share of the publishing company Mondadori, which controlled an important national newspaper, Rome's *La Repubblica*, some popular weekly magazines, and other media. When a conflict emerged between the two for control of the company, they decided to submit the dispute to an arbitrage, which ultimately handed the company to De Benedetti. Unhappy with the result, Berlusconi decided to sue and this time obtained a favorable outcome. Once again, however, it seems that the judge, Vittorio Metta, was convinced not so much by the facts of the case and the arguments of the attorneys, but more by about $200,000 in cash that he received from Berlusconi's lawyer. This particular lawyer, Cesare Previti, was a long-time Berlusconi associate, who served as senator for Forza Italia and even as defense minister in one of his administrations. He was ultimately convicted of bribing the judges of the Mondadori trial, was expelled from the Senate, and had to serve time in prison. Berlusconi was also found guilty in the first-degree trial for the corruption of the judge in the case, but ultimately the statute of limitations, once again, saved him from a prison sentence; it was quite clear from the trial that he was the beneficiary of the bribe and that he was fully aware of the corruption scheme. A significant appendix of this criminal trial was a civil lawsuit started by De Benedetti to get compensation for the corrupted deal. The civil court of Milan awarded De Benedetti's companies a significant amount of money (initially about 750 million euros) to be paid by Berlusconi's corporations. Following a pattern, the judge in this civil case became familiar to Italians: shortly after the sentence, a team from Canale 5, one of Berlusconi's TV channels, went after the magistrate in the streets of Milan with a camera, trying to ridicule him in any possible way. The crew highlighted, among other things, the color of his socks, the fact that he was smoking in the street, or that he occasionally changed his directions while walking. Most journalists' associations harshly condemned the program as a gratuitous smear.

The habit of corrupting public officials, it seems, started quite early during Berlusconi's career. At the end of the 70s the construction company he controlled, Edilnord, was subject to a tax inspection by the Guardia di Finanza. The inspection found nothing, but the officer in charge, a Captain Massimo Berutti, resigned shortly afterward and joined the Berlusconi staff as a consultant and then as a lawyer. When Berlusconi founded Forza Italia, Berutti became a member of the House of Representatives, but he also became the subject of the attention of the prosecutors. He was indicted and convicted (both in the first degree and the appeal trials) for money laundering, but by the time the procedure got to the Court of Cassation, the statute of limitations got rid of the charges. Later, he was also indicted, and this time convicted in all degrees, for obstructing justice:

he had attempted to convince law enforcement officers not to testify in a trial against Berlusconi's companies.

The whole saga of Berlusconi's indictments and trials started in 1994 and just went on endlessly for the whole time he was Italy's central political figure. In fact, it continues to this day. In 2013 he ultimately had his full conviction (confirmed in the Court of Cassation this time) and he was sentenced to 4 years for tax fraud as the judges found that he had set up a scheme to evade taxes while, at the same time, defrauding some of his business partners. An offshore company of his would purchase movies and other TV products from US companies, to then sell them to his official Italian corporations with a significant mark-up, thus hiding the profit from the authorities (and from the other shareholders). Ultimately, the sentence was reduced due to an amnesty and he went on to serve a little less than a year of civil service in a home for the elderly in the Milan area. Because of the sentence, he had to leave Parliament and could not be elected in the following round, in 2018.

* * *

It is quite evident from this brief description of some of Berlusconi's legal troubles that many aspects of his conduct as a businessman and as a politician could be quite damaging to his reputation; in fact, it seems amazing that he managed to achieve various electoral successes notwithstanding the uncovering of his corrupted deeds. What he did was to adopt a twofold strategy of defense. On one side, he would organize the best possible team of lawyers to set up a technical defense within the proceedings. He publicly claimed, repeatedly, to have paid his legal team fees in excess of 600 million dollars over the years[7], a sum which is enough to retain hundreds of excellent lawyers for a couple of decades. Besides virtually unlimited resources, Berlusconi's lawyers could often count on the support of Parliament to approve laws that favored him. We already mentioned two cases: the laws that grant immunity for the highest offices in the Republic, which were both found unconstitutional, but other laws were quite effective. For instance, a bill passed by Parliament in 2001, which made non-admissible in trial several documents obtained by the Milan prosecutors from international sources, such as foreign courts; or another law passed in 2002 that limited the criminal cases of accounting fraud. Both laws had a direct impact on Berlusconi's trials. Another law, also in 2002, introduced additional instances in which a party could file a motion to transfer a criminal trial from one jurisdiction to another in the presence of a "legitimate suspect of bias" of a judge. Additional legislation, approved by Parliament in 2005, reduced even further the terms for the statute of limitations, with a direct impact on the Mills trial. In 2006, the Forza Italia-controlled Parliament passed a law that was later found unconstitutional; it prevented prosecutors from appealing when the defendant was acquitted in the first-degree trial. In some cases, Forza Italia only floated bills. For example, one limiting the possibility for magistrates to resort to wire-tapping; ultimately no working solution was ever found to limit the eavesdropping capabilities of the courts in a way that could be understandable to the public and the project was dropped. Besides benefiting from laws seemingly promulgated for his benefit, Berlusconi could, of course, use the levels of the executive branch while in office. Consequently, many requests for documents from Milan prosecutors to foreign courts, a frequent practice in cases of international money laundering or tax fraud, which had to be administered by the Ministry of Foreign Affairs, were slowed down, or virtually stopped, for years. In addition, curiously, many inspections were ordered by the Ministry of Justice[8] in those prosecutors' offices, like the ones in Milan, where the magistrates had proved particularly dangerous for the head of the executive branch.

Berlusconi's second line of defense is beyond the strictly legal jeopardy, it concerns the impact of what he perceives as judicial attacks on the public perception of his persona, and how the disclosure of the criminal investigations may affect it. His defense, on this front, is, fundamentally, his communication technique. The support of his enablers and the media favorable to him managed to frame all these episodes as a chapter of the political struggle between the leader and some other entity presented as hostile. At times, it is Berlusconi against the left, a political party that uses the judicial branch as a weapon. Other times, it is Berlusconi against the media, which take advantage of the initiative of a few judges to smear a politician they do not like, or it is Berlusconi against the judiciary, a power biased against him for political reasons; or, again, Berlusconi against De Benedetti, a competitor. Ultimately, it was and is much more about the public perception of the investigations and trials, rather than the prospects of actually being sentenced. The public perception in these cases is obviously very significant: when a newspaper runs a story alleging wrongdoing about a politician, it is one thing to rely on statements by other people or even anonymous sources, quite another to cite judicial documents that explain how a crime was uncovered and the details of the evidence found. The dynamics between judicial proceedings and the media are rather powerful, and, if one believes in the fundamental importance of keeping empowered individuals, especially politicians, accountable, they should be. If someone were to study today the history of Berlusconi's wrongdoings from the documents of the various trials that had him as defendant it would be very difficult not to conclude that Berlusconi committed several crimes against the society and had his enablers help him get away with most of the accusations. However, for so many years, the public debate about this subject went on, almost on a daily basis, representing a fight between powers, more or less equally legitimate, where the moral standing seemed almost irrelevant. Most influential media do not want to appear as biased and an easy and comfortable way not to appear biased is to have a controversial issue presented by the two sides involved. So, for example, the promulgation of a law that could have a clear impact on one of Berlusconi's trials would be presented in a TV talk show by having someone from the right, a supporter of Berlusconi, explain how the law was intended to reform the process in a way that was more respectful of the guarantees of the accused. And even if the representatives from the left would point out how such a law was an evident attempt to tamper with the system to help the head of the conservative party accused of crimes, it remained a debatable issue, a matter of political leaning. Conservative citizens could listen to respected politicians and officials defend it, and that seemed to be good enough for them, at least for most of them.

* * *

Anyone who followed the debate about justice in Italy around Berlusconi's indictments in the last 2 decades would find highly familiar the public perception of the Russia investigation or the impeachment proceedings during the first 3 years in office of Donald Trump. However, while the dynamics of the public debate seem very familiar, the institutions at play are quite different and they may lead to very different outcomes. How do prosecutors, officials of the executive branch of government, act in the US when there are credible grounds for investigating a representative of the same branch, or even its head, the President of the United States?

This issue became urgent, of course, during the Nixon administration with the development of the Watergate scandal, which ultimately brought that presidency to an early end. The facts are well known: in May 1973, after the possibility of an involvement of the White House in the covering up of the

Watergate burglary was publicly floated, the nominee for Attorney General, Elliot Richardson, asked Archibald Cox to accept the job of Special Prosecutor in charge of the case. It was rather clear to Richardson that the Senate, at that time with a Democratic majority, wouldn't confirm him without solid guarantees that the role of members of the executive branch in the scandal would be thoroughly investigated. We will never know if a GOP majority would have confirmed Richardson with no such commitment, but the Senate was satisfied with the appointment of Cox and the terms of his engagement: he could be fired, other than that, he could proceed as he thought fit. However, in October that same year, the Special Prosecutor was terminated during what is known as "the Saturday Night Massacre": Richardson refused to follow the president and chose to resign rather than fire Cox, as Nixon wanted. The Deputy Attorney General also resigned rather than carry out Nixon's order, and ultimately, the Solicitor General fired Cox under tremendous pressure. These events left an open, very important, question: if the president is in charge of the prosecution of federal crimes through the Department of Justice, how can he, or high officials he may want to protect, be held accountable when a credible hypothesis of wrongdoing is on the table?

The answer was the Independent Counsel Provision within the Ethics in Government Act of 1978, during the Carter administration. In the following years, Congress modified the statute multiple times in the search for an optimal balance between the actual effectiveness and independence of the prosecutor holding the executive branch accountable on one side, and the necessity to allow the government to function regularly without the threat of, potentially, an aggressive, partisan, investigation on the other. Certainly, the best-known case of prosecution under the Independent Counsel Statute was the investigation of President Bill Clinton by Ken Starr, which led to articles of impeachment for obstructing justice and other counts. Such an investigation, which started as a probe of Clinton's involvement in the Whitewater real estate deal in Arkansas many years before, and ended up investigating the president's encounters with Monica Lewinsky, was perceived, not without solid grounds, as highly partisan. There are few doubts that Starr's performance contributed to the final decision by Congress not to renew the provision of the Independent Counsel, which expired in 1999.

So, what happens now when there are credible allegations that the president or high executive officials committed a crime? Well, the Attorney General tends to nominate a Special Counsel in order to appoint a prosecutor who, to some degree, is (and appears) as independent from the executive branch she or he is supposed to investigate. This was the case when acting AG James Comey appointed Patrick Fitzgerald to probe the Valery Plame affair in 2003, or, more relevant for us, when acting AG Rod Rosenstein nominated Robert Mueller to head the Russia investigation for the Department of Justice. It is rather evident that these appointments do not quite solve the basic problem: the Special Counsels are still working for the DOJ and are therefore subject to the supervision of the AG and, ultimately, of the president. In fact, many conservative politicians and pundits during the Mueller investigations underscored that had Trump fired the Special Counsel or the AG, he was well within his rights to do so. Moreover, regulations of the Department of Justice state that a sitting president cannot be indicted and a Special Counsel should be expected to abide by such regulation. In fact, this is precisely what Robert Mueller did: he followed the Office of Legal Counsel memo from 1973 and abstained from charging Trump with obstruction of justice, even though there was ample evidence to make a case for the accusation.

In the US, of course, the judiciary does not incorporate prosecution, which is exercised, at the federal level, by officials appointed by the president. Nevertheless, within the administration of criminal justice, the prosecution is precisely the activity that can be, arguably, the most effective in making officials from the executive branch accountable.[9] So what happens in the US when a president, or someone the president wants to protect in pursuit of his interests, is the target of a criminal investigation? What restrains the chief executive from exercising his constitutionally given powers and ordering the prosecutors to shut down an investigation? Nothing, seem to argue many Trump-supporting pundits in these last few years: he has the legal right to do it. They may just have a point; he is, after all, the boss of the Attorney General and, indirectly, of all federal prosecutors.

Though frequently used in the public debate, the concept of "rule of law" may have different meanings depending on the context. Sometimes it is intended as the strict application of the text of the law to a specific instance; in other cases, more relevant to our point, it underscores the rule by the laws as opposed to the rule by empowered individuals, when public matters are settled based on the arbitrary will of someone in control. This general principle can be considered as the origin of several norms that are at the core of the political culture of the West: for example, the one that prevents the head of the executive branch from prosecuting his political opponents (outside of the standard, impartial procedures put in place to investigate all crimes). A second example could be the norm that prevents all presidents from interfering with an investigation or judicial proceeding in which he has a clear personal interest. Such norms may even be codified and written down as regulations of the DOJ or other institutions, but, unless they are made into enforceable legislation, how effective can they be if a president is willing to disregard them? We know that Trump had no problem whatsoever in contacting directly US attorneys, even in districts in which he owns businesses and has clear personal stakes. The best-known example of such possible interference is probably the firing of Preet Bharara, former US Attorney of the Southern

District of New York. According to Bharara's statements, after being assured personally by Trump that he would continue to hold that office, he was contacted multiple times by phone by the president, he refused to take some of the calls and he was quickly and unceremoniously fired. Later, Trump, as reported, personally interviewed lawyers to fill that same position. Of course, he also publicly encouraged his justice department to go after his political opponents and he fired justice officials who would not plead loyalty to him personally.

If the president has a legal right to do all this, what is left to keep him in check are only norms; but again, norms are effective only insofar as the public expects officials to adhere to them. As far as the law goes, the only mechanism to make the president accountable is impeachment, a rather extreme remedy. Pundits often stress the fact that impeachment is a political process, not a legal one. They underscore the fact that, unlike an ordinary criminal trial, both the indictment and the verdict are decided by members of Congress based on a definition of the crimes that is so vague ("bribery, treason…high crimes and misdemeanors") as to allow the maximum latitude to members of Congress, who will inevitably vote based on political considerations. In the context of our discourse, however, impeachment is a legal process, in the sense that it is defined by written law, the US constitution, and attributes clearly the responsibility to carry it through to specific actors and in a specific enough frame. Nevertheless, it can be argued, the impeachment process is also an exercise in ethics. Members of Congress are expected to attend to the proceedings in a fair-minded way and examine all the evidence presented and not pursue the interests of the party they belong to regardless of facts. Ultimately, they should vote for impeachment and removal of the president if, in fact, they believe in good faith that he committed the wrongdoing he is charged with and that such wrongdoing is grave enough to justify the extreme measure. No law compels members of Congress to behave in such a manner, they are simply expected to do so.

In practice, however, a major factor that will determine the actual behavior of members of Congress in an impeachment proceeding is the way they believe their attitude and vote will be perceived by their constituency (which ultimately gets to decide whether members of Congress keep their job). In the case of Trump, if there is a large enough base that supports the president no matter what he does or says, Republican members of Congress will not be inclined to confront the president with impeachment and removal proceedings, as they will be concerned about their own political prospects. Ultimately, the problem seems to be that the president's political base, this significant part of the electorate, do not regard as important that Trump refuses to follow long-standing norms, just as many Italians did not seem to care about Berlusconi's ethical standards.

When an institution or a system is based on norms as opposed to the law, a condition for it to function properly is that the actors that have a role in it must, mostly, abide by the norms; they may do so either because they feel compelled by their moral values, or because they feel they will be judged negatively if they do not. In the case of both Berlusconi and Trump, moral values count little against their personal advantage, and they both found ways to impose narratives that largely allow them to remain immune from public judgment. In cases such as these, only the law can effectively prevent empowered individuals in office to seek their advantage instead of that of the public.

An enlightening example of the different effectiveness of the law compared to norms refers to public statements. We can conceive that an empowered individual, say a government official, can be held accountable in two different settings: by the press or in a public hearing, where she testifies under oath (for example in a criminal trial or a congressional investigation). In the first instance, the only restraint from lying for her own benefit are norms, in the second, lying under oath can lead to indictment, conviction, and possibly prison. The obvious difference is very clear to the US president. In 2018 Trump offered a few remarks to the press shortly after his return from the Singapore meeting with North Korea's Kim Jong-un:

> The other most notable moment came during the gaggle, when reporters asked Trump about a statement to The New York Times concerning a June 2016 meeting at Trump Tower between Donald Trump Jr., Jared Kushner, and campaign chairman Paul Manafort, along with a Russian lawyer. The President dictated the statement, as his lawyers acknowledged in a letter to special counsel Robert Mueller. That statement was false and quickly debunked.
>
> "That's irrelevant," Trump said Friday. "It's a statement to The New York Times, the phony, failing New York Times. That's not a statement to a high tribunal of judges. That's a statement to the phony New York Times."
>
> In short, the President is saying that it's totally acceptable to lie to the press, and by extension the public, as long as he is not under oath in the justice system. (As I've reported, Trump is far more honest under oath.) As a matter of law, this is true, but as a matter of character and leadership, it is not. The President is freely telling the public that he has no compunctions about lying through his teeth. Why does anyone still debate whether he means it?[10]

The conclusion seems quite clear: when lying implies breaking the law and committing a crime Trump is perfectly capable of restraint. When it is just the violation of a norm, there is no point in observing it, as there will be no negative consequence. The maxim reported at the beginning of this chapter, "It is better to be red with shame than green with rage," maybe the most telling rule reportedly adopted by Berlusconi in conducting business. Meaning that being shamed for violating a norm is not a big deal, what is important is to get the upper hand.

An interesting New York Times article in March 2019 focused on the different performance by right-wing publicist Alex Jones depending on the settings: his TV show or a courtroom:

…in the On camera and in public, the stocky Texan is famous for his meandering soliloquies and belligerent, occasionally violent verbal outbursts. The Alex Jones persona orbits around his volatility, keeping audiences entertained and colleagues on their toes. It's never quite clear whether he'll laugh and burst into song, pound the table in a fit of rage or begin dramatically weeping.

The deposition video features Mr Jones from the waist-up, sitting at a table—a camera angle similar to his online broadcasts. However, unlike an Infowars episode, the host is not in control. Instead, Mr Jones is peppered with aggressive questions from an attorney. His confidential sources are exposed to be message board trolls and cranks. He's made to read from a disturbing police report, chronicling the testimony of emergency medical workers who attended the shooting at Sandy Hook, and then immediately watch footage of his past broadcasts, in which he declares that elements of the violence were part of a "false flag" operation.

In the video, Mr Jones occasionally attempts to slip into his Infowars persona. But his digressions are dismissed by lawyers as "nonresponsive." At one point, Mr Jones, evidently weary from questioning, asks for clarification of the lawyers' meaning of the word "staged." His question is cut off. "I'm not here to answer your questions," the lawyer says. "You're going to tell me what staged means when you said it."

…the deposition highlights a troubling reality: The legal system may be the only way to defang a well-known conspiracy theorist at the height of his powers.[11]

Courts are kryptonite for people who wish to confuse reality and dismiss facts because they have procedures in place that tend not to allow people to use nonsense to escape scrutiny. Exactly for this reason, plausibly, Trump did not testify with Mueller. A couple of decades before, Bill Clinton understood he was expected to clarify his situation before the American people and ultimately accepted to be questioned under oath. He could not ignore that such a step involved many risks and possible legal jeopardy, but he did it anyway, most likely because he calculated that voters would have sanctioned his refusal to be held accountable. Trump, having learned that his voters did not really care enough about, for example, his refusal to disclose his tax returns, rightly thought he could get away with refusing to testify and, if necessary, fight it in the court system.

This is what potentially makes a justice system based, in significant part, on norms vulnerable. As David French wrote, "It's the formulation that renders the government primarily responsible for safeguarding liberty, and the people primarily responsible for exercising that liberty for virtuous purposes. As John Adams said, 'Our Constitution was made only for a moral and religious people. It is wholly inadequate to the government of any other.'"[12] Which can be another way of saying that if the citizens of a country wish to have a Republic, they must be "able to keep it."

It has been argued by Trump's supporters that the president can fire officials who are investigating crimes in which he (or members of his family, or his cronies) has some kind of stake and thus terminate his legal jeopardy. Some pundits on the right also argue that he cannot be indicted in any case, even that he can pardon his potential accomplices and even himself: he could be bribed by someone and then instantly pardon himself and make the crime go away. As William Barr writes in the infamous memo he sent to the White House before he was nominated as AG (and which had most likely a significant role in getting him this nomination in the first place):

> "Constitutionally, it is wrong to conceive of the President as simply the highest officer within the Executive branch hierarchy. He alone *is* the Executive branch. As such he is the sole repository of *all Executive powers* conferred by the Constitution." Thus, "the Constitution vests *all Federal law enforcement power,* and hence prosecutorial discretion, in the President." That authority is "necessarily all-encompassing," and there can be "no limit on the President's authority to act [even] on matters which concern him or his own conduct[13]"

All these arguments, though contrary to the concept of the rule of law and distant from the liberal-democratic tradition of government, are, to a good extent, founded in the law of the United States. Berlusconi's base, just like Trump's, was ready to justify whatever he did. However, the big difference is that he could not pardon himself, or any other person for that matter; he could not fire or interfere with any prosecutors in any criminal proceedings, because the law prevented him from doing it. Today, in the US, norms and ethical values may not be enough to prevent the abuses by empowered officials.

* * *

If the institutional systems of Italy and the US concerning the effectiveness of the judicial function to check the executive branch are different, the ways Berlusconi and Trump shaped the public debate around the possibility that he committed crimes is quite similar. The very first thing both Berlusconi and Trump do when accused of wrongdoing is to seek something they can accuse the accuser with. Their preferred modus operandi is to find a possible reason for the accuser to be biased against them and then insist on it, and have their political allies amplify the message so that the public understands that the accusation is being presented as instrumental to getting the leader, not because of actual wrongdoing. Berlusconi would mostly accuse the prosecutors that investigated him, as well as the judges that ruled against him, to be communists, or at least left-leaning, and to act for a political reason. In the same fashion, Trump accused the "angry democrats" from Special Counsel Robert Mueller's team of seeking to undermine him politically. In another instance, he famously accused a judge of being biased because of his Hispanic heritage, after he ruled against him in the Trump University case.[14] When there are no plausible reasons for the accusers to be biased, both Berlusconi and Trump simply attack their credibility, or their mental ability, or both. Alternatively, they simply mock and insult them.

In other instances, Trump and Berlusconi complain about the process. In Italy, as we have seen, there has been a long-standing debate about the judicial process, at least since the beginning of the 80s, dating back to the times of the contrast between the judiciary and part of the politicians from the ruling parties, especially the socialists. During these years, the prosecutors from various cities indicted a significant number of local officials from the Socialist and the Christian Democratic parties; the resulting proceedings obviously had an impact on the reputation of the politicians involved in the scandals. One of the reactions from the socialists, rather than responding to each accusation with facts, was to point out how, in their opinion, the judiciary was interfering with the executive branch and that it was necessary to introduce new legislation to better guarantee the rights of the accused. Among the many legislation proposals, there was also a nuclear option: an amendment to the constitution that would reduce the number of members of the Superior Council of the Judiciary elected among magistrates and increase the number of those appointed by the parties. The debate ultimately led to the introduction of a new criminal procedure, in the late 80s, that was supposedly more attentive to the rights of the defendant; nevertheless, not surprisingly, it did not affect the ability of the prosecutors to investigate and indict politicians. In fact, any effective measure to ensure such an outcome would also cripple the criminal-justice system overall, thus affecting the prosecution of ordinary crimes, probably with the resulting backlash from the public. As we have seen, if anything the Italian justice system guarantees the right of the indicted in excess, especially in white-collar cases, and even more when the defendant has the means to hire a good law firm to take full advantage of all the loopholes of the law. Berlusconi brought back the due process debate for his benefit in the 90s and in the following decades, usually by claiming that the combined effect of a prosecutor's indictment and the reporting of the news by the press would result in significant damage to the politician's reputation, a violation of the principle of due process. A public figure, he complained, could face smearing with no effective defense. The Republicans, following the accusation of sexual misconduct by Supreme Court appointee Brett Kavanaugh, used a similar argument. As they did during the handling of the impeachment inquiry by the House Intelligence Committee in 2019. Such claims, of course, are unfounded. Due process is a fundamental principle of the liberal political philosophy, it informs the institutions of contemporary Western democracies and it was conceived to prevent the government from inflicting incarceration or other penalties in an arbitrary way. It has nothing to do with one's reputation. If Berlusconi felt that he was unfairly indicted for some crime and that he was publicly smeared as a result, he had all the means to explain to the public that he did not commit such actions: due process is a principle to be activated in court, not in the public debate. In the same way, Judge Kavanaugh wasn't facing legal jeopardy, he wasn't in front of a jury which might have convicted him. He was simply to be evaluated by senators who would form an opinion about his character and decide whether to confirm him as a Supreme Court Justice. There is no issue of due process violation there, just the opinion of the senators and their accountability with their constituency.

All in all, something the two leaders seem to have in common is an apparent preference toward a justice system with two levels: the first one is for ordinary crimes, it should be swift and "not too mindful" of the rights of the defendant. The second one should be applied to white-collar crimes, especially those committed by the cronies of the two leaders, where prosecutors are found to be always too aggressive and the judges frequently biased. Trump made it obvious that he thinks the police should not bother too much about the accused in custody: "Please, don't be too nice," when handling someone in custody, he publicly said to police officers. Trump's statement is suggestive of a strange inclination toward the use of violence, or, possibly, he finds that such inclination will portray him as tough, a feature he seems to deem important as it relates to the public perception of his persona. He famously and repeatedly said, during the 2016 presidential campaign, that he would bring back waterboarding, because "torture absolutely works, believe me," and in fact he would "bring back a hell of a lot worse than waterboarding."

Trump's record with the use of presidential pardon also enlightens his disregard for the rule of law. Of course, from a legal standpoint, the president's discretion in this area is very wide, and many of his predecessors also made questionable choices, but Trump's decision, for example, to pardon Arizona sheriff Joe Arpaio, convicted of disobeying a lawful order by the judiciary, makes it very clear where Trump stands in terms of legal culture, or lack of it. Again, as with his support for waterboarding (or worse), his main concern seems to be his desire to appear tough: Arpaio famously adopted very harsh, even, reportedly, inhumane, methods with the prisoners in his care; so, supporting the sheriff, by extension, makes Trump strong, he seems to calculate. A similar pattern was likely in action when he decided to pardon soldiers suspected of war crimes and found guilty of atrocities. Roy Moore, a former judge, and a candidate for the Alabama Senate seat, is another case of an individual who benefited from Trump's support even though he had been removed from the office of State Justice for defying a court order. Moore won the nomination of the GOP but went on to lose the Senate election to the Democratic candidate, largely because credible allegations of sexual assault on his part were made public.

Another area in which the US system, largely based on norms, seems to be ineffective under Trump concerns the difficulties in having the White House cooperate with congressional investigations and oversight. In many cases, particularly during the impeachment proceeding in the House of Representatives, Trump's White House has asserted an unprecedented claim of general and absolute immunity from the obligation of testimony or producing documents, even when ordered by a subpoena. Past administrations, in many instances, have proved reluctant to have officials testify on certain issues, or hand over requested documents. However, all these cases were usually the subject of negotiations between Congress and the executive to find some middle ground that would enable the administration to maintain a reasonable amount of confidentiality or executive privilege, while allowing Congress to exercise its oversight. With Trump, the attitude of the executive is to completely stonewall Congress; he seems to be saying: "you want documents? Make me if you can..." While in business it can occasionally be considered "smart" to resort to such methods, in politics the traditional ethics imposes on executive officials a high level of transparency so that they can be accountable before the people.

The behavior of the president is generally expected to adhere to norms also in those instances in which a conflict of interest may prevent the head of the executive from seeking solutions for the benefit of the public because he might be inclined to pursue his personal gains. Previous presidents, especially those with significant business engagements, have put their investments in a blind trust to prevent any possible question of corruption. Of course, Trump did nothing of the sort: he placed his business on a revocable trust managed by his children, a solution that hardly prevents him from knowing which policies might benefit his particular corporate interests. After all, what Trump really thinks about a possible conflict of interest in the executive branch became quite clear during his first 2 years in office, after Jeff Sessions as Attorney General recused himself from matters relating to the Russia investigation. Session's decision was fully consistent with the regulations of the department he was heading, nevertheless, because of this recusal, Trump repeatedly and publicly attacked and humiliated him, and never forgave him for what he must have seen as a pointless weakness and ultimately fired him right after the mid-term elections. Berlusconi's attitude toward all possible conflict of interest has been very similar. When he won the elections he would not sell his businesses or resort to an effective blind trust; instead, he did exactly the same as Trump: he put his children in charge. Except in his case, the stakes were even higher as he owns large corporations with thousands of employees and some of them belong to the politically sensitive sector of mass media.

But the most striking similarity between Berlusconi and Trump is the way they were able to shape the public debate in such a way as to escape accountability from their unprecedented, unethical, and illegal behavior. The report prepared by Special Counsel Mueller describes very clearly various instances of obstruction of justice by the commander in chief, as a public statement signed by thousands of lawyers, from both sides of the political spectrum, testifies. Nevertheless, after the release of the report a great part of the American public could spend hours:

watching pundits engaged in that most modern of activities:

grappling with revelations that manage to be at once outrageous and...thoroughly predictable. *Shocked, but not surprised*. It might be the defining emotion of the politics of 2019, and it lurks, among the shaded legalese, in the Mueller report. The person leading the American government lies, with regularity and impunity? It's outrageous, but widely known. His agents *do the same*, on his behalf? Scandalous, and also a bit tedious. The White House, populated by several beneficiaries of nepotism and headed by someone whose mentor was a lawyer for the mob, has a dull tint of corruption? Shocking! But no longer surprising.

Trump is exceptionally skilled at separating people from their outrage, and one of his most common rhetorical tricks is his use of repetition as incantation. Whether it's 'U-S-A' or 'Lock her up' or 'No collusion, no obstruction,' his catchphrases have the effect not only of imposing his version of reality on audiences with blunt-force insistence, but also of lulling them into complacency. The refrains here function in the way refrains usually do: They become so familiar as to stop being questionable. And the Mueller report, so long in the making, has succumbed in its own way to that dynamic. A document making similar claims about a different president would be eye-popping; this particular report, however, about this particular president, simply confirmed that Donald Trump is the same person the American public—his supporters and his dissenters alike—has known him to be all along: venal, self-absorbed, unprepared. The report was metabolized accordingly. As MSNBC's Chris Hayes summed it up on Thursday evening, it "isn't a bombshell so much as a compendium and confirmation of who the man is and how he conducts himself."[15]

While Trump's ability to shape the desired narrative was fundamental in allowing him to steer clear of the consequences, another factor was just as necessary: the unconditional support from fellow politicians and pundits from the conservative sides, of which AG William Barr was only the most egregious example. The support of enablers was even more important for Trump in the impeachment proceedings: ultimately, 52 of 53 Republican senators voted to acquit him from the charge of abuse of power (the only exception being Mitt Romney).

Chapter 6

Policy, or the boring side of power

As a rule, all individuals who reach high positions of power in modern democracies are highly ambitious people with a strong need for self-actualization; it is very hard to imagine that a person without this quality can accomplish being elected to the highest level of government. However, some of these individuals also have a vision for their country, a goal they want to achieve to improve, in their assessment, the society they are part of. Others simply seek power for the sake of it, because of their need to be at the center of things or to feel they are winning. Based on the considerations of the previous chapters, it should be clear that both Trump and Berlusconi belong to this latter category of politicians, and their general attitude toward policy implementation makes that quite evident. This doesn't mean that these two leaders are always completely indifferent to policy-making. In many cases, these activities may have a significant impact on the approval by the electorate, something that they obviously care deeply about as a means to achieve or maintain office. However, it should be evident that they lack a vision and a passion for the implementation of legislation, or executive actions, which may change society in some desired direction. The exception to this general rule is Trump's apparent obsession with the US being ripped off by other countries, either by accepting trade deals that lead to US trade deficits or because of its willingness to provide security at its own expense for some allies. Trump appears to feel a genuine passion in this regard because he has stated publicly these concerns many times over the decades (even long before the 2016 campaign) and because he seems to have personally pushed policies in this direction while in office, even, arguably, at the risk of losing support from part of the conservative public. Mainly this passion has translated into his many demands that NATO allies spend more on defense and the many instances in which he imposed tariffs on other countries to achieve some trade advantages. Critics say that these policies are shortsighted and can be considered the result of a deep misunderstanding of international trade dynamics as well as international strategic and security issues, but they appear to have been actively pursued by the US president. In the case of Berlusconi, it is hard to detect any sign of genuine interest toward any policy whatsoever during his administrations.

Trump has profited a lot in terms of public support from the economic performance of the US during his years in office, that is until the Covid-19 health emergency; was such praise really deserved? In general, whatever the voters might think, presidents do not have a strong impact on economic growth and job creation, at least not in the short run. There may be a couple of exceptions: in times of depression, such as during the 2008-2009 collapse of the financial system and the resulting rise of unemployment, the administration has a fundamental role in doing a couple of things. First, reassuring the financial markets that the government is willing to take any necessary measure to avoid the kind of panic that leads to bank runs, or its contemporary equivalents. Second, increase public spending in order to offset the reduction of consumption by families and lack of investment by corporations to boost the economy and reduce unemployment. Another thing administrations can do to improve short-term economic prospects is to spark optimism in the business community: improved expectations by the actors that make investment decisions can indeed have an immediate positive effect on growth. Other than that, policies typically affect the long-term economic performance; they are programs such as infrastructures, research and development, education that have an impact on production only after years, which is why it is often difficult to put them in place: the politicians who implement them don't get to benefit from the results in terms of public recognition. While it is certainly possible that Trump's declarations and general attitude have stimulated the expectations of many business people, his handling of the economy seems to have been adopting the standard GOP policies, including meeting the expectations of Republican donors. In many cases, the policies implemented have little to do with the commitments during the presidential campaign. While during the campaign he mostly announced economic policies that could be defined as populist, in several cases belonging more to the tradition of the Democratic Party than the Republicans[1], when in office he made a rather sharp right turn.[2] This seems to suggest that his economic policy platform responded more to political marketing needs than actual elements of a vision for economic development.

Trump's signature achievement in the realm of the economy is probably the tax cut bill, skewed toward higher incomes and the earnings of corporations. While the measure was substantially not in line with the policy he ran on, it has significantly increased the US public debt, with no plausible justification in a cycle of economic growth. A frequent claim by Trump and his supporters contemplates the benefits for business coming from the deregulation policy that his administration implemented. In this case, too, the White House adopted the standard position of the Republican Party, particularly after the Tea Party movement, though it remains to be seen whether these policies will benefit the public overall. To stick to the financial system, appointing Mick Mulvaney, a former member of the Freedom Caucus and someone who seems to oppose regulations in principle, to the direction of the Consumer Financial Protection Bureau will probably not boost the effectiveness of this agency, designed to pursue the interests of consumers. At the same time, the bill passed by the House of Representatives in 2017 that constitutes a rollback of the Dodd-Frank Act (a law designed to avoid some of the financial practices that caused the 2008 meltdown) did implement a significant amount of deregulation. Even though the Senate limited its scope, it may allow financial institutions to engage in risky practices in future years.

Possibly, one of Trump's most characteristic interventions in the economy is a series of attacks on the chairman of the Federal Reserve System, Jerome Powell, someone he had nominated, for pursuing a policy, in his opinion, of excessively high interest rates. The FED runs the US monetary policy. In most Western countries, the monetary authorities have been shielded from interference by the executive for a rather important reason: administrations know that a growing economy is a much better situation than a recession for its electoral prospects and may be inclined to pressure central banks to lower rates and thus increase the chances of fostering economic growth. However, while low rates may boost growth and be beneficial in the short run, they might also cause a rise of inflation. Knowing how the temptation of governments to achieve short-term growth at all costs in order to gain popular support may also bring big problems to economic stability, most countries have an independent monetary policy. In many cases, the officials in charge of central banks cannot be fired, if not in very special circumstances, and established norms strongly suggest that the executive not interfere with decisions concerning interest rates. Of course, Trump couldn't care less about a norm and, when he sensed that the economy might be slowing down in 2019, he began attacking Powell with a series of public statements evidently designed to bully him into reducing the rates and achieving his electoral objective.

In a way, Trump's more astounding declarations during the 2016 campaign dealt with the health care policy, a sector that, it is often remembered, represents about a fifth of the overall economy in the US. On various occasions, he pledged to repeal the Affordable Care Act, or Obamacare, and replace it with something "wonderful," with no hints whatsoever of what it would be. Today we can quite confidently say he had no plan at all since the "wonderful" thing was never disclosed, let alone made part of an actual bill, or even a memo. Famously, after the inauguration, Trump also said that "nobody knew health care could be so complicated," making it quite evident that he had not approached the subject at all before the election, or afterward. While the GOP-controlled Senate did not manage to repeal Obamacare, the Trump administration hit the ACA with a couple of blows. The first one was included in the tax cut bill approved in 2017, a provision that repeals one of the major elements of ACA, the so-called individual mandate, the tax penalty to those individuals who refuse the required health coverage (this mechanism ensures that younger, and typically healthier, persons be part of the overall risk pool). The second one deals with pre-existing conditions: perhaps the most popular element of Obamacare, it prevents insurance companies from denying coverage (or charging more) for individuals who have a condition before purchasing the policy. In 2018, the Department of Justice would not enforce that part of ACA, claiming it was dependent on the individual mandate, already repealed by Congress.

An area in which Trump seems to have pressed to get results is immigration and border security, his signature campaign pledge. However, many of the policies executed in this regard were poorly planned, often mitigated by the courts, and sometimes resulted in public opinion debacles (as with the images of children in cages shown in the TV networks, after the government implemented the separation of families entering the US from the southern border.) Trump's eagerness to bring some results to his voters, especially the famous, "beautiful" wall on the border with Mexico, also made evident how the negotiation skills he bragged about so much were rather overestimated, to say the least. A few days before Christmas of 2018, the US government went into shutdown mode, as Congress had not granted funding for several executive departments; the shutdown lasted over a month and was the longest in US history. In the preceding days, the Senate had passed an appropriation bill that seemed on its way to getting the vote of the House and the president's signature. However, a few conservative pundits and right-wing media noticed with disappointment that the bill did not include funding for the famous wall, so Trump immediately declared he would not sign it. Usually, the shutdown comes with a blame game between the two parties over which one is mainly responsible for it. However, in this case, Trump had a meeting with the Democratic leaders broadcast on TV where he clearly assumed all responsibility for the shutdown, saying: "I am proud to shut down the government for border security." He evidently wanted to pose as a resolute defender of the wall, but in the process, he completely accepted the blame for the shutdown, leaving the Democrats in the very comfortable position of waiting for the inevitable caving by the president. Trump implicitly surrendered about a month later, after needless damage was done to thousands of US employees and to those citizens who needed the public services.

* * *

While Trump seemed to genuinely care for "fixing" international trade deals and he did push, though in an amateurish way, to implement the immigration policies he announced during the campaign, Berlusconi never seemed to be interested in any policy whatsoever. The only exception being those that affected a specific interest of his: usually having to do with his trials or with his business. Not that Italy did not need reforms during the Berlusconi era; in fact, it desperately needed many, in different areas of government. The Italian economy, though very dynamic in the north of the country thanks to the entrepreneurial spirit of its small and medium companies and particularly its local clusters, had many problems dating back decades.

One of these problems, as we have seen, was the difference in terms of economic development between the South and the North. Actually, the difference went beyond the purely economic realm, and included social issues such as organized crime, a long-standing problem especially in Sicily and other regions, which had become a phenomenon so embedded in the social fabric as to constitute a serious obstacle to social development and even the standing of the rule of law. The lower presence of corporations, big and small, in the South meant, of course, lower employment opportunities, in great part compensated by the public sector. However, more public employees in the South did not provide better or more services: quite the opposite. For example, the public health services provided in the South were more expensive but of lower quality, as demonstrated by the significant "migration" of patients to the North in search of better health care. The main reason for the electoral rise of the Northern League, starting in the late 80s, was precisely what was perceived as a drain of resources from the North to the South in exchange for little results. The solution, according to many, was to implement a more federalist system of government, particularly from a fiscal standpoint, where local politicians who wanted to distribute more services would also have the burden of asking voters to pay for them. By the late 90s, the introduction of federalist elements in the country's institutions had become one of the most urgent political topics in the public debate. The left-leaning government, worried that it may lose the support of voters who favored federalism, introduced a constitutional reform to shift the authority over many policy areas from the central state to the regions; at the same time, it also introduced legislation[3] to achieve a higher level of financial accountability for local governments. Shortly after, in 2001, Berlusconi won the elections again and headed a government with the support of the Northern League, the party that had made federalism its main issue. Neither Berlusconi's party, nor the Northern League supported the federalist reforms, while also refusing to implement the measures of fiscal responsibility previously approved.

Another urgent problem during Berlusconi's tenure was the extent of the Italian public debt. To be sure, it was not his fault; the debt started growing in the 70s and the 80s due to a very generous pension plan system for public employees and other expenditures not balanced by appropriate taxation. By the 90s, the public debt had become a huge problem and it was arguably one of the main causes of the 1992 financial troubles. In 2001, with the start of the second Berlusconi government, the conditions were ideal to lower the debt. After the entry of Italy into the Eurozone, inflation was not a problem and interest rates were at an all-time low, largely thanks to the center-left governments that had put some order into the public finances to meet the Maastricht criteria. One of the main elements of Berlusconi's campaign in 2001 was his pose as defender of free markets and his pledge to reduce useless spending in the public administration while reducing taxes. However, one of Berlusconi's allies, National Alliance, the party that had its roots in the fascist ideology, had a constituency that believed in, in fact praised, public intervention in the economy and public spending provided an opportunity to pay off political debts and generate a certain amount of gratitude in some voters. In exchange for a significant increase in public spending, Berlusconi could count on the help of the National Alliance to vote for the laws he needed for his trials and for the re-organization of the public broadcasting system, which of course directly affected his own media empire. According to most independent observers, the broadcasting statute approved by Parliament in this period is a gift to Berlusconi's media companies: it does not provide clear criteria for the selection of the companies to which the authorization to broadcast should be granted and it does not prevent the concrete possibility of dominant position by certain corporations. For these reasons, once Parliament passed the law, the President of the Republic refused to sign it, and later the European Court of Justice found it contrary to European principles.

The important thing for Berlusconi, not unlike Trump, is how things look, rather than how they actually are. One of his brilliant initiatives in the electoral campaign of 2001 was the signing of the "Contract with the Italians," resembling the "Contract with America" proposed a few years earlier by Newt Gingrich in the US. He went on a popular talk show with a friendly host, the long-time public television journalist Bruno Vespa, and staged the signing of a sheet of paper in which he pledged to pursue a number of policies if elected. According to most observers, the sham was highly successful, just as the "Contract with America" had been for the Republicans. Many Italians read it as an actual commitment to policy-making and gave him credit for it. The substance of the "contract" dealt with reducing taxes, enforcing security, reducing unemployment, increasing minimum retirement pensions, and building infrastructures. During the campaign for the following elections, in 2006, a great part of the debate revolved around whether Berlusconi had managed to meet his commitments during his time in office. Probably, he mostly did not, but a final judgment depends on how the policy goals are interpreted, given the lack of details. The larger point is that nowadays, in the highly specialized societies of the West, public policy on economic matters, in fact on nearly all matters, is so sophisticated that it is very difficult to state detailed policies on hundreds of pages, let alone on a one-page contract.

When it comes to foreign policy, a comparison between the governments led by Trump and Berlusconi has to take into account the much different positions of the US and Italy on the international stage. Though the relative weight of the economy of Italy declined in the last couple of decades, the country is still one of the ten most important ones in the world. On the contrary, Italy was never very relevant, at least since the end of the Second World War, on the political level. Militarily it is not a significant factor; even though it participated in many UN-led or NATO-organized units for peacekeeping or other purposes in many parts of the world, including, Iraq and Afghanistan, it spends a lower percentage of its GDP on defense than most other NATO members. The US, of course, is the world's leading superpower, with enormous responsibilities all over the planet. Even though in the near future this position might be challenged by China and other countries, there seems to be no question that the US is the biggest economy of the world, can count on a strong technological edge, and has the most powerful army. These two different positions on the world stage have obvious significant implications for the countries' foreign policies. Having said that, there certainly are various similarities between the two leaders.

The first one that may come to mind is their puzzling deference toward Russia's Vladimir Putin. Both Trump and Berlusconi always seemed to have a soft spot for strong men, but Putin seemed to have a very special place for them. Berlusconi did everything he could to develop a personal relationship with him and his family and, even when he was not Italy's prime minister, he managed to be invited to special state occasions by the Russian autocrat. Putin's reputation as an enemy of the basic principles of Western liberalism, such as the rule of law and free press, did not prevent the two leaders from praising him. During an international press conference with Putin and Berlusconi, a reporter asked the Russian leader a question that was found uncomfortable; Berlusconi's reaction was to mime the firing of a machine gun in the direction of the press core while smiling to Putin. Most of the American public who watched footage from the 2017 Helsinki summit meeting between the US and Russia might never forget the strange sensation after Trump's public declarations in favor of Putin and his dismissing of the findings of his own intelligence agencies regarding the meddling in the 2016 elections. For a few hours, maybe for a day or two, the public, including conservatives, seemed stunned and in disbelief of what had just happened, a few commentators said out loud what many had only thought within themselves: "what does Putin have on him?" As that was the only explanation that made some sense, that could provide a rationale for such a display of weakness in a man who made a point of appearing strong at every chance he got. When WikiLeaks disclosed a large number of files from the US intelligence and foreign service in 2010, some documents indicated that the US government was concerned, puzzled, and suspicious about Berlusconi's closeness to Putin; agents were tasked with finding out the reasons behind the friendship. In both Berlusconi's and Trump's cases, we know that there might have been business-related motives for them to go to such lengths to cultivate their relationship with the Russian President. Many Italian companies have an interest in Russia, particularly the oil and energy company ENI that has a strong stake in the South Stream enterprise together with Gazprom, a Russian state-owned corporation. According to a Georgian diplomat quoted in a WikiLeaks document, Berlusconi was promised a percentage of the business generated by the cooperation between the Italian and Russian companies. We also know from the Mueller investigation that the Trump organization was negotiating a real estate deal in Moscow and was seeking the approval of that government. It would hardly be surprising if hidden business deals with Russia that involve the Trump organization will be unearthed in the future.

While Berlusconi's coziness with Putin could be troubling to some extent for other European leaders and may cost the Italian taxpayers if the wrong business deals were made, Trump's actions toward Russia are far more consequential. Since the end of World War II, the US has had more than one general addresses of foreign policy; sometimes more inclined toward what is usually called "realpolitik," the actual power relations in the international arena, and some other times in which moral standings have had a more salient role. However, in all cases, the US was always conscious of its preeminent role of bastion for the values of the West, of its responsibility as the "leader of the free world," as it is commonly defined in America. As such, the US always was a major shareholder of NATO, the member with the controlling stake in fact. All this changed with Trump, and it seems to have changed mostly because of his desire to please Putin. Other elements may play a role in Trump's attitude, perhaps his obsession with other countries not paying their "fair share," but there is little doubt that the country that benefits the most from the downgrading of NATO and from the generation of a wedge between the US and Europe is Russia.

If Putin is Trump's and Berlusconi's best friend on the international stage, he certainly hasn't been the only one; many others can be identified among the dictators and strongmen of the world. Berlusconi went to great lengths and efforts to cultivate a personal relationship with Colonel Gaddafi of Libya, with Turkey's Erdogan, Egypt's Mubarak, and others. Trump also enjoys cultivating a personal relationship with other strong men, often in a rather weird way. Probably the most notable examples come from his interactions with North Korea's Kim Jong-un: after threatening "fire and fury" in the aftermath of a few menacing missiles launched by the Asian country, Trump sought in every way to get close to him . They even reached the point of writing each other letters with the US president declaring to the press: "We are in love, OK?" The administration even accepted to participate in two summit meetings, something no prior president had done; the results were not up to the expectations. A point Berlusconi and Trump have in common in all these interactions is how important it is to them to stress the personal relationship they establish with foreign leaders: when describing the relations with a particular country they always insist on their personal role, and how their interactions with the other leaders conduct to positive results. It is never about the institutions or the economic and strategic alinements; it is always about them personally. This need to portray international relations as heavily dependent on the friendship of their leaders takes us back to the diplomacy of the eighteenth and nineteenth centuries, when relations among powers depended heavily on the personal relationship between the kings and emperors, frequently also connected through family relations. This inclination by Trump and Berlusconi may be one of the reasons they seem to dislike multilateral settings, such as the meetings of the G7 or NATO summits, in which they usually stand out as the odd ones. Trump manifested uneasiness when meeting with several other heads of state or of government for celebrating an event or defining a common goal, often leaving the summits well before the scheduled closing and leaving the others to wonder. One of the most famous pictures of Trump participating in an international meeting is one taken at the G7 summit in Canada in June 2018. Germany's Angela Merkel stands up before him with the other Western leaders by her side while Trump is the only one sitting down with his arms crossed as to signal that he is not really ready to be part of the group. Berlusconi had an additional feature to display at international events: his habit of downgrading the gravitas of the meetings by setting up clownish shows. In Italy, this side of Berlusconi's international activities has been dubbed the "diplomazia del cucu," an expression that could be translated as the "diplomacy of the peekaboo," from the time he hid behind an object and, when Angela Merkel was approaching, jumped out saying "peekaboo," or something to that effect.

Both Trump and Berlusconi stated on many occasions that, before they took office, their countries had been often disrespected and occasionally laughed at. However, they would assure voters that, with them as leaders, things would change and they would restore the international prestige to which the US and Italy were entitled. The truth, in fact, is quite the opposite. Berlusconi in Europe was widely considered an untrustworthy populist who managed to be elected to the highest office thanks to his media empire (which stretched also to Spain and France, where he owned TV channels). The Economist, perhaps one of the most reputable magazines in the world, published a series of articles in 2001 detailing the reasons why the leader was "unfit" to lead Italy[4], an unprecedented stand. The reputation of Trump is not much better among Western nations. Possibly it is more sinister, as to reflect the much more consequential role of the US for the international community as well as a hint of cruelty, or at the very least, a lack of compassion that can be easily identified in his character, probably emanating from his desire to appear tough at all costs. Hence, it is not a coincidence that the two leaders achieved exactly the opposite of what they had claimed they would, that is prevent other leaders from laughing at their countries. In 2011, Angela Merkel and the French president Nicholas Sarkozy were asked on camera about their opinion on Berlusconi's reliability during a financial crisis: they looked at each other and smiled for an instant. The Italian TV news programs showed these images repeatedly for days and it was perhaps the most revealing sign of the political decline of the Italian tycoon: he had to resign shortly after and, while he retained a political role as head of his party, he never had a chance to become the head of government again. Trump was also the evident object of a few laughs in 2019 at an event at Buckingham Palace following a NATO summit, when Canada's Justin Trudeau, the UK's Boris Johnson, and France's Emmanuel Macron were caught on video commenting on his awkward manners and disregard for etiquette and visibly laughing about it. As on past occasions, Trump abruptly left the meeting early, skipping the final events.

As regards the policies that Trump seems to be passionate about, namely the US not being "ripped off" by other countries, his years in office can hardly be declared a success story. The wedge he managed to create with NATO's allies, particularly because of the bullish way he sought to get some countries to pay more for defense spending (which is very different from paying the US back, as Trump sometimes claimed) will hardly be beneficial to the US and their leading role in the world. The trade wars with China, the European Union, and other trading partners did not help at all in reducing the trade deficit of the US (on the contrary, it increased even further) while it seriously hurt many US exporting sectors, starting with products of farming. The North American Free Trade Agreement with Mexico and Canada, which he had attacked relentlessly during the 2016 campaign, had to be renegotiated by the three countries at Trump's request only to be restored in what appears to be, for all practical means, the same deal. As National Review's Kevin Williamson summarizes:

> Trump promised Americans sustained 3-percent economic growth, but the economy has not met that standard. He promised a shrinking trade deficit, but the trade deficit has grown. He promised to build a wall along the southern border and to make Mexico pay for it, which he has not done. Which is to say, on the core issues of economic growth, trade, and immigration, President Trump is a failure by his own criteria.[5]

The lack of interest of Berlusconi in actual policy is quite evident based on the people he recruited to implement it. While he valued personal competence in his corporations, he seemed to care almost only about loyalty in his political appointments. Trump adopted a very similar attitude. In the beginning of his administration, while pricing loyalty above other qualities, he seemed to realize that he needed professionals with experience to avoid mistakes and embarrassing instances of failure. But, as he gained more confidence, he felt less compelled to rely on policy professionals in the White House and tended to surround himself with aides who would execute whatever he said. As Paul Krugman wrote, "Trump...wants people who will be personally dependent on him, who don't have any kind of professional reputation to defend and therefore won't take a stand on principle. That is, he only wants hacks."[6]

But probably the biggest damage brought by Berlusconi and Trump to policy implementation in their countries derives not from specific measures that they pushed or even the appointment of incompetent officials, but is rather a consequence of the level of distraction from important public matters that they brought with them. The controversies, the outrageous statements, the attacks on the enemies, whether real or manufactured: it has all been a major distraction that made it impossible to properly develop a public debate on actual policies. To some extent, in modern democracies policy and politics are always mixed and interlaced, but under these two leaders, politics is all that matters, and very little space is left for policy.

* * *

Traditional marketing textbooks used in business schools identify at least four elements that should be taken into account to design a sound and effective business strategy, the famous four Ps: Product, Price, Place (intended as distribution channels), and Promotion. While an ideal company should be strong in each one of the Ps to ensure long-term success, it is conceivable that businesses can achieve good results, especially in the short run, if they are particularly effective just in some areas, though weak in others. For example, a company may have a mediocre product but it is promoting and distributing it so well, and at a reasonable price, that it may pull off satisfactory sales results for a while, at least until most of the customers, initially attracted by the effective advertising, realize the product is not good. A similar characterization could be used for the political market and, using this analogy, it seems fair to say that Berlusconi's and Trump's policies (their "products") are mediocre, at least insofar as they have been implemented by their administrations, but their promotional strategies have been extremely effective, thus allowing them to win elections, at least for some time. Of course, a complication is that the assessment of the "product" by voters, that is the implementation of public policies, is far more difficult as opposed to most actual products in the market. However, at least in Berlusconi's case, this depiction seems to be confirmed by the fact that he never won two consecutive elections: after trying his "product" for a while, Italians always voted for the other side.

Chapter 7

"Believe me!" Sex scandals in the age of populism

The romantic and sexual deeds of Berlusconi and Trump occupied a significant part of the press coverage of their personas during their tenure and, it seems, having multiple affairs is an important part of their need for self-expression and self-actualization. This is hardly a new phenomenon: sex scandals have been associated with many politicians of all leanings for as long as one can remember, but it is worthwhile noting that this kind of scandal has quite a different impact on the public in the US as opposed to Europe. In the old continent, the press assumes that voters are not particularly concerned about, say, a minister's private life and, as long as his or her sexual encounters do not involve wrongdoing or interfere with official business, the affairs should not damage their career. Things can be quite different in the US, particularly since the Gary Hart affair in 1987, when the press dedicated a lot of the coverage of the presidential candidate to his romantic life, ultimately leading to him leaving the race. During the previous decades, politicians' sex lives were widely absent from the public debate and even when presidents were considered womanizers, such as the case with John F. Kennedy, the mainstream press would not usually go there. Arguably, the biggest sex scandal of all in recent times was President Bill Clinton's affair with White House intern Monica Lewinsky, certainly made worse by his misleading statements, which ultimately led to his impeachment in the House of Representatives. In Italy, or other European countries, the press would hardly cover events such as the Clinton affair in the same way; however, Berlusconi's adventures in the aftermath of his separation and divorce from his second wife, Veronica Lario, appeared flamboyant and coarse to a degree that could not pass unobserved by the media and the public.

Berlusconi and Trump seem to display similar patterns of behavior in their personal romantic lives. They were both married multiple times and created relatively large families maintaining, apparently, strong bonds with the children from all marriages, who are involved in the family businesses. While these marriages did not prevent the two from evidently having occasional affairs, there seem to be a few differences between Trump and Berlusconi as regards to the attitude toward women and the way to approach them. Perhaps the most significant one is that there are signs that Trump may show a proclivity toward aggressiveness, perhaps even violence that seems to be absent from Berlusconi's modus operandi in this realm. Multiple women have quite credibly and publicly accused Trump of sexual misconduct and even rape, and according to his own statements in the infamous Hollywood tape with Billy Bush, he brags about how his star status allowed him to behave very aggressively with women. Berlusconi, on the other hand, vulgar as the representations of some of his romantic deeds appear to be, does not seem to display a similar inclination toward violent acts directed at women, quite the contrary in fact, and no allegation of him being involved in a sexual assault has ever been made. Another difference is that there are no hints of sexual scandals involving Trump while in office: all his alleged affairs happened before his inauguration in 2017, while Berlusconi, particularly after his divorce, engaged in all sorts of encounters with multiple women while he was the head of the government, even in official residences. Having said that, for both politicians sex scandals have been a significant part of their press coverage and the public debate on their personas, for both leaders such scandals are interlaced with possible crimes.

The romantic life of Berlusconi and Trump is obviously affected by the way they see women and their role in society, which in turn has a significant political impact, both in terms of how the female electorate perceives these leaders (and their political party), and the cultural influence that such perception has in their countries. Scholars that study sexism usually make a distinction between hostile sexism and benevolent sexism.[1] The former exhibits explicit antipathy toward women, often in an aggressive way and an urge to dominate them. The benevolent form of sexism tends to represent women as pure and ethically superior on condition that they behave according to traditional cultural patterns, especially gender norms. Benevolent sexists often emphasize the need to protect women. Given this distinction, it seems an intuitive conclusion to include Trump in the first category of sexists and Berlusconi in the second. During the 2016 presidential campaign and while in office, Trump exhibited a particular resentment of what he perceived as attacks by women: he often used the word "nasty" to describe women who did not support him or that simply asked him questions he did not like. More than once he seemed to refer in some way to the menstrual cycle as a negative; for example when claiming that Fox News reporter Megyn Kelly had "...blood coming out of her...wherever..." after she had questioned him about his attitude toward women in a primary debate. He also used a blood reference when attacking Morning Joe journalist Mika Brzezinski, after what he thought was unfavorable coverage on her part. Many times, he used the physical appearance of women to attack them and, reportedly, he was particularly disturbed by the act of Melissa McCarthy in the Saturday Night Show impersonating and mocking press secretary Sean Spicer; not because it highlighted the weaknesses of Spicer's performance in the White House, but because he couldn't conceive of a woman mocking a man on his team. Berlusconi, too, is and was perfectly able to attack women he perceived as enemies. More than once he referred to the "angry and resentful," and often "ugly," feminists. He famously once attacked a prominent politician from the left, the former Christian Democrat Rosy Bindi, whom he considered unattractive, describing her as "prettier than intelligent" (she then responded that she would not dignify Berlusconi's attack by saying that he was taller than polite). Nevertheless, the general attitude of Berlusconi, unless he perceives to be directly attacked, is that of the traditional family man from the 50s, who expects women to conform to traditional gender norms, possibly be pretty, and have a role as housewife and as a mother or a mistress; a role, in short, measured against her male partner. Berlusconi always bragged about his courting abilities and the pleasure of protecting and escorting women.

The general attitude of these two leaders toward women, of course, has significant political consequences. As far as the US electorate is concerned, it is fair to remember that there was a huge gender gap (usually measured by the sum of the differences between the inclinations of each gender to vote for a given party) long before his participation in the race for president. Women have been more inclined to vote for Democrats since about the 80s and this gap has slowly grown ever since. However, with Trump, the trend accelerated and things got worse for the GOP. In the 2016 election, women supported Hillary Clinton by 14 points, but by the end of 2019 polling showed a significant increase in the gap: in a hypothetical race where the president is running against Joe Biden women would prefer the latter by a whopping, and unprecedented, 24 points. Another thing that should worry Trump is that his numbers have not dropped with women of color or white women with a college degree, but mostly with poorly educated white women, who voted in favor of Trump by 23 points in 2016, but now seem willing to vote in his favor only by a margin of 4 percent.[2] In Italy, there never was a significant gender gap between the center-right and the center-left, and, in general, women seemed to behave electorally in a slightly more conservative fashion if compared to the US. Nevertheless, as the sexual scandals of Berlusconi increased and gained more coverage in the news, starting in 2009, it appears that the Italian leader lost some support from female voters (as well as from religious individuals).

* * *

The scandals that involved Trump during his political tenure are very well known: the first major one is the unearthing of the "Hollywood tape," where he brags about his very aggressive approach (if not outright assault) toward women with TV host Billy Bush. This moment marks the low point of his campaign, when he lost the support of many of his prominent allies (even Mike Pence, who disappeared from the scene for a while, seemed on the verge of making some negative comment on this matter) and seemed doomed to lose the election overall. It also constitutes the only instance in which he publicly apologized to the public for something. The second scandal, or set of scandals, is the reporting of two affairs he allegedly had with women from show business. The first one is Playboy playmate Karen McDougal, with whom he apparently maintained an intimate and lasting relationship while married to his third and current wife. The second one involves adult film actress Stormy Daniels, who claims Trump had sex with her and then, shortly before the 2016 elections, sent his lawyers to get her to sign a non-disclosure agreement so that she would not divulge the affair. Though Trump has denied both affairs, after listening to the statements of the two women and the objective facts, it is very hard to believe that they made up everything, in fact, even Trump's ardent supporters tend to avoid defending his version on this issue. A third significant group of scandals of a sexual nature is the one represented by several accusations, usually quite credible, by more than a dozen women alleging sexual misconduct and even, in at least one case, rape.

By comparison, the sex scandals of Berlusconi are many more and quite more colorful; also, many of them refer to his behavior while he was the head of Italy's government. While there was always talk and innuendo concerning his relationships with women other than his wife, things precipitated after his separation from Veronica Lario, a theater actress whom he had married after divorcing his first wife. In 2009, about a year after he won the general elections for the third time, Veronica Lario made a few public statements that seemed to damage Berlusconi. In April, she published an open letter to her husband on a left-leaning newspaper expressing her anger about the candidacy of several young and attractive women, with little or no political experience, to members of the European Parliament in the lists of Forza Italia. She explained that "someone has written that all this has been done to entertain the Emperor. I agree, what emerges from the newspapers is garbage without decency."[3] Just a few weeks later, the media reported that Berlusconi participated in the birthday party of an unknown 18-year-old girl from Naples and gave her a 6000 Euro neckless as a present. Berlusconi came up with a number of innocent explanations for his attendance at the party, but the media easily showed many inconsistencies in his version and, a few days later, Veronica Lario announced that she was filing for divorce. Berlusconi's separation was something of a turning point: before that moment, the Italian media tycoon may have had a number of affairs, but he did it privately and handled them in a rather discreet way which did not affect his official business. After Lario's announcement, however, Berlusconi seemed to lose all restraint and the press began to narrate all the Boccaccio-like stories of his long nights of parties filled with young girls, prostitutes in many cases, dressed up as nurses, or nuns, or simply naked, dancing and entertaining the "Emperor" in all sorts of ways. One of the many sex scandals deserves a special mention because of its legal repercussions: the story of Ruby, the "Hearts-stealer."

On May 27, 2010, the dancer—and, likely, occasional prostitute—Karima El Mahroug, born in Morocco and aged 17 at the time, was taken into custody by the Milan police on charges of theft of 3000 euros. As she had no ID with her, she was escorted to the police station to confirm her identity, according to laws and standard procedures. Since she was a minor, the magistrate ordered her into the custody of an institute for the underage. However, that night, Berlusconi himself called the chief of the Milan police and pressured him to release Karima to the care of Nicole Minetti (a young girl, very close to Berlusconi and frequent guest of the Arcore parties). The prime minister told the official that the girl was the nephew of Egypt's President Hosni Mubarak, and that a diplomatic crisis would be avoided by abiding by his request. Karima was released to the care of Minetti, but Berlusconi's friend left her to the custody of Michelle, another acquaintance of Berlusconi and an occasional prostitute herself, and with whom Karima was already living (she was also the person from whom Karima had allegedly stolen the 3000 euros). Karima, also known as Ruby the "Hearts-stealer," later declared that she had participated in hardcore parties in Berlusconi's estate together with other girls from show business and, in some cases, professional prostitutes. The main outcome of the incident was that Berlusconi was indicted for abuse of power, for having pressured the Milan police to release Ruby, and for abusing a minor. Immediately, the case became political. The House of Representatives, where Berlusconi and his allies could count on a majority, filed a motion with the Constitutional Court claiming that, when Berlusconi leaned on the Milan chief of police, he was exercising a duty of his office and therefore should be tried in the Special Court (the Ministers' Court) set up for these cases. It was a rather embarrassing instance for the House, as the majority of its members implicitly accepted Berlusconi's version that he called the police because he believed that Ruby was the nephew of the Egyptian president. Of course, there were no grounds whatsoever for such a claim and it defied logic, as well as common sense, to think that Berlusconi's intervention was anything other than an attempt to avoid having Ruby disclosing his sexual adventures and abusing a minor. The general mood in the House during the debate and vote was rather similar to the one in the US Senate in January and February 2020, at the hearings following Trump's impeachment. During the debate and vote, the members of the chamber were in a position of having to defend a proposition that was implausible and embarrassing. The Italian Center-right Deputies declared that they believed Berlusconi acted to defend a person he believed to be the nephew of a foreign head of state, while the Republican US senators decided that it was not worthwhile to hear from direct witnesses about Trump's extortive request of dirt on a political opponent to a foreign government.[4] This, of course, after repeated complaints from the GOP that the witnesses heard in the House did not have direct knowledge of the president's acts. However, the Constitutional Court rejected the motion, and Berlusconi was prosecuted in Milan and then convicted in the first-degree trial. Later, also thanks to a change in the criminal code following a law passed by his allies, he was acquitted in the appeal, when the judges verified that even though there had been prostitution, it was not adequately proven that Berlusconi knew about Ruby's age. But this trial, like many others described in Chapter 6 of this book, had a significant appendix: during the hearings, many of the girls that used to participate in the spicy parties at Arcore were called to testify. It was later found that Berlusconi was paying Ruby and the girls millions of euros, so the prosecutors started another trial accusing him of obstruction of justice and witness tampering. As of the beginning of 2020, the trial is still pending.

It is a rather typical situation in the realm of politics: a sexual scandal that evolves into a criminal issue largely because of the attempts of the politician to cover up the embarrassing facts. A similar pattern led to the impeachment of President Clinton in the 90s. In Berlusconi's case, of course, he could have also been guilty of abuse of a minor if he knew about Ruby's age. We can find the same pattern in one of Trump's scandals: the Stormy Daniels payoff, performed so that she would sign a non-disclosure agreement, though in this case, the possible crime is campaign finance violation rather than obstruction of justice. What is more surprising about Trump's instance is the relatively little coverage the press dedicated to the whole case. After all, his attorney, Michael Cohen, was indicted — and later pleaded guilty — for that same crime and, considering that the real beneficiary of the operation was no one other than Trump, who also ultimately paid the actress, it defies reason and common sense to think that he had no knowledge of the deal. As stated multiple times by many commentators during Trump's political tenure: any other politician would have been crushed by the same circumstances.

* * *

The sexual scandals of Trump and Berlusconi could be considered simply as additional instances in which the two leaders proved their disregard for the law and their determination to use any possible means to claim victimhood, and dismiss the accusations as an attack from some sort of enemy: the deep state, the left, the press, etc. However, their public behavior and statements in this regard also provide an additional window in their worldview and the standards by which they measure one's success. The basic standard, of course, is the individual achievements in the most material elements of life: wealth, power, status, and sex. If one analyzes most of their public statements, it is rather clear that these values are the ones they think are worth fighting for: not some vision for the development of the society of their countries, not some long-term policy goal, just politics for the sake of maintaining power. This confirms what the US president seems to think each individual should adopt in life: use all the leverage one can get to win, with little or no regard to long-term reputation and moral standing. According to many observers, a central element of Berlusconi's self-representation is his physical body, to which the leader obviously dedicates a lot of time and attention: his strange hair, the height of his heels, the tanning of his face, etc. Traditional politicians, for example, those of Italy's First Republic, tended to hide their physical beings and self-represent as "pure discourse," political ideas and principles that would guide the implementation of policies. Of course, this does not mean that some, or even most, of those politicians did not act out of personal ambition, in the search of power for its own sake. But the fact that they thought it necessary, or at least useful, to represent ideas and principles is a significant indication of the evolution of politics and how Berlusconi either helped to generate or accompanied a shift in the political culture.

Berlusconi's exposure of his body, according to one author, is pre-modern, in that it "may recall the certain features of the body of the king, who must never die because it reflects the strength of its people. A sanctity that can go as far as martyrdom (for a time the man has defined himself as 'touched by God')."[5] Berlusconi, for years, was quite skillful in promoting his body as a necessary part of his political relevance for the country, for his voters. He mixed a slightly self-ironic attitude with subtle and more serious claims in order to represent his physical attributes, as when he offers his hand to Bruno Vespa while being interviewed on TV, and asks him to smell... "It is the scent of sanctity," he says as the friendly journalist smiles. Or, when he explains that, "Pregnant mothers ask me to place my hand on their wombs..."[6] as a lord or a bishop from the middle ages would do with his peasants. A similar pattern is apparent with Berlusconi's sicknesses, which he always managed, in a non-trivial way, to transform into actual media events and as an opportunity to foster consent.[7] The same can be said of the display of bodily transformations designed to make his body look younger: the hair transplant and the strange look of his head, or the heavy and often awkward use of products to tan his face. "However, it is not only the body of the leader that counts in Berlusconism," says cultural studies scholar Fabio Dei, "In media representations, it is also always combined with female bodies: his wife's, or mistresses', his political fans, the female officials of his cabinets, journalists and show-girls from his TV networks...These bodies, differently from the male body, must be beautiful..."[8] The documentary *Videocracy*, by the Swedish-Italian director Erik Gandini, also strongly suggests that the representation of the female body is an essential element of the aesthetic of Berlusconism, as it associates the beginnings of the leader's TV career with the first strip-tease broadcast on TV. Another author[9] indicates the origins of this aspect of Berlusconi's representations in the TV program *Drive-in*, one of the first and most popular programs of *Italia 1*, one of Berlusconi's national networks. The show displayed a group of beautiful women, usually in bikinis or other attires that would allow them to show their bodies abundantly, in roles that underscored their physical essence; they almost never talk, while middle-aged males would deliver punchlines alternating their role of devout fathers and husbands with the search for an adventure with one of the models. In the 80s *Drive-in* became a cultural phenomenon: not that there had not been TV shows that had used the female body as a central element of appeal, even on the state-owned channels, but now these bodies were being aired on prime time instead of late at night and they were being displayed without any amount of subtlety.[10]

The last sex scandals, the prostitutes, the wild parties, and the people around Berlusconi with the task of organizing them, they all participated in promoting the association between Berlusconi and the female body in the public representation of the leader. A similar pattern can be observed in Donald Trump before he entered the political arena. His multiple, and very public, marriages and divorces, his bragging about his ability to get the best looking girls and supermodels, his self-representation in the Miss Universe pageant...it all points to an effort to associate himself to beautiful women's bodies and project the image of a winner.

Chapter 8

Conclusions: extracting lessons about the importance of norms

For anyone wondering what the aftermath of Trump's political tenure will look like, be it in 2021 or 2025, it may be an interesting exercise to look at what happened in Italy after the decline of Berlusconi as a political leader. The two countries are different in numerous regards, but considering the many similarities between Trump and Berlusconi, the effect of the latter on the political culture of Italy might provide some hints as to what the current US president will leave behind.

There are few doubts that historians will record the period between 1993 and the early 2010s in Italy as the age of Berlusconi. He won the general elections in 1994, 2001, and 2008, but lost them in 1996, 2006, and 2013. In the following ones, in 2018, at the age of 81, he no longer had a central role in politics; in fact, he could not even be elected as a member of Parliament due to his prior conviction. In 1994, his government lasted only a few months as he quickly lost the support of the Northern League; in 2001, he was sworn in office again and managed to keep his job of head of the government for the whole 5-year duration of Parliament, whereas in 2008 he would last only a little more than 3 years. All in all, during the 2 decades or so after 1993, he was in office for less than half of the time. Even when he was prime minister, he did not have absolute power: in this parliamentary system, his party never achieved a majority in the House or the Senate and therefore he had to rely on his allies, who were not always ready to maintain him in power at all costs. Lack of support from his allies is why he had to resign in 1994 and 2011, and even between 2001 and 2006, arguably the height of his power, he had to resign and form a new government, due to his allies' pressure. Nevertheless, there are few doubts that he was constantly the central figure of the political system, a presence that had always to be taken into account. From the very beginning of his career in politics, he kept surprising all Italians—outraging many of them—with controversies and norm-breaking behavior and each time many citizens would think something along the lines of: "Ok, this is too much, even for him…this time he will go down." Others would add: "finally he will be unmasked…he will be exposed for what he really is, and it will be apparent to the whole country that we followed an impostor, a conman, for years." Nevertheless, it never really played out that way. The closest it came to it was in 2011, during his last period as prime minister. In the spring of that year, the Ruby sex scandal was on the front pages of most newspapers, triggering critics from sectors of the Church and harsh attacks by Berlusconi to the prosecutors, labeled as communists, who "cannot remain unpunished." In the meanwhile, local elections in many cities signaled that the center-left was in clear advantage, even though Berlusconi's party and his allies could dominate the airways, in fact, all of Berlusconi's networks plus two out of three public TV channels were found in violation of electoral campaign laws by the governmental agency in charge of monitoring telecommunications. In this period, Forza Italia was proposing a reform of the justice system that many viewed as, once again, instrumental to solving Berlusconi's personal problems. Within the legislation being floated, a provision would make payments following a civil lawsuit mandatory only after the last degree of the judgment, by the Court of Cassation, something that would benefit Berlusconi's company, already sentenced to pay De Benedetti for the Mondadori deal.[1] In the meantime, the economic situation was beginning to deteriorate: the spread between the interest rates of the Italian bonds with the German ones (a significant indicator of how the markets view the prospects of the Italian economy) passed the mark of

300 points in July. In November it widened to over 500 points, a strong sign of the government's perceived inability to put some order into the public finances. The international credibility of the Italian leader, never very high, was declining to an all-time low: just a few months before, the release of documents of the US embassy in Rome by WikiLeaks exposed the judgment of American diplomats: "Berlusconi's will to put his interest before those of the State damaged the reputation of the country." In November, Italy's European partners grew highly worried about Italy's situation and particularly about the leadership of Berlusconi. According to former US treasury secretary Timothy Geithner, they sought the participation of the US in a plot to push for Berlusconi's resignation.[2] In one famous instance, during a joint press conference, a journalist asked French president Nicolas Sarkozy and German chancellor Angela Merkel if they had confidence in Berlusconi; they looked at each other and ostensibly smiled. By mid-November, Berlusconi realized he could not count on a majority in Parliament and resigned. Spontaneous and hostile rallies in Rome, broadcast by all TV channels, saluted his departure as head of the Italian government.

After that, Berlusconi still maintained control over Forza Italia, but lost the support of other center-right parties, and the share of the vote of Forza Italia declined year after year. In 2008 Berlusconi had run with the party "Popolo delle Liberta" (Peoples of Freedom), a union of Forza Italia, National Alliance, and some minor allies, which achieved 37 percent of the votes in the elections for the House of Deputies, enough to win the elections. However, in 2013 he only won 21 percent and in 2018, back with Forza Italia, he only achieved 14 percent of the votes. In 2011, to use the words of Paolo Mieli, former editor of the *Corriere della Sera*, "the cork has popped," which is another way of saying "The dam has broken." In a way it was true, the shortcomings of this leader and his failure to work for the policy goals he set himself was apparent as never before. However, there wasn't really a common acknowledgment of the deterioration of the public debate during the previous 18 years, wasted around a person who seemingly had no real interest in the development of actual policies, besides the ones that affected him directly. There was no public recognition of the lost occasions missed while arguing about the empowerment of one person, instead of the country's problems. The result was a progressive and generalized loss of confidence in the ability of the elite to govern the country effectively. Right after Berlusconi's resignation, the President of the Republic chose Mario Monti as the person who would seek the confidence of Parliament and form a new cabinet, resorting to an Italian habit of last resort: appointing esteemed technicians perceived as "above the parties" in times of crisis. An economics professor and former member of the European Commission, where he had managed anti-trust proceedings against Microsoft and other big corporations, Monti received the confidence vote of all parties except the Northern League. Once the crisis was over, however, governmental affairs went back to professional politicians, who presented themselves to voters again in 2013.

* * *

Though the center-left won the elections and could achieve a plurality in the Senate and the House, a new party (which would not call itself a party, to underscore its break with traditional politics) had a massive success: the Five Stars Movement. Founded officially just 4 years before by comedian Beppe Grillo and internet entrepreneur Gianroberto Casaleggio, the movement is not easy to characterize based on the traditional political divide. Since the very beginning many of its militants can be identified as left-leaning, while others sympathize with the right, and, in a few cases, members of its elite have been characterized as fans of fascism. Perhaps the most salient element of the "Five Star" group is the heavy resentment toward the political elites: certainly toward Berlusconi and his enablers and supporters, but also, to some degree, toward the center-left. Grillo spent years explaining how corrupt and inept the politicians were and one of his most effective communication initiatives was the "Vaffanculo day," yes, the "Fuck you day." During these events, Grillo would rally the crowds of Italian cities condemning the system, particularly the parties' habit to have convicted felons among the candidates (even though this was a feature of the right a lot more than the left), and raising support for referendum initiatives to abrogate certain laws. Other than that, the main themes of the "Five Star" rhetoric were the preservation of the environment and the need to exploit the full potential of the web. The movement held its primaries online, often with debatable results in terms of internal democracy; for example in 2013, when many of the candidates managed to get a place high on the party's list, and consequently got a seat in Parliament, with just a few hundred votes cast online, with little scrutiny from anyone. However, direct democracy is another important talking point of the movement and online systems would especially contribute to its enforcement. The rhetoric on democracy notwithstanding, the elite of the group proved rather intolerant of internal debate and tended to expel whoever protested the "official" discourse. The movement also did not seem to appreciate scrutiny from the press, mostly regarded as an enemy that colluded with the traditional elite.

A striking feature of the 2013 general elections, besides the impressive success of the Five Star Movement, was the extent to which the parties that had inherited the system in the early 90s, were already worn-out after 2 decades of the public debate revolving around the leader of the right. Berlusconi lost about 6 million votes, but the left did not do much better, and, though it came out of the elections as the winner, it lost close to 3 million votes if compared to the previous results. While many voters left the traditional parties and chose the Five Star Movement, many others simply decided not to vote. The participation in elections is historically much higher in Italy than the US: in 2006 almost 84 percent of the adult citizens voted, but the percentage decreased to 80 percent in 2008 and 75 percent in 2013, an additional sign of the voters' increasing dissatisfaction with the state of public life. In the following years, the parties that identified with the traditional left and right of the political spectrum became even weaker and the political system based on the competition between, essentially, two-party coalitions seemed to, progressively, fade away. A situation that became evident with the outcome of the last elections, in 2018, which made it very difficult to form a new government with the necessary confidence of Parliament. The Five Star Movement became the first party, with almost 33 percent of the votes, while the rest went to the center-left and center-right coalitions, thus creating three poles, ideologically incompatible and none with enough strength to support a cabinet. A further complication was that within the center-right of the spectrum, the first party was now the Northern League, with a renewed rhetoric and populist leadership that proved electorally rewarding but hardly an effective platform for policy-making. After lengthy negotiations, the Five Star Movement and the Northern League formed an alliance that would support a government headed by a university professor and public servant outside of active politics, Giuseppe Conte. However, the disagreements between these two parties eventually led to the implosion of the coalition, after just a little more than one year. The Northern League bet on the possibility of new elections as the polls indicated they could significantly increase their votes, but the Five Star Movement reached a new agreement with the Democratic Party to support a new, slightly left-leaning, cabinet, still headed by Conte. All these evolutions were not easy to follow for the non-initiated public and certainly contributed to the fatigue of the average citizen and the growing distrust of politicians in general. To complicate things even further, the electoral law kept changing[3], not allowing voters to get used to the rules and therefore affecting their ability to express their preferences with some awareness, while the people's confidence in the political elite and its ability to implement long-term necessary policies was diminishing more than ever.

* * *

Before Berlusconi, Italian politicians were mostly hesitant to expose their persona when communicating with the public. Possibly, because of a less than great experience with the last leader who had done so, Benito Mussolini. But to a good extent, also because the political culture of the country after the war conceived the parties as the main reference for leadership; everyone seemed to think that ideology and cultural identity counted much more than the single empowered individuals. It is not a coincidence that with the "descent" of Berlusconi, many observers started talking about a cult of personality when referring to him and his followers. This expression, "cult of personality," became widespread in the world political lexicon after Khrushchev's 1956 famous speech at the 20th Congress of the Communist Party, the one in which he condemned several of Stalin's deeds. "Cult of personality," as National Review's Jonah Goldberg notes, "is synonymous with 'cult of the individual' — indeed, Khrushchev used the phrases interchangeably in his speech. Both terms refer to the idea that a single person can be greater than the party, or wiser than the ideology the party stands for. Think: 'I alone can fix it.' Such a mindset is a threat to the power of the party and the legitimacy of its doctrines."[4] In August 2015, during a GOP primary debate, Fox News journalist Brett Baier asked the participants whether they would plead to support the party's nominee, whomever it turned out to be. Sixteen candidates accepted, Trump was the only one who did not. In the following months, at times, he reversed that statement, but it remains significant in that it underscores how he sees himself and how he wants to be seen by the conservative electorate: as something separate and more important than the party. His persona is above all and nothing else really matters; not a party, not an ideology, not even a policy. It is just about him, Trump. This frame of mind has the additional advantage of not requiring ideological consistency:

> ...there's a simpler reason for a cult of personality: It's the only sustainable line of defense. Stalin violated party ideology all the time. He contradicted his past positions cavalierly, adopting and discarding ideas on a whim. He would even change his views to test his loyalists. Today, insist that chocolate ice cream is the best flavor and get everyone to agree with you. That way, if anyone disagrees tomorrow when you say it's vanilla, you'll know who the potential traitors in your midst are. This is where Trump's cult of personality comes in. For several years there's been a kind of competition on the right to come up with a coherent intellectual or ideological framework to support Trump's presidency. Every single one that comes out of the clouds of theory to get close to the reality on the ground has crashed. He's a nationalist who puts America first but says we'll await Saudi Arabia's say-so on a military strike against Iran. He says he wants free trade but also thinks tariffs are good. There's no halfway defensible ideological, intellectual, or moral standard that Trump doesn't violate, often routinely. A cult of personality that replies "Trump's right" or "his enemies are worse" before the question is even asked is the only place to hide.[5]

These considerations work perfectly for Berlusconi as well.

The party he set up from scratch in 1993, Forza Italia, mostly by recruiting among the executives of his companies, made some sense only in regards to enhancing his political fortunes and power. Its ideology was the result of carefully performed polls that told Berlusconi exactly what would impress clusters of voters and could be sold, with a minimum of consistency, in association with his life's story. Had the situation of the country provided some opportunity for a political proposition on the left, there is little doubt that Berlusconi would have taken the opportunity and presented himself as a socialist, maybe an heir to his friend Bettino Craxi. A telling, if somewhat embarrassing, sign of the central role of Berlusconi's persona are the lyrics of the song used at the party gatherings: "President, we are with you, Thank God Silvio is here!"

In the political trajectories of both Trump and Berlusconi, the evident crucial role of their personas for the political systems in which they operated brings us to the problem of the relevance of accidents in historical evolutions, where the "accidental" includes the specific features of the character of individuals that are relevant for certain societal developments. The significance of accidents is a problem to which historians occasionally refer to as the "Nose of Cleopatra." Had the Egyptian ruler had a different nose, not as attractive, Roman leaders such as Julius Caesar or Marc Anthony would possibly not have fallen for her, the struggle for power in the empire would have led to different outcomes and the whole world would have evolved in a different direction. In a similar line of hypothesizing, we can wonder what would have happened in Italy if the politician who more than any other contributed to its formation, Camillo Benso di Cavour, had not suddenly died of a disease in 1861, just days after Italy was unified? What about Lenin's early death in 1923, which ultimately cleared the way for Stalin's rise? Are historical developments dominated by random accidents? This problem has puzzled many thinkers at different times, particularly historians who proved to have a strong interest in the methodology of their science. The British historian Edward H. Carr proposed an interesting and reasonable solution. He recognized that accidental things such as the nose of Cleopatra or the character of an empowered individual may have a significant impact on events; however, such things are not usually those recognized as "causes" by historical interpretation. In order to make his point he offers a thought experiment: Mr Jones, driving after a party where he had large amounts of alcohol, runs over and kills a Mr Robinson, who was crossing the street with the intention to purchase cigarettes. Now, it wouldn't be false to state that Robinson died, in part, because he craved for tobacco, but is this causation useful in any way? Would it make sense to prevent people to go to buy cigarettes to make traffic safer? Alternatively, would it make more sense to prevent drunk people from driving? Therefore, the criterion Carr suggests, following a strong British intellectual tradition, is utility. That is, the "causes" that are helpful in conceiving significant interpretations of historical events are the ones that help us to better understand how society works.[6] Of course, understanding historic developments is key to understanding our present; as philosopher Benedetto Croce famously said, ultimately, "all history is contemporary history." So, as Carr also recognized, the character of empowered individuals, such as Berlusconi and Trump, may be considered among the accidental facts of history that are also consequential. Nevertheless, the bigger question, rather than their character and personal inclinations, is why a significant number of the citizens of Italy and the United States chose to support them electorally thus enabling them to create some serious problems for their societies.

* * *

But what are the main troubles that these two leaders created in their respective countries? We can probably identify six groups of long-term damages that are results of Berlusconi's and Trump's political actions.

One of the most evident problems caused by these two leaders to the political systems as well as to the societies in their countries is the extreme polarization within both the political elite and the electorates. Of course, we know that the wedge in the US and Italy was significant even before the "descent" of the two politicians, but the presence of Berlusconi and Trump increased the polarization to a degree unseen in a very long time: possibly since the final phase of World War II in Italy and the Civil War in the US. This evolution did not happen by chance. One of the most relevant narratives that both Berlusconi and Trump were able to impose, for the purpose of improving their electoral prospects, was the framing of the political arena as an "us against them" struggle, where the stakes are very high and where "them" is not just an adversary with a different political agenda, but, rather, an enemy that must be defeated at all costs. One big difference between the polarization they encouraged and the pre-existing one is that the latter evolved largely around policy matters, while the former was, and is, essentially about their personas, at least for the strongest supporters, the base, of these leaders. Many within the "base" rationalize their support in several ways, but often enough they simply love these two politicians, they feel attracted to them at an emotional level and just want to see them succeed. The exacerbation of the degree of polarization makes it difficult for the parties' elites to cooperate in pushing bipartisan policies in Congress or elsewhere, which, especially in the US system of government, can cause serious damages and slow down, or outright stop, the implementation of policies. It came as no surprise that, under Trump, the US experienced the longest government shutdown of its history, just to cite an obvious example.

A second significant problem that can be associated with the political trajectory of Trump and Berlusconi is the deterioration of the so-called administrative state if with that expression we mean the bureaucracy of professionals (some would call it technocracy) that takes on the task of actually implementing the policies set by Congress or by the Administration. While some people, almost exclusively on the right[7] tend to loath the "administrative state," this is essentially made up of the public officials and employees who take care of such things as diplomacy, law enforcement, environmental protection, crisis management, education, development of knowledge, fostering economic growth, and many other things. All the people engaged in these, at times difficult, tasks may be either right or left-leaning, but their primary goal is to enact effective and, possibly, efficient systems that are beneficial to the vast majority of citizens. There may be a healthy debate over whether, say, the use of marijuana should be legalized or how to pay for health assistance, but once such matters are settled by politicians, these people, the bureaucrats, are the ones that make everything work. Well, to some extent, for these public employees, particularly those that care deeply about delivering a valuable service to fellow citizens, a clash with bosses such as Trump or Berlusconi is inevitable. What these leaders want is a state that makes them look good, with little regard for any other criteria, certainly not the effectiveness of the offices. Hence, in all those cases in which the optics of the administration conflict with the official objectives of the administrative states, friction is to be expected. When Trump falsely claimed that Hurricane Dorian was on its way to, among other states, Alabama, the technical staff from the National Weather Service in charge of predicting the course of the hurricane had to face the choice between the wrath of the president and a technically correct assessment. When the NWS chose to do its job, that is to inform the public based on the scientific data available, the dissatisfaction of the president was inevitable. Or, more consequentially, when Trump had his lawyer Rudy Giuliani stir up the Ukrainian officials to look for dirt on Joe Biden, the US ambassador to that country evidently faced a similar choice. Distancing herself from the administration and doing her job on behalf of the American people, or just accepting that the president's aides used the power of the office for partisan advantage in the upcoming elections? Of course, the difference between Trump and Berlusconi, as far as their ability to do damage is concerned, regards the different quality of the state in the two countries. While the US is mostly effective and can count on a well-motivated workforce that, to a significant extent, sees its job as public service, Italy has a big, largely inefficient, machine. While there are areas of excellence in its administration—parts of the armed forces and law enforcement, traditionally the central bank, certain research institutions—a significant part of it is a bureaucratic apparatus mainly dedicated to its preservation and maintenance rather than providing services to the citizen. This situation, of course, makes the damage that Trump is causing in the US government much worse and more consequential.

As noted by many observers in both countries, institutional damage is another inheritance of these two leaders that the US and Italy will have to live with. Possibly, the most apparent dents inflicted regard the law enforcement institutions these leaders choose to denigrate in order to bully their way out of criminal investigations: so Trump had to attack the intelligence community, the FBI and, at times, his own Department of Justice, while Berlusconi harshly savaged the magistrates, especially, of course, those in charge of investigating and prosecuting his deeds. However, the institutional damage does not stop there. Again, the extreme polarization and the rhetoric that comes with it are significant obstacles to an orderly institutional reform. In the year 2000, during the last year of a center-left government in Italy, a constitutional reform voted by Parliament introduced many federalist elements into the country's institutions. The reform was far from perfect but Parliament controlled by Berlusconi, starting in 2001, could have adopted and eventually corrected it. Instead, the new administration simply criticized the reform, at times as too federalist, at others as not sufficiently federalist, and made no efforts to make it work. A later attempt by the center-right government to reform Italy's institutions also failed, largely because of the reluctance of the opposing parties to cooperate in any way. In just over 3 years, Trump managed to leave institutional scars that will last for a long time, starting with the degrading of the presidency. The conclusion that can be drawn from, "Unmaking the Presidency," the recent book by the editors of Lawfare[8], seems to be that the president's continuous effort to avoid accountability by Congress, by the press, by the judiciary, or by any other power converts this office into something much different from what the founding fathers had in mind: something more similar to the absolutist monarchies of different centuries.

An additional negative effect on the political system that both Trump and Berlusconi brought in their countries is the corrosion and decline of the right side of the political spectrum, at least the decline of the values of conservatism that are most consequential for the development of society. In both countries, the right, or center-right, was already on its way to some kind of decline. In Italy, it had been subject to deterioration because of decades of holding power with no perspective of transition with the other political forces. While in the US, a gloomy cycle that progressively radicalized the conservative electorate and the candidates at each election, distanced the GOP from a significant part of its potential voters, especially the demographic groups that are growing more and that are more dynamic. By using populist tactics, Trump and Berlusconi managed to preserve, at least in part, the electoral strength of the right in the short or medium term. However, in Italy, Forza Italia ultimately maintained only a fraction of its votes, and conservatives have struggled to find a party and an elite to lead them. In the US, the GOP is looking at the progressive distancing of its more sophisticated voters. While the center-left may salute such an evolution as a win, there are reasons to think that a very weak right side of the spectrum is not at all beneficial to the system, and for the citizens altogether. In both countries, the conservative parties at their best have often fostered the principle of personal responsibility, which can be a healthy counterweight to the principles of solidarity and equality generally affirmed by the left. The weakening of the principle may be detrimental to the development of these societies in the long run.

Among the damages brought by these two leaders that are probably not recognized enough is the unprecedented level of distraction that they forced on the public debate about important and, at times, urgent affairs. Practically since 2015 in the US and from late 1993 until recently in Italy, Trump and Berlusconi have forcibly occupied most of the public debate, almost monopolizing the first page of the newspapers and magazines, the time of TV news and talk shows, and the space of most media dealing with politics and policy. For years, it has been mostly about them, rather than about issues of importance to the citizens. Such a distorted debate made it extremely difficult to dedicate the necessary attention to other, much more consequential, matters.

Last but not least, we should consider the damage done to ethics, possibly the most important, and long-lasting heritage of the Trump and Berlusconi time at the center of the political arena. Pundits, politicians, and journalists have underscored the possible negative consequences of these politicians' style of leadership on ethics in editorials and statements many times. But how does it work? What is the mechanism based on which the two leaders could damage recognized social norms? Even before Peter L. Berger and Thomas Luckmann's landmark book *The Social Construction of Reality* was published in 1966, several social scientists realized that the world we live in is largely man-made.

We do not mean, of course, the physical infrastructure, things such as building, roads, and bridges, but rather the institutions that characterize our culture and make our society what it is: things such as governments, money, families, and the like. In the same way, we, as humans, provide the legitimation of these institutions, which, using the terminology introduced by Berger and Luckmann, generate the "Symbolic Universes" that largely characterize our way of life. Arguably, the choice of the word "Creation" of reality could be slightly misleading as it suggests intentionality; "Generation" of reality could be preferable. However, it remains a fact that culture, intended in the broadest possible way, is made by man; as is ethics, an important part of culture itself. Throughout face-to-face interactions (or other types facilitated by technology), people continuously seek clues from the behavior of their fellow citizens in order to understand what should be considered appropriate or wrong. The behavior and statements of each observed individual have an impact, large or small, on the understanding of the difference between right and wrong of other members of society. People in the media or with public exposure have the opportunity to disseminate clues of this kind to large audiences and therefore have a prominent role in the definition of what is to be considered ethical. Individuals such as Trump and Berlusconi not only have large audiences that listen to them, but they are, or have been, almost continuously at the center of the public debate and their statements and attitudes are exposed to the public at large on a daily basis, thus empowering them with a relatively strong impact over the shaping of "Symbolic Universes." Of course neither of the two, by themselves, has the power to generate, or significantly modify, moral values. Nevertheless, it is quite plausible that the combination of their constant presence as powerful voices in the political debate and a strong, though embraced by a minority, subculture that proves emotionally attached to these leaders, all supported by a significant part of the elite (the "enablers"), may lead to an actual change of shared values.

This does not mean that either Trump or Berlusconi had the urge or the ambition of promoting a new ethics or any new idea whatsoever, as they seem to have no interest in such things and there are little doubts that they can state something one day and the opposite the next day without much thought. As Jonah Goldberg noticed about Trump, "Contrary to the myth that he opposes political correctness, he will even use progressive weapons against his enemies when the opportunity arises. In 2015, he badgered Jeb Bush for being insensitive to women and women's health. Yes, Trump's got bigoted ideas, but like all ideas, they take a back seat to his narcissism and glandular impulsiveness. My unified theory of Trump is that he's a person with little to no interior life who responds to flattery and criticism with Pavlovian predictability." Berlusconi similarly used political correctness when it suited his narrative, for example in 1997, when he condemned Romano Prodi's Center-left government for being too harsh on Albanian migrants that were trying to enter Italy. Of course, he would justify and promote the toughest measures toward migrants later, when he thought it would bring him votes. But, like Trump, his most apparent feature as it relates to his relationship with ethics is an astounding indifference. As The New Republic's Lidija Haas writes, reviewing Paolo Sorrentino's movie on Berlusconi:

...that's what he enjoys: More than the ephemeral pleasures of the notorious bunga-bunga festivities, it's that feeling of other people compromising themselves for him, knowing just what he is and going along anyway. This is perhaps the closest thing to an identifiable human emotion Sorrentino grants him. 'Do you know what happens when someone uses psychology on me?' he genially warns a guy who's just made a pathetic, doomed gesture at standing up to him. 'Nothing. Absolutely nothing happens.'[9]

* * *

Both Trump and Berlusconi have been, at times, characterized as fascists. The word fascist has been used and misused so frequently in the political rhetoric that it has lost part of its meaning. A prominent scholar of fascism, the late historian Renzo de Felice, said that fascism should be regarded as a phenomenon that is limited in time and space: the period between the two world wars of the last century, and Western Europe. Outside of these bounds, there may have been regimes or parties with some elements of fascism, but nothing that can be accurately identified as such. Having said that, the politics of Berlusconi and Trump may have in common more than one element with fascism. Perhaps the most evident one is the communication style and the self-representation of the leader. Mussolini was a journalist before becoming the leader of fascism and had a talent, an intuition we may say, for forging messages that would be readily received by an audience and stimulate action. He also clearly saw the advantages of portraying the political struggle as an "us-versus-them" situation. Some scholars noted that fascism lacks a coherent and rational political ideology if this word is to indicate a clear doctrine for the establishment of a regime, in the way liberalism and communism do. However, we can identify several elements of the fascist political culture: for example, a strong contempt for Marxism and liberalism, especially the parliamentary aspect of the latter, with all its lengths, discussions, and even corruption practices in the decision-making process. The decisions should be taken hierarchically, with a strong leader, the "Duce," at the top, ruling the state and society. However, as De Felice noted, it would be a mistake to confuse fascism with prior types of dictatorship: the latter typically encourages masses to passiveness, while fascism wants its followers to mobilize and participate actively in the social struggle to defeat common enemies and promote the development of civilization.

A major instrument of mobilization of the people for Mussolini was a direct communication channel between the duce and the crowd, which is Trump's and Berlusconi's preferred way to convey messages: direct, unfiltered, and possibly unquestioned. Mussolini did not have twitter, but we can guess he would have loved it. One of the pillars of the Fascist regime was the governmental propaganda program and censorship designed to keep Italians in a bubble. Of course, there is nothing like it in Italy or the US; nevertheless, in both cases, several outlets appear to be concentrated in downplaying facts that may damage the perception of the leader, while overemphasizing those that may enhance their public perception.

A second important aspect of fascism that we can also find in the style of government of Berlusconi and Trump is the dismissal of the rule of law. Of course in the case of fascism, this principle was outright declared obsolete and incompatible with the standard of hierarchy (though it was in fact applied in many instances by the regime: Mussolini, his propaganda notwithstanding, trusted the old administrative state a lot more than his party to rule society). In the aftermath of World War I, while the movement was becoming an electoral phenomenon, squads of fascists, in a militia fashion, would go on expeditions to beat opponents, trash newspaper offices, or socialist meetings and other gatherings perceived as adversarial. In many, if not most, of these instances, the police would not intervene to restore the law and many members of the liberal bourgeoisie would turn a blind eye. The threat of violence by the squads was also a factor in inducing the king to offer Mussolini the possibility to form a government in 1922: the leader of fascism became the head of the government following the constitutional procedures and achieved the confidence of Parliament, but he did so while threatening a "March on Rome" by his militias. Many of the politicians from the traditional liberal elite, while they mostly despised Mussolini, concluded that he could be kept under control. In a parallel way, many Italian and American conservatives looked the other way when Trump or Berlusconi attacked the judiciary or law enforcement representatives. Of course, the high and medium bourgeoisie in the 1920s could justify risking the rule of law with the fear of socialism, a concrete threat back then, with the Bolsheviks seizure of power in Russia just a few years back.

Fascism gained a certain amount of consent among all social classes; from the beginning of the movement, in 1919, among its followers there were factory workers as well as teachers, artisans, farmers, soldiers, lawyers, and other social groups. However, the class that was overrepresented in fascism, especially during its beginnings, was the petty bourgeoisie. Many within this group did not feel represented by the previous political elites, they found them inadequate with their corruption and ineptitude, and were eager to have a voice of their own in public affairs: the rise of fascism provided an opportunity. Many supporters of Trump and Berlusconi, possibly their very base, likely felt and feel in a similar fashion. While it was positioned far to the right of the political spectrum, fascism was not meant to simply constitute a barrier for bolshevism, it wanted to change things; its announced role was to lead a revolution of the society and of the state. Those who despised the liberal politicians who had governed Italy since its very beginnings and who, at the same time, saw socialists as a dangerous threat, were attracted to fascism as a modern and possibly effective way to move the society forward. From this perspective, it is possible to conceive of fascism as an attempt to modernize society at a time when it wasn't quite clear if socialism, in accordance with the Marxist doctrine, could be a natural evolution of capitalism in the Western world. If classic liberalism was on the descending side of its historical curve, possibly fascism could be a valid alternative to socialism. It would provide a different political culture; it would mobilize the whole of the society, not one class against the other, and would end the endless talks and the corrupted deals of the politicians controlling Parliament: a strong leader would take control and lead the nation toward development and greatness. Nowadays fascism is considered, almost universally, one of the great recent catastrophes of humanity, and a few countries belonging to the liberal-democratic group even banned fascism, as a unique exception to the freedom of expression. However, between the two great wars of the twentieth century, this movement was able to stimulate large popular support in Italy, Germany, and other countries, in Europe and beyond. One way to look at this political phenomenon is temporary deviance from the political values that the West had embraced since the end of absolutism: rule of law, equal rights before the law, democracy, etc. How could it happen? In short, we can accurately summarize its origin with the coincidence of three elements: an empowered man desperately searching for a political space; a society with large groups of citizens resentful of traditional elites, which sought representation and new values to follow and, finally, the occasionally reluctant support of large parts of the political and economic elites. All three elements may sound familiar nowadays in the US and Italy.

Endnotes

Introduction

1 Larry M. Bartels, "What's the Matter with *What's the Matter with Kansas*?" Presentation at the Annual Meeting of the American Political Science Association, September 2005.

2 http://www.pewresearch.org/fact-tank/2018/11/08/the-2018-midterm-vote-divisions-by-race-gender-education/

3 Norberto Bobbio, "Destra e Sinistra. Ragioni e significati di una distinzione politica," Donzelli Editore, 1994.

Chapter 1

1 Nick Tosches, "Power on Earth," Arbor House, 1986.

2 Lorenzo Ruggero, "Dossier Berlusconi. Anni Settanta," 2016, Kaos Edizioni.

3 Mario Guarino, "Fratello P2. L'epopea piduista di Silvio Berlusconi," Kaos Edizioni, 2001.

4 Marco Travaglio, Elio Veltri, "L'odore del soldi. Origini e misteri delle fortune di Silvio Berlusconi," Editori Riuniti, 2001.

5 Michael D'Antonio, "The Truth about Trump." Thomas Dunne Books, 2016.

6 David Barstow, Susanne Craig, Russ Buettner, "Trump engaged in suspect tax schemes," The New York Times, October 2, 2018.

7 Ibid.

8 Lee Wohlfert-Wihlborg, "In the Manhattan Real Estate Game, Billionaire Donald Trump holds the Winning Cards," People's Magazine, November 16, 1981.

9 Michael Kruse, "The Final Lesson Donald Trump Never Learned from Roy Cohn," Politico, September 19, 2019.

10 Ibid.

11 Michael Hirsh, "How Russian Money Helped Save Trump's

Business," Foreign Policy, December 21, 2018.

12   In order to build Trump Tower in Manhattan, Trump had to demolish the 1929 Bowit Teller building. A face of the building featured two big friezes which, according to the metropolitan Museum of Art, had a significant artistic value. At first Trump agreed to donate the friezes to the museum but as the cost of preserving them was apparently very high, they were destroyed, causing a public relations debacle for the New York developer. See Michael D'Antonio, Ibid.

13   Peter Fritsch, Glenn R. Simpson, "The Business Deals that Could Imperil Trump," The New York Times, April 21, 2018.

14   Ibid.

15   Jennifer C. Manion, "The moral relevance of shame," American Philosophical Quarterly, Vol 39, N. 1, January 2002.

16   Mona Charen, "Does Trump Understand Corruption?" National Review, September 27, 2019.

17   Drew Westen, "The Right Analogy on Impeachment," The Hill, November 18, 2019.

18   Mary Brenner, "How Donald Trump and Roy Cohn's Ruthless Symbiosis Changed America," Vanity Fair, June 28, 2017.

19   Jeffrey Toobin, "The Dirty Trickster," The New Yorker, May 23, 2008.

20   Peter York, "Trump's dictator chic," Politico Magazine, March/April 2017.

21   Paul Ginsborg, Enrica Asquer, "Berlusconismo. Analisi di un Sistema di potere," 2012, Laterza Editore. Author's translation.

22   Mark Seal, "How Donald Trump Beat Palm Beach Society and Won the Fight for Mar-a-Lago," Vanity Fair, December 27, 2016.

Chapter 2

1   Robert Putnam, "Making Democracy Work," Princeton University Press, 1994.

2   Gustavo Zagrebelsky, "Le istituzioni di governo" in AA.VV. "La scienza politica in Italia. Materiali per un bilancio," Franco Angeli, Milano 1984.

3   Edoardo Fracanzani, "Le origini del conflitto," 2014, Rubbettino.

4   A typical case is that of Mario Sarcinelli, a high-ranking officer of Italy's central bank who was indicted and jailed in 1979 under what seemed a fabricated charge (he was quickly exonerated after resigning his office). Most believe his legal jeopardy was caused by his refusal to accept the request by P2 members not to oppose financial arrangements favorable to Michele Sindona and other members of the lodge. He was often addressed as "communist" by some politicians and journalists from the conservative side.

5   See Chapter 3.

6   Gary Miller, "The Transformation of the Republican and Democratic Party Coalitions in the US," Perspective on Politics, September 2008.

7   Jason M. Roberts, Steven S. Smith, "Procedural Context, Party Strategy and Conditional Party Voting in the US House of Representatives, 1971-2000," American Journal of Political Science, Vol. 47, N. 2, April 2003.

8   For example Jason M. Roberts, Steven S. Smith, "Procedural Context, Party Strategy, and Conditional Party Voting in the US House of Representatives, 1971-2000," American Journal of Political Science, April 2003.

9   Edward G. Carmines, "Political Issues and Party Alignments: Assessing the Issue Evolution Perspective," Annual Review of Political Science, January 2008.

10 Mark D. Brewer, "The Rise of Partisan Conflict within the American Electorate," Political Research Quarterly, June

2005.

11 Jacob S. Hacker, Paul Pierson, "The Dog that Almost Barked: What the ACA Repeal Fight Says about the Resilience of the American Welfare State," Journal of Health Politics, Policy and Law, Vol. 43, N. 4, 2018.

12 Paul Pierson, "The New Politics of the Welfare State," World Politics 48, N. 2, 1996.

13 Paul Pierson, "Dismantling the Welfare State? Reagan, Thatcher and the Politics of Retrenchment," New York, Cambridge University Press, 1994.

14 Jeffrey Frankel, "Republican and Democratic Presidents have Switched Economic Policies," Milken Institute Review, N. 5, First Quarter, 2003.

15 Theda Skocpol and Alexander Hertel-Fernandez, "The Koch Network and Republican Party Extremism," American Political Science Association, September 2016, Vol. 14, N. 3.

16 James G. Capretta, "The GOP's ongoing Health-Care Confusion," The New York Times, July 7, 2017.

17 Kevin D. Williamson, "Health-Care is the Opposite of a Right," The National Review, February 27, 2019.

18 James E. Dalen, Keith Waterbrook, Joseph S. Alpert, "Why Do So Many Americans Oppose the Affordable Care Act?" The American Journal of Medicine, 2015.

19 See notes 27 and 28 in this chapter.

20 Brian F. Schaffner, Matthew J. Streb, "The Partisan Heuristics in Low-Information Elections," Public Opinion Quarterly, Vol. 66, 2002. Geoffrey L. Cohen, "Party over Policy: The Dominating Impact of Group Influence of Political Beliefs," Journal of Personality and Social Psychology, 2003, Vol. 85, N. 5.

21 Jonah Goldberg, "Today's Conservative Divide Pits Anti-State against Anti-Left," The National Review, January 24, 2020.

22 George Will, "Tripping over the Inevitable. The Coming

Backlash against the Clintons," The Washington Post, March 4, 2007.

23 Seth E. Masket, Joanne M. Miller, Michael T. Heaney, Dara Z. Strolovitch, "Networking the Parties: A Comparative study of Democratic and Republican National Convention Delegates in 2008," paper presented at the 105th Annual Meeting of the American Political Science Association, Toronto, Ontario, Canada, September 3-6, 2009.

24 Paul J. Maher, Eric R. Igou, "Brexit, Trump, and the Polarizing Effect of Disillusionment," Social Psychological and Personality Science, January 2018.

25 Marco Tullio Liuzza, Valentina Cazzato, Michele Vecchione, Filippo Crostella, Gian Vittorio Caprara, Salvatore Maria Aglioti, "Follow My Eyes: The Gaze of Politicians Reflexively Captures the Gaze of Ingroup Voters," Plos One, 6(9) e25117. doi:10.1371/journal.pone.0025117, 2011.

26 Jason M. Roberts, Steven S. Smith, "Procedural Context, Party Strategy and Conditional Party Voting in the US House of Representative 1971-2000," American Journal of Political Science, Vol. 47, N. 2, April 2003.

27 Steve Kornacki, "The Red and the Blue. The 90s and the Birth of Political Tribalism," Harper Collins Publishers, 2018.

28 Joseph Bafumi, Robert Y. Shapiro, "A New Partisan Voter," The Journal of Politics, Vol. 71, N.1, 2009.

29 Mark Brewer, "The Rise of Partisan Conflict within the American Electorate," Political research Quarterly, June 2005.

30 Edward G. Carmines, "Political Issues and Party Alignments: Assessing the Issue Evolution Perspective," Annual Review of Political Science, January 2008.

31 Tim Alberta, "American Carnage. On the Front Lines of the Republican Civil War and the Rise of President Trump," Harper Collins Publishers, 2018.

32 Darrel Enck-Wanzer, "Barack Obama, the Tea Party and the

Threat of Race: On Racial Neoliberalism and Born Again Racism," Communication, Culture and Critique, N. 4, 2011.

33 Theda Skocpol, Vanessa Williamson, "The Tea Party and the Remaking of Republican Conservatism," Oup USA, 2012.

34 Alan I. Abramowitz, "Partisan Polarization and the Rise of the Tea Party Movement," paper presented at the Annual Meeting of the American Political Science Association, Seattle, Washington, September 2011.

35 Tim Alberta. Ibidem.

36 Jonathan Haidt, "The Righteous Mind. Why Good People are Divided by Politics and Religion," 2012, Vintage Books.

37 Ibidem.

38 Jacob S. Hacker, Paul Pierson, "The Dog that Almost Barked: What the ACA Repeal Fight Says about the Resilience of the American Welfare State", Journal of Health Politics, Policy and Law, Vol. 43, N. 4, 2018.

39 Jacob S. Hacker, Paul Pierson, Ibidem

40 Sohrab Ahmari, "Against David Frenchism", First Things, May 29, 2019.

Chapter 3

1 See note n. 4 in this chapter.

2 Michael Wolff, "Fire and Fury. Inside the Trump White House," Henry Holt and Co., 2018.

3 Olwen Bedford, Kwang-Kuo Hwang, "Guilt and Shame in Chinese Culture: a Cross-Cultural Framework from the Perspective of Morality and Identity," Journal for the Theory of Social Behavior, Blackwell Publishing, 2003.

4 Durante R., Pinotti P. and Tesei A, "The political legacy of entertainment TV," 2019, The American Economic Review.

5 Yasha Mounk, "The more you watch the more you vote populist," The Atlantic, July 6, 2019.

6 P. Mancini, "Challenges between commodification and lifestyle politics. Does Silvio Berlusconi provide a new model

of politics for the 21st century?" 2011, Oxford University, Reuters Institute for the study of journalism.

7   Shira Gabriel, Elaine Pavarati, Melanie C. Green, Jason Flomsbee, "From Apprentice to President: The Role of Parasocial Connections in the Election of Donald Trump," Social Psychology and Personality Science, 2018.

8   One of the first scholarly works to analyze the complexity in the definition of organizations' objectives is "The Economic Theory of Managerial Capitalism" by Robin Marris, Macmillan, 1967.

9   Matthew Pressman, "On press: The liberal values that shaped the news," Harvard University Press, 2018.

10   Cited in Eric Alterman, "Newt Gingrich 2012: Liberals should Root for Him," The Daily Beast, October 8, 2010.

11   Starting in 1969 with the explosion of a bomb in a bank in the center of Milan which left 17 dead and 88 wounded.

12   Shafer, J., "The surprising reason the right doesn't trust the news," Politico, September 26, 2018.

13   For example Tim Groseclose, Jeffrey Milyo, "A Measure of Media Bias," Quarterly Journal of Economics, 2005 or Matthew Gentzkow, Jesse Shapiro, "Media Bias and Reputation," Journal of Political Economy, 2006.

14   Ceren Budak, Sharad Goel, Justin M. Rao, "Fair and Balanced? Quantifying Media Bias Through Crowdsourced Content Analysis," Public Opinion Quarterly, Vol. 80, 2016.

15   Hans J.G. Hassel, John B. Holbein, Matthew R. Miles, "There Is No Liberal Media Bias in Which News Stories Political Journalists Choose to Cover," Science Advance, April 2020.

16   David Domke, Mark D. Watts, Dhavan, V. Shah, David P. Fan, "The Politics of Conservative Elites and the 'Liberal Media' Argument," Journal of Communications, Autumn 1999.

17   "This Article is Full of Lies. You Can Really Fool Some of the People All of the Time," The Economist, October 31, 2019.

18 Stefano della Vigna, Ethan Kaplan, "The Fox News Effect: Media Bias and Voting," NBER, Working Paper N. 12169, April 2016.

19 Clay Ramsay, Steven Kull, Evan Lewis, Stefan Subias, "Misinformation and the 2010 Election. A Study of the US Electorate," WorldPublicOpinion.org, Program on International Policy Attitudes at the University of Maryland, December 2010.

20 Harshdeep Kaur, March 1, 2018, https://www.vcestu dyguides.com/blog/the-political-correctness-debate

21 https://www.youtube.com/watch?v=8wLCmDtCDAM

22 Peter A. Lawler, "Trump, the Cubs and political correctness," National Review, November 3, 2016.

23 https://www.youtube.com/watch?v=phsU1vVHOQI

24 Robert Westbrook "Anti-Intellectualism in American Life Revisited," Paper presented at a conference on "The University in the Public Eye," Whitney Humanities Center, Yale University, 29 September 1995.

25 Fabio Dei, "Pop politica: le basi culturali del berlusconismo," Studi culturali, anno VIII, N. 3, dicembre 2011.

26 Actually, the expression, it seems, was first used by members of the special assault units of the Italian Army in World War I, who used to write it on the bandages that covered their wounds. It was later celebrated by Gabriele d'Annunzio, a poet and soldier, who, after the war, was considered for a time as a competitor of Mussolini and a possible leader of fascism. One of his best-known endeavors had been the occupation of Fiume, a city with a significant Italian-speaking population previously part of the Austrian-Hungarian Empire, defeated by Italy in 1918. The phrase highlighted the dismissal of fear of death by soldiers, but it was later adopted by fascism and it seemed to fit well in light of the movement's occasional disregard for rational analysis and study as well as its anti-intellectualism. It is probably

not a coincidence that a similar phrase was also, apparently, the favorite of Trump's would-be ideologue Steve Bannon and his praise of the honey badger because it "doesn't give a shit."

27 Quoted in Nicolas Baer, "American Idiot. Rethinking Anti-Intellectualism in the Age of Trump," posted in opendemocracy.net, August 25, 2017.

28 Mark Bauerlein, "The Dumbest Generation," Tarcher Perigee, 2009; Susan Jacoby, "The Age of American Unreason," Vintage, 2009; Charles Pierce, "Idiot America; How Stupidity Became a Virtue in the Land of the Free," Doubleday, 2009; Tom Nichols, "The Death of Expertise; the Campaign Against Established Knowledge and Why it Matters," Oxford University Press, 2017.

29 Morning Joe, MSNBC, November 1, 2019. https://www.youtube.com/watch?v=SQTmYTDx-VE

30 Thomas Patterson, "Pre-primary news coverage of the 2016 presidential race: Trump's Rise, Sanders' emergence, Clinton's struggle," Shorenstein Center, June 13, 2016. Cited in Regina G. Lawrence, Amber E. Boydstun, "What We Should Really be Asking About Media Attention to Trump," Political Communication, December 29, 2016.

31 While director of the TG1, Minzolini proved his ethical standards by inflating his expense account and committing other crimes for which he was prosecuted and sentenced. As a further reward, he was included in the Forza Italia Senate list in the 2013 elections and became a Senator.

32 Interview aired on May 23, 2019 on CNN, https://www.youtube.com/watch?v=VgqyrkJaXY0

33 Charles Sykes, "The Humiliation of Lindsey Graham," Politico, October 8, 2019.

34 According to CNN's Chris Cillizza, the award for best performance should have gone to Vice President Mike Pence for his praise of Trump: "It is just the greatest privilege of my

life to serve as the—as vice president to the President who's keeping his word to the American people and assembling a team that's bringing real change, real prosperity, real strength back to our nation," Chris Cillizza, "Donald Trump's Cabinet Members, Ranked by Their Over-The-Top Praise of Trump," CNN, June 13, 2017.

35 Johnathan V. Last, "Trump is Waging War on the GOP. He is Winning," Washington Examiner, November 9, 2018.

36 Richard C. Fording and Sanford F. Schram, "The Cognitive and Emotional Sources of Trump Support: The Case of Low-Information Voters," New Political Science, October 2017.

37 John F. Harris, "One Big Thing that Dems Get Wrong About Warren," Politico, November 7, 2019.

38 Alex Shepard, "How the GOP Bamboozled The New York Times' Political Desk", The New Republic, December 17, 2019.

Chapter 4

1 Stephen Hawkins, Daniel Yudkin, Miriam Juan-Torres, Tim Dixon, "Hidden Tribes: A Study of American Polarized Landscape," More in Common, 2018.

2 Daniel Elazar, "American Federalism, a View from the States," Harper and Row, New York, 1984.

3 Patrick I. Fisher, "Definitely Not Moralistic: State Political Culture and Support for Donald Trump in the Race for the 2016 Republican Presidential Nomination," Political Science and Politics, October 2016.

4 Pew Research Center, "Wide Gender Gap, Growing Educational Divide in Voters' Party Identification," March 2018.

5 Richard C. Fording, Sanford S. Schram, "The Cognitive and Emotional Sources of Trump Support: The Case of Low-Information Voters," New Political Science, Vol. 39, 2017.

6 An interesting book on this subject is Drew Westen's "The

Political Brain. The Role of Emotions in Deciding the Fate of the Nation," published by Public Affairs in 2008.

7   Thomas B Edsall, "The Contract with Authoritarianism," The New York Times, April 5, 2018. The authors of the study "use a long-established authoritarian scale—based on four survey questions about which childhood traits parents would like to see in their offspring—that asks voters to choose between independence or respect for their elders; curiosity or good manners; self-reliance or obedience; and being considerate or well-behaved. Those respondents who choose respect for elders, good manners, obedience and being well-behaved are rated more authoritarian." The correlation between inclination toward authoritarianism and Trump support was confirmed by, for example, B. Choma, Y Anoch, "Cognitive Ability and Authoritarianism. Understanding support for Trump and Clinton," Personality and Individual Differences, N. 106, 2017.

8   Roberto Biorcio, "Democrazie e Populismo nella seconda Repubblica," in M. Maraffi, "Gli italiani e la politica l," Bologna, Il Mulino, 2007.

9   Mario Caciagli, Piergiorgio Corbetta, "Le ragioni dell'elettore. Perche ha vinto il centro-destra nelle elezioni italiane del 2001," Il Mulino, 2002.

10   Thomas B. Edsall, "We aren't seeing White Support for Trump for what it is," The New York Times, August 28, 2019.

11   John F. Harris, "He is Our O.J. Politico's readers explain why they are standing with Trump during Impeachment," Politico, January 9, 2020.

12   Chris Cillizza, "The Greatest Trick Donald Trump ever pulled," CNN, January 7, 2019.

Chapter 5

1   Both election systems were based on lists, whose positioning within the political spectrum was very well known: The list

named "Magistratura Indipendente," for example, was more appealing to conservative judges and closer to the Christian Democrats, while "Magistratura Democratica" was closer to the Communists and the Socialists.

2   The Secretary-General of the party, Enrico Berlinguer, famously stated that "the propulsive force of the October revolution had come to an end."

3   The Rome offices of prosecution during the late 70s and 80s, called "the harbor of fogs" by members of the press, had the reputation of being very close to the parties in office, occasionally doing their bidding by dismissing cases that could damage them and by actively promoting others that could work in their favor.

4   Ken White, "6 Reasons why Paul Manafort Got Off so Lightly," The Atlantic, March, 9, 2019.

5   The four officers identified in the law are the President of the Republic, the President of the House, the President of the Senate, and the President of the Council of Ministers, which is the official designation of the head of the government.

6   "Berlusconi, Lodo Alfano è il minimo per una democrazia" Reuters Italia, July 24, 2008.

7   Berlusconi states as much, for example, in the documentary "Berlusconi. The Epic Story of a Billionaire who Took Over Italy" produced by journalist Alan Friedman and released in 2015.

8   While the Italian Ministry of Justice cannot interfere with the merit of judicial cases or with the career of magistrates, it can supervise and inspect the administration of offices within the judiciary.

9   As was already apparent in the 30s: "In every way the Prosecutor has more power over the administration of justice than the judges, with much less public appreciation of his power. We have been jealous of the power of the trial judge, but careless of the continuous growth of the power

of the prosecuting attorney." (National Commission on law observance and enforcement, Report on Prosecution. Washington DC. Government Printing Office, 1931).

10 David A. Graham, "Trump's Remarkable Admission About Dishonesty," The Atlantic, June 15, 2018.

11 Charlie Warzel, "Why Courtrooms are Kryptonite for Alex Jones," The New York Times, March 31, 2019.

12 David French, "What Sohrab Ahmari gets wrong," The National Review, May 30, 2019.

13 Quoted in Donald Ayer, "Bill Barr's Dangerous Pursuit of Executive Power," The Atlantic, June 30, 2019.

14 At this point, before Trump became president, the GOP still had ethical concerns and Speaker Ryan called out the statement as a "textbook example of racism."

15 Megan Garber, "The Perverse Paradox of the Mueller Report," The Atlantic, April 19, 2019.

Chapter 6

1 Amber Phillips, "A short list of economic issues on which Donald Trump sounds more like a Democrat than a Republican," August 8, 2016, Washington Post.

2 Matthew Yglesias, "Goodbye Populism. Hello Plutocracy," Vox.com. December 29, 2017.

3 Especially the Decree n. 56 issued in 2000.

4 Before the 2001 elections, in April, the Economist published a cover story with the title "Why Silvio Berlusconi is unfit to lead Italy."

5 Kevin D. Williamson, "Trump isn't a Nazi. He is a Failure," National Review, December 27, 2019.

6 Paul Krugman, "Donald and the Deflationists," New York Times, February 14, 2019.

Chapter 7

1 Peter Glick and Suna T. Fiske, "The Ambivalent Sexism

Inventory: Differentiating Hostile and Benevolent Sexism," Journal of Personality and Social Psychology, 70, 1996.

2   Harry Enten, "A Historic Gender Gap is Possible in 2020," CNN online, December 27, 2019.

3   "Veronica Lario: Le veline candidate? Ciarpame senza pudore per il potere," La Repubblica April 28, 2009.

4   There were, however, some exceptions, in the case of the US Senate they were Susan Collins and Mitt Romney, who refused to vote against calling additional witnesses.

5   Dei, "Le basi culturali del Berlusconismo," Ibid.

6   Filippo Ceccarelli, "La biopolitica del corpo," June 8, 2008, La Repubblica.

7   Boni, "Il superleader. Fenomenologia mediatica di Silvio Berlusconi," Melteni edizioni.

8   Fabio Dei, "La Pop-politica. Le basi culturali del Berlusconismo," Studi Culturali, 2011.

9   Massimiliano Pananari, "L'egemonia sottoculturale. L'Italia da Gramsci al gossip," Einaudi 2010.

10   Elisa Giomi, "Da Drive-in alla Make-over television. Modelli femminili e di rapporti tra i sessi nella TV belusconiana (e non)", Studi Culturali, April 2012.

Chapter 8

1   See Chapter 5.

2   Timothy Geithner, "Stress test. Reflections on the Financial Crisis," Broadway Books, 2015.

3   After the 2005 electoral reform introduced by the Berlusconi Administration, which eliminated the uninominal districts and went back to a proportional system based on blocked lists (blocked in the sense that they are prepared by the party's oligarchy and the voters do not have a say), there was another reform in 2015, though it was never actually used in elections. Before the general elections of 2018, another law instituted the electoral system now in force: a

peculiar combination of majoritarian and proportional votes that, with the current political supply, created a confusing outcome. Three parties, ideologically incompatible (or seemingly so) roughly gained a third of the votes each, with no clear winner and no solution for the creation of a government with some chance to stay in power for long-term policy development.

4   Jonah Goldberg, "Trump's Defenders Have Adopted a Doctrine of Infallibility," National Review, October 4, 2019.

5   Ibidem.

6   Edward H. Carr, "What is History," Vintage, 1967.

7   Steve Bannon, Senior Advisor to Trump at the beginning of his presidency, famously stated that one of his objectives was the "deconstruction of the administrative state."

8   Susan Hennessey, Benjamin Wittes, "Unmaking the Presidency. Donald Trump's War on the World's Most Powerful Office," Farrar, Straus and Giroux, 2020.

9   Lidija Haas, "Paolo Sorrentino's 'Loro' will Make You Feel Complicit," The New Republic, September 19, 2019.

Author biography

Edoardo M. Fracanzani, Ph.D., studied Political Science, Economics, and Business Administration. He lived and worked in Italy, the USA, and Latin America. He participated in researches on economic, political, and social subjects, published and edited the Rome-based magazine Analisi Italia, and is the author of many articles and books on contemporary Italian politics and society. In 2009 he published, "A letter to Cavour. Anomalies of a Nation" and in 2014 "The origins of the conflict," a historical account of the relations between Italian political parties and the judicial branch. He also worked as an executive and business consultant.

From the author

Thank you for purchasing *Norms Under Siege*. My sincere hope is that you derived as much from reading this book as I have in creating it. If you have a few moments, please feel free to add your review of the book to your favorite online site for feedback. Also, if you would like to share your opinion about the topics discussed in the book please write to e.fracanzani@gmail.com.

Sincerely,
Edoardo M. Fracanzani

CULTURE, SOCIETY & POLITICS

The modern world is at an impasse. Disasters scroll across our smartphone screens and we're invited to like, follow or upvote, but critical thinking is harder and harder to find. Rather than connecting us in common struggle and debate, the internet has sped up and deepened a long-standing process of alienation and atomization. Zer0 Books wants to work against this trend. With critical theory as our jumping off point, we aim to publish books that make our readers uncomfortable. We want to move beyond received opinions.

Zer0 Books is on the left and wants to reinvent the left. We are sick of the injustice, the suffering and the stupidity that defines both our political and cultural world, and we aim to find a new foundation for a new struggle.

If this book has helped you to clarify an idea, solve a problem or extend your knowledge, you may want to check out our online content as well. Look for Zer0 Books: Advancing Conversations in the iTunes directory and for our Zer0 Books YouTube channel.

Popular videos include:

Žižek and the Double Blackmain

The Intellectual Dark Web is a Bad Sign

Can there be an Anti-SJW Left?

Answering Jordan Peterson on Marxism

Follow us on Facebook
at https://www.facebook.com/ZeroBooks and Twitter at https://
twitter.com/Zer0Books

Bestsellers from Zer0 Books include:

Give Them An Argument
Logic for the Left
Ben Burgis
Many serious leftists have learned to distrust talk of logic. This is
a serious mistake.
Paperback: 978-1-78904-210-8 ebook: 978-1-78904-211-5

Poor but Sexy
Culture Clashes in Europe East and West
Agata Pyzik
How the East stayed East and the West stayed West.
Paperback: 978-1-78099-394-2 ebook: 978-1-78099-395-9

An Anthropology of Nothing in Particular
Martin Demant Frederiksen
A journey into the social lives of meaninglessness.
Paperback: 978-1-78535-699-5 ebook: 978-1-78535-700-8

In the Dust of This Planet
Horror of Philosophy vol. 1
Eugene Thacker
In the first of a series of three books on the Horror of Philosophy,
In the Dust of This Planet offers the genre of horror as a way of
thinking about the unthinkable.
Paperback: 978-1-84694-676-9 ebook: 978-1-78099-010-1

The End of Oulipo?
An Attempt to Exhaust a Movement
Lauren Elkin, Veronica Esposito
Paperback: 978-1-78099-655-4 ebook: 978-1-78099-656-1

Capitalist Realism
Is There No Alternative?
Mark Fisher
An analysis of the ways in which capitalism has presented itself
as the only realistic political-economic system.
Paperback: 978-1-84694-317-1 ebook: 978-1-78099-734-6

Rebel Rebel
Chris O'Leary
David Bowie: every single song. Everything you want to know,
everything you didn't know.
Paperback: 978-1-78099-244-0 ebook: 978-1-78099-713-1

Kill All Normies
Angela Nagle
Online culture wars from 4chan and Tumblr to Trump.
Paperback: 978-1- 78535-543-1 ebook: 978-1-78535-544-8

Cartographies of the Absolute
Alberto Toscano, Jeff Kinkle
An aesthetics of the economy for the twenty-first century.
Paperback: 978-1-78099-275-4 ebook: 978-1-78279-973-3

Malign Velocities
Accelerationism and Capitalism
Benjamin Noys
Long listed for the Bread and Roses Prize 2015, *Malign Velocities*
argues against the need for speed, tracking acceleration
as the symptom of the ongoing crises of capitalism.
Paperback: 978-1-78279-300-7 ebook: 978-1-78279-299-4

Meat Market
Female Flesh under Capitalism
Laurie Penny
A feminist dissection of women's bodies as the fleshy fulcrum of
capitalist cannibalism, whereby women are both consumers and
consumed.
Paperback: 978-1-84694-521-2 ebook: 978-1-84694-782-7

Babbling Corpse
Vaporwave and the Commodification of Ghosts
Grafton Tanner
Paperback: 978-1-78279-759-3 ebook: 978-1-78279-760-9

New Work New Culture
Work we want and a culture that strengthens us
Frithjoff Bergmann
A serious alternative for mankind and the planet.
Paperback: 978-1-78904-064-7 ebook: 978-1-78904-065-4

Romeo and Juliet in Palestine
Teaching Under Occupation
Tom Sperlinger
Life in the West Bank, the nature of pedagogy and the role of a
university under occupation.
Paperback: 978-1-78279-637-4 ebook: 978-1-78279-636-7

Ghosts of My Life
Writings on Depression, Hauntology and Lost Futures
Mark Fisher
Paperback: 978-1-78099-226-6 ebook: 978-1-78279-624-4

Sweetening the Pill
or How We Got Hooked on Hormonal Birth Control
Holly Grigg-Spall
Has contraception liberated or oppressed women?
Sweetening the Pill breaks the silence on the dark side of hormonal
contraception.
Paperback: 978-1-78099-607-3 ebook: 978-1-78099-608-0

Why Are We The Good Guys?
Reclaiming Your Mind from the Delusions of Propaganda
David Cromwell
A provocative challenge to the standard ideology that Western
power is a benevolent force in the world.
Paperback: 978-1-78099-365-2 ebook: 978-1-78099-366-9

The Writing on the Wall
On the Decomposition of Capitalism and its Critics
Anselm Jappe, Alastair Hemmens
A new approach to the meaning of social emancipation.
Paperback: 978-1-78535-581-3 ebook: 978-1-78535-582-0

Enjoying It
Candy Crush and Capitalism
Alfie Bown
A study of enjoyment and of the enjoyment of studying. Bown
asks what enjoyment says about us and what we say about
enjoyment, and why.
Paperback: 978-1-78535-155-6 ebook: 978-1-78535-156-3

Color, Facture, Art and Design
Iona Singh
This materialist definition of fine-art develops guidelines for
architecture, design, cultural-studies and ultimately social
change.
Paperback: 978-1-78099-629-5 ebook: 978-1-78099-630-1

Neglected or Misunderstood
The Radical Feminism of Shulamith Firestone
Victoria Margree
An interrogation of issues surrounding gender, biology,
sexuality, work and technology, and the ways in which our
imaginations continue to be in thrall to ideologies of maternity
and the nuclear family.
Paperback: 978-1-78535-539-4 ebook: 978-1-78535-540-0

How to Dismantle the NHS in 10 Easy Steps (Second Edition)
Youssef El-Gingihy
The story of how your NHS was sold off and why you will have
to buy private health insurance soon. A new expanded second
edition with chapters on junior doctors' strikes and government
blueprints for US-style healthcare.
Paperback: 978-1-78904-178-1 ebook: 978-1-78904-179-8

Digesting Recipes
The Art of Culinary Notation
Susannah Worth
A recipe is an instruction, the imperative tone of the expert, but
this constraint can offer its own kind of potential. A recipe need
not be a domestic trap but might instead offer escape – something
to fantasise about or aspire to.
Paperback: 978-1-78279-860-6 ebook: 978-1-78279-859-0

Most titles are published in paperback and as an ebook.
Paperbacks are available in traditional bookshops. Both print and
ebook formats are available online.
Follow us on Facebook
at https://www.facebook.com/ZeroBooks
and Twitter at https://twitter.com/Zer0Books